The Making of Shareholder Welfare Society

The Making of Shareholder Welfare Society traces and accounts for the debates and discussions between law and economics scholars and mainstream legal scholars, management theorists, and economic sociologists. This is done in detail to demonstrate that the shareholder welfare society was built from the bottom up, beginning with theoretical propositions regarding alleged market efficiencies and leading all the way to the idea that a society characterized by economic freedom and efficiency maximization paves the way for uncompromised shareholder welfare, in turn, being good for everyone.

This book is of relevance for a variety of readers, including graduate students, management scholars, policy-makers, and management consultants, as well as those that are concerned about how the economic system of competitive capitalism is now in a position where it is riddled by doubts and concern, not the least of which are the levels of soaring economic inequality. It addresses the topics with regard to corporate governance, accounting, and society and will be of interest to researchers, academics, students, and members of the public who are concerned about the economic system of competitive capitalism.

Alexander Styhre is Chair of Organization Theory and Management, Department of Business Administration, School of Business, Economics and Law at the University of Gothenburg, Sweden.

Routledge Studies in Corporate Governance

1 **Corporate Governance Around the World**
Ahmed Naciri

2 **Behaviour and Rationality in Corporate Governance**
Oliver Marnet

3 **The Value Creating Board**
Corporate Governance and Organizational Behaviour
Edited by Morten Huse

4 **Corporate Governance and Resource Security in China**
The Transformation of China's Global Resources Companies
Xinting Jia and Roman Tomasic

5 **Internal and External Aspects of Corporate Governance**
Ahmed Naciri

6 **Green Business, Green Values, and Sustainability**
Edited by Christos N. Pitelis, Jack Keenan and Vicky Pryce

7 **Credit Rating Governance**
Global Credit Gatekeepers
Ahmed Naciri

8 **Mergers and Acquisitions and Executive Compensation**
Virginia Bodolica and Martin Spraggon

9 **Governance and Governmentality for Projects**
Enablers, Practices, and Consequences
Edited by Ralf Müller

10 **The Making of Shareholder Welfare Society**
A Study in Corporate Governance
Alexander Styhre

The Making of Shareholder Welfare Society

A Study in Corporate Governance

Alexander Styhre

LONDON AND NEW YORK

First published 2018
by Routledge

2 Park Square, Milton Park, Abingdon, Oxfordshire OX14 4RN
52 Vanderbilt Avenue, New York, NY 10017

Routledge is an imprint of the Taylor & Francis Group, an informa business

First issued in paperback 2019

Copyright © 2018 Taylor & Francis

The right of Alexander Styhre to be identified as author of this work has been asserted by him in accordance with sections 77 and 78 of the Copyright, Designs and Patents Act 1988.

All rights reserved. No part of this book may be reprinted or reproduced or utilised in any form or by any electronic, mechanical, or other means, now known or hereafter invented, including photocopying and recording, or in any information storage or retrieval system, without permission in writing from the publishers.

Notice:
Product or corporate names may be trademarks or registered trademarks, and are used only for identification and explanation without intent to infringe.

Library of Congress Cataloging-in-Publication Data
Names: Styhre, Alexander, author.
Title: The making of shareholder welfare society : a study in corporate governance / by Alexander Styhre.
Description: New York : Routledge, 2017. | Includes index.
Identifiers: LCCN 2017025253 | ISBN 9781138636040 (hardback) | ISBN 9781315206257 (ebook)
Subjects: LCSH: Finance—United States—History. | Capitalism—United States—History. | Corporate governance—United States—History.
Classification: LCC HG181 .S835 2017 | DDC 338.60973—dc23
LC record available at https://lccn.loc.gov/2017025253

ISBN: 978-1-138-63604-0 (hbk)
ISBN: 978-0-367-88644-8 (pbk)

Typeset in Sabon
by Apex CoVantage, LLC

Contents

Preface

"Out of sheer rage, I've begun my book on Thomas Hardy," D.H. Lawrence wrote in his journal on September 5, 1914 (cited in Dyer, 1997: i). This is arguably not a recommendation widely endorsed in all the world's "creative writing" courses, to get started on basis of strong affect. Instead, at least academic writing is understood as what is pursued *sine ira et studio*, "not allowing personal motives or temper influence conduct, free of arbitrariness and unpredictability," in Max Weber's (1999: 100) formulation. On the other hand, rage and anger are trustworthy emotional responses to perceived injustices or difficulties, and they offer the benefit of not easily being mistaken for any other emotional state. More specifically, rage and anger can fuel scholarship over considerable periods but only as long as it can be contained within the individual author's writing practices, to serve the end as give expression to an extended argument. What speaks against rage and anger as what propels a scholarly pursuit is that it may blindfold the writer and turn him or her into a revenge-seeking renegade, a crusader, and a vigilante that fails to oversee the entire field of the operations. That would be a terrible squandering of useful energy, capable of being canalized into worthwhile contributions.

In Samuel Taylor Coleridge's *Biographia Literaria*, he distinguished between *fancy* (from Greek, *Phantasia*) and *imagination*. Fancy is here the lower-order thinking, essentially being "a mere assemblage of data," while imagination is what locates "the poet by the harder route to a higher end" (Watson, 1953: 211). More explicitly, Coleridge saw imagination as an "an *active* power," independent of the "fixed associations of memory and experience," and was also "the *unifying* power" in the poet's work (Hardy, 1951: 336). Therefore, fancy, the lower-order cognitive process, "[c]an never do the job of imagination" (Hardy, 1951: 340). For Hegel (1999: 299), "imagination" (*Einbildungskraft*), is the process where the human consciousness produces "representations" (*Vorstellungen*) of object before it is capable of formulating "concepts" (*Begriffe*) that apprehends the representations. Unfortunately, the German term *Begriffe* and its connotations with actual handling and manual operations—in short, its tactile qualities—pertaining to theorizing is lost in the translation, but for Hegel the practice of *philosophieren* is largely a matter of making the world manageable on basis of imaginative processes and accompanying practices. For Alfred North Whitehead, another thinker who was no enemy of thinking that seeks to grasp the outer limits of human consciousness, imagination "[i]s not to be divorced from the facts: it is a way of illuminating the facts" (Alfred North Whitehead, cited in Bennis and O'Toole, 2005: 102). In Whitehead's view, one of the tragedies of this world is that "those who are imaginative have but slight experience, and those who are experienced have feeble imagination," a condition that risks to condemn humankind to only a cursory and incomplete understanding of the world it inhabit.

Why all this talk about dead poets' and philosophers' affective states and their theories of imagination? Business school research is rarely portrayed as a creative act engaging the scholars' *Einbildungskraft*, but is more commonly associated with the dry amassing of data and theorizing. Introducing yet another "great-thinker-since-long-dead-and-almost-forgotten," Giobattista Vico, the renowned Neapolitan intellectual and historian, Vico argued in his *New Science* that history rarely reveals itself in its full complexity to its analysts. Instead, it is only possible to understand history in a piecemeal and incomplete fashion, unfolding as the process of carefully forging fragments from a distant past together. In Vico's view, this predicament should not be presented as an embarrassment for the historian or (what we today refer to as) the social scientist as this may not be much, but that is all there is. Addressing institutional and political changes over six decades of corporate governance practices is to become aware of the magnitude of Vico's insight. There are few comprehensive and conclusive stories to be told, but instead the analyst needs to cobble together a variety of resources and fragment to be able to tell, for example, a story of how the *ancien régime* of the managerial capitalism was increasingly running out of steam and thus discredited by free-market protagonists, eager to advance their view of the unregulated market as the most efficient mechanism not only for determining prices but also for monitoring insiders in the firm. That these insiders hold unique and specialized skills and know-how in how to best optimize the resources mobilized in the firm did no longer matter. In order to be able to pursue this project, a certain degree of anger or frustration (still kept under full control) may be helpful.

The events of 2008 and the great recession that followed has spawned a great deal of scholarly writing as these events apparently indicated that much of the free-market ideology that was advanced on broad basis in the period after around 1980 were mistaken or otherwise underrated or ignored the risks involved in permitting markets to monitor themselves. The lack of prudence and proper risk assessment and moderation on part of finance industry professionals have in some cases been mind-boggling (I don't want to regress to speak about greed, but some commentators think otherwise). In order to emotionally and intellectually cope with the magnitude of this collective failure to see how incomplete these free-market stories were, a little element of anger may be permitted and indeed even helpful in canalizing affect into scholarly practices and writing. In addition, to have a fair share of imaginative capacities is helpful in being able to see the connections between all the fragments and elements that have been scattered all over the scene before and after 2008. Now, it is commonplace to address the role of the finance industry, the political bodies, the regulatory control executed by the state and the government, credit rating agencies, neoclassical economic theory, certain algorithms and calculative practices and esoteric innovations such as the Gaussian copula and robot trading, and a long series of additional actors, tools, conditions, and events that all contributed to what can perhaps best be described in vernacular terms as "a real mess." To impose some kind of coherent and linear narrative on all these factors worthy of being considered and taken into account certainly demands some kind of imaginative skills.

At the same time, to recourse to major thinkers and theorists is not a sufficient strategy for bringing order in the complexity now being produced on industrial and everyday basis in the finance industry and elsewhere. While we may use Hegel or Whitehead (or anyone else) to shed light on the operations of the finance industry or changes in corporate governance practices, such "grand thinkers" are not likely to offer the tools needed to accomplish such an analysis, regardless of their merits. We can here cite the anthropologist Paul Rabinow, pointing at the need to combine social theory and more detailed empirical data with more recent theoretical development to accomplish the social and economic theorist's work:

> Today, the pedagogic challenge is to rethink the established combination of fast and slow operations that remains at the core of what inquiry should be. One may say, 'Let's go to Chernobyl, but don't let [Max] Weber behind.' Of course, Weber is not going to tell you directly what's going on there—that would be ridiculous to expect. But surfing the internet is no going to tell you what is significant, either.
>
> (Paul Rabinow, cited in Rabinow, Marcus, Faubion, and Rees, 2008: 56)

What we can learn from Coleridge, Hegel, Whitehead, and Vico is that the conditions under which humanity seek to make sense out of their life world are bound up with our very own capacities to participate in self-reflexive and critical thinking, but the very tools needed to say something meaningful about contemporary conditions, Paul Rabinow adds, need to be sought elsewhere. Thus, to participate in the work to make sense out of the changes in corporate governance means to demonstrate a fair share of *sang froid* inasmuch as all the pieces of the puzzle is unlikely to be available (or to collect them would require substantial amounts of time and resources), and yet the image that can be visualized justifies the work actually accomplished as it indicate something of significance. As another noted anthropologist,

Clifford Geertz (1975), have remarked, just as one should be aware of the lure of common sense thinking, taking the whole world as a matter of what epistemologists refer to as "face validity"—in short, common sense assumed that the world essentially is precisely as it appears at first sight—the other epistemic vice is to *overtheorize*: "The world is what the wide-awake, uncomplicated man takes it to be. Sobriety, not subtlety, realism, not imagination, are the keys to wisdom; the really important facts of life lie scattered openly along its surface, not cunningly secreted in its depths," Geertz (1975: 22) says. That is, Geertz (1975: 22) continues, "[s]ome of the most crucial properties of the world are not regarded as concealed beneath a mask of deceptive appearances, things inferred from pale suggestions or riddled out of equivocal signs." On the contrary, these most crucial properties of the world "are conceived to be just there . . . invisible only to the clever" (Geertz, 1975: 22). Needless to say, there is a very delicate balance between under- and overtheorizing that the practicing researcher needs to be aware of; in many cases, this sense of overstepping a boundary, to venture too far inlands reveals itself only as a vague intuition that perhaps, after all, this was a bit too far-fetched? On the other hand, to just look at what is at hand without even trying to connect the parts, that is, to give voice to what is "inexpressible" in Henri Bergson's formulation (1999: 23–24), is equally unsatisfying. In this zone between the absolute certainty of common-sense thinking and the relentless anxiety regarding the actual state of things, imagination may be the practicing scholar's guiding principle, setting a boundary for what may be said without every taking anything for granted. A wisely executed imaginative text is after all pointing at both factual condition and possible solutions; it ventures in the zone wherein what is known and what appear to be likely are the outer limits.

This book is part of a wider project to understand how competitive capitalism have changed since the early 1970s—that is, a period that by and large coincides with my own lifetime—from being an economic system that generated economic growth and well-being without amplifying economic inequality to unreasonable levels to an economic system with lower growth but with higher economic inequality, a shift that arguably would undermine the economic well-being of many citizens in Western advanced and democratic welfare states. In order to reduce the sheer complexity of such a venture, different aspects of this institutional change needs to be targeted at the time. The question of corporate governance, one of the most centrally located practices in the corporate system of competitive capitalism, determining how the firm's accumulated residual cash is to be distributed or invested, is of key importance for how the corporate system, developed over time since the eighteenth century, operates. In this volume, the question of corporate governance is not only a matter of how the corporate system is optimized and managed but takes on a wider political significance as the critics of the regime of managerial capitalism introduce the term *efficiency* as the sole legitimate measure of the performance of the corporate system. The innovation of the business charter, granted by the sovereign state to promote business venturing while minimizing the risk of opportunistic behaviour that would undermine the enterprise, was originally developed as a legal vehicle that bridged and balanced a variety of interests, which the sovereign state had to consider. Consequently, the business charter and the firm as an autonomous legal entity was never intended to serve the one-dimensional goal of maximizing its efficiency; instead, the efficiency criteria was considered along a variety of performance measures that the firm's board of directors, endowed with decision-making authority, would recognize.

The change in corporate governance over the last five decades have systematically discredited this legal view of the firm and have overtly ignored the historical roots of the corporate system. Instead, orthodox neoclassical economic theory has been advanced as some kind of neutral and inherently rational model for determining how corporate governance practices *should* be conducted. Unfortunately, this economic model is neither neutral (it is highly politicized and serve certain ends and interests), nor inherently rational (at least as long as rationality is no longer defined as self-referential consistency but is defined in substantial terms and measured in terms of desirable outcomes and accomplishments). As a consequence, the shareholder welfare governance model that has been proposed on basis of free-market theories has led to lower growth, highly leveraged risks, rising unemployment, and not least to soaring economic inequality in systematic ways. It is always possible for the shareholder welfare governance crusader to articulate counterfactual hypothesis ("What if . . .") to buffer such criticism, but as a matter of fact, such objections cannot mute the economic fundamentals that speaks against the model they have proposed and campaigned for. That is, it is possible that the continuation of the managerial capitalism model would have led to a similar decline in performance of the corporate system, but we can never tell. Instead, what is at hand are the new economic realities wherein the shareholder welfare corporate governance model has played a decisive, even central role in creating economic inequality and slower economic growth. Free marketeers have been fond of saying that "economic freedom" is the root of any great society, but the economic freedom their reforms and campaigns have produced seems quite unattractive now once it is enforced. Formulated in essentially negative terms (i.e., what political scientists refer to as a "negative freedom") as "the absence of state regulation," when all is said and done, it appears as if such economic freedom was beneficial to only the top-notch income groups, while for the rest, the retrenching state basically brought unfavourable consequences. In other words, the bundling of the efficiency criteria and the political campaign to establish economic freedom on basis of corporate governance reforms was arguably never, despite all the tedious talk about the need for "increased efficiency," about making the corporate system more vital or competitive from the view of the legislator, that is, the sovereign state, but had no other objective or ulterior motives than to benefit the finance capital owners who were ready to fund the free-market crusade that continued for most of the second half of the last century. In the pursuit to create economic freedom "for all," a very small minority was, in fact, better off. By default, economic freedom is thus another way to speak about economic inequality. Thus, the basic claim made by the proponents of shareholder welfare governance, that "What is good or the finance capital owners is good for everybody and for society," repeated over and over, simply proved to be not true; it was part of the free-market mythology contained within orthodox neoclassical economic theory and that serves to block and neutralize empirical evidence that falsifies some of the elementary assumptions made in this theoretical framework. This volume is an account for how this mythology was part of the work to reform the corporate governance practices in the corporate system, a most successful project whose consequences we are now set to handle.

Acknowledgements

I would like to thank David Varley, Commissioning editor, Routledge/Taylor & Francis, for providing me with the opportunity to write and publish this book, I would also like to thank Brianna Ascher and Megan A. Smith, editorial assistants, Routledge/Taylor & Francis, for their support in the process.

In the academic community in inhabit, there are numerous scholars, practitioners, and other colleagues that are worth thanking for making everyday life inspiring and even occasionally quite exciting. My colleagues at the School of Business, Economics, and Law, and especially at the Section of Organization and Management are the first to thank, but also the wider and much more geographically dispersed community of scholars with whom I am lucky to collaborate with and who engage on everyday basis in the study of managerial practices and their implications.

In the end, the capacity to have the ambition, will, and endurance to embark on a book-writing project is dependent on family: Sara, Simon, and Max. Even through academic life essentially unfolds as a matter of learning a trade, to pursue a career (i.e., to "keep afloat"), to mimic the stars and the heroes of your targeted discipline while trying to say something original or even personal, and to earn a bit of credentials, in the end you realize, after years or even decades, as David Foster Wallace once put it, that "[y]ou end up becoming yourself." So, in the end, there's no use in chasing the rainbow as you may find precisely what you are looking for exactly where you are. But such small-time discoveries demand their own idiosyncratic courage and sacrifices, and barely do we realize the importance of such virtues until it is too late. In private life too, the owl of Minerva takes off at dusk.

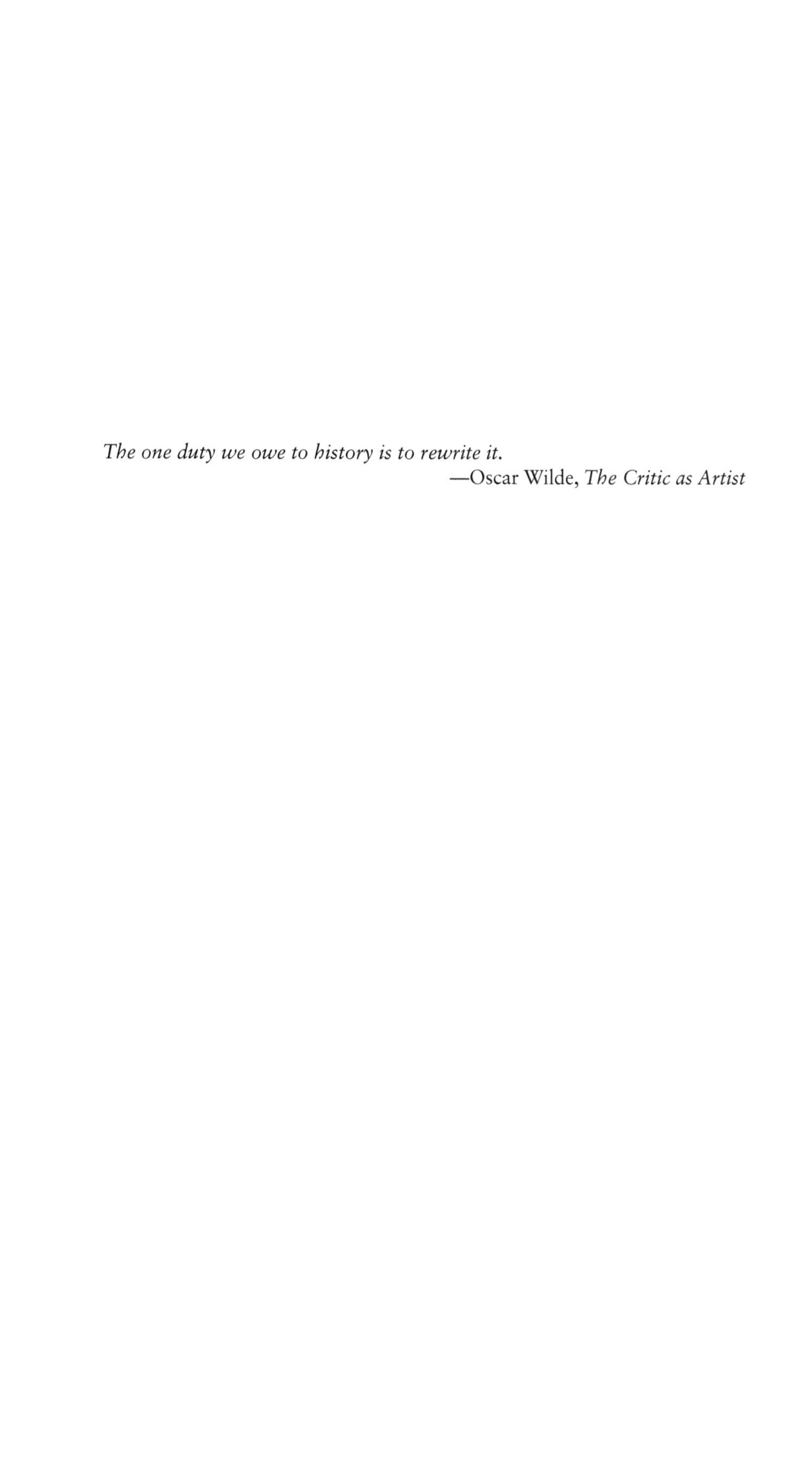

The one duty we owe to history is to rewrite it.

—Oscar Wilde, *The Critic as Artist*

Introduction

The Financial Crisis, the Great Recession, and the Question of Corporate Governance

Elementary Definitions and Research Problem

In this volume, a few quite straightforward definitions are applied. First, a firm is defined as "[a] collection of resources embedded in a network of relationships among stakeholders" (Aguilera and Jackson, 2003: 450, Footnote 5). A firm, essentially a collection or bundle of illiquid production factors (machinery, patents, co-workers, brands, etc.), is aimed at producing economic value. This economic value can be further separated into user-value (i.e., the value that the firm's consumers and clients can realize when they use the firm's goods or services) and economic value (i.e., financial value) that is being transferred to stakeholders, most notably as salaries to employees as a compensation for their work and dividends to shareholders to compensate for the risk they have carried. The firm is thus an economic and legal entity that produces economic value that to varying degree can be extracted from the firm. As there is a tradeoff between distributing economic value and investing in future production factors (e.g., technology, Research and Development [R&D], human resources), directors—who *de jure* are given the right to make such decisions—need to strike a balance between a series of objectives and interests, not the least between long-term performance and firm viability and see, for example, short-term responses to the claims of compensation of, for example, employees and shareholders (Zhang and Gimeno, 2016). Such decisions are labeled *corporate governance decisions*.

Corporate governance is a wide and in many ways disputed term and practice, but for the sake of simplicity, it is here defined, following Aguilera and Jackson (2003: 450), as "the relationships among stakeholders in the process of decision making and control over firm resources." Corporate governance is therefore highly politicized, addressing questions such as "Who owns the firm?" "Who have the right to the economic value generated by the firm?" and "What role do salaried managers play in determining how firm resources are invested?" An accompanying but less widely used term is *corporate control*, which Jensen and Ruback (1983: 5) define accordingly: "We define corporate control as the rights to determine the management of corporate resources—that is, the rights to hire, fire and set the compensation of top-level managers."

Corporate governance decisions are subject to scholarly research within a series of disciplines including management studies, economics, legal studies, and economic sociology. Competitive capitalism, an economic system based on private ownership and accompanying defined ownership rights (Appleby, 2010; Ingham, 2008; Goody, 2004), monitored and regulated by the sovereign state (Commons, 1924), have enacted the legal entity of the firm as its principal vehicle for enterprising and economic value generating activities. Corporate governance consequently addresses a series of issues being at the very core of the economic system. The corporate governance of the firm is legally prescribed by *corporate law*, which is a *constitutional law* that describes and determines a set of mandatory rules that needs to be followed in the governance of the firm. Moreover, the sovereign state grants business charters to economic ventures that include both privileges and responsibilities, and therefore, the firm is embedded within the wider institutional framework of the sovereign state. This means for instance that the firm is a free-standing legal entity that owns itself, and the board of directors, the firm's principal corporate governance mechanism, have the authority to make business judgement decisions including decisions regarding, for example, what managers to hire and how much of the economic value generated that should be paid out to shareholders.

As being an internal, yet elementary process within the corporate system of competitive capitalism, corporate governance is not so frequently addressed in the wider public. Much of what happens in the boardrooms, the executive suites, and during the annual meetings basically follows the conventional wisdom, and little drama is the rule rather than the exception. Yet, at the same time, to be able to influence and modify corporate governance practices of the firm is to some extent comparable to modifying the DNA, the genetic code, of an organism: if the carefully developed corporate governance practices, enshrined by corporate law and rooted in widely shared business judgement principles, are altered, the entire corporate system may change, with significant implications for competitive capitalism and its surrounding society. This volume examine how free-market protagonists, adhering to orthodox neoclassical economic theory, have managed to slowly modify corporate governance practices over the last six decades so that the original idea of the chartered business venture, enacting the firm as a team production effort embedded in the heterogeneous interests of stakeholders, recognized by the sovereign state, is now more focused on creating economic value to be distributed to the owners of stock, that is, the finance capital owners. This is not a trivial modification of corporate governance practices but represent a pervasive institutional, political, and cultural change over the last half-century of the increasingly financialized corporate system. To some extent, this is precisely an analogy to the "knock-out gene mice" that today populate life science laboratories worldwide, the genetic modification of the innermost and most elementary process of the corporate system, leading to the shift from treating the firm as a team production entity to enacting it as a shareholder-controlled economic production and extraction entity. Before proceeding into further details, some illustrative cases of this systemwide and comprehensive change are provided.

The Problems of Shareholder Welfare and Economic Inequality

As a being a corporate governance matter, the firm has been enacted in at least two ways, Tomaskovic-Devey, Lin, and Meyers (2015: 531) argue. First, the firm is visualized as a "production machine," in which "inputs of materials, capital and labour lead to outputs, and value added is the residual value after production costs." In addition, the firm is understood as an "accumulator of profits," an entity that controls significant economic resources:

> In this formulation firms do not add value so much as accumulate it, from both internal production relations and external relationships with suppliers, customers, and the state. Similarly the value accumulated by a firm is distributed to stakeholders inside the firm (labour, direct owners), those in a liminal position (e.g. equity holders, sub-contractors, leased labour), and external stakeholders (e.g. the state, creditors, charities).
>
> (Tomaskovic-Devey et al., 2015: 531)

For a management researcher, being concerned with the internal workings of the entity of the firm, the former view is taken. In this view, managerial skills and acumen add to the overall efficiency of team production efforts, and mangers are both incentivized and socialized to act in accordance with professional standards to optimize (but not of necessity maximize) the efficiency of the operations. In contrast, economists tend to ignore the firm as a meaningful entity of analysis. For economists, it is the *market* that is the arbiter of economic exchanges and what most effectively prices commodities, goods, and services, and therefore, the firm is merely regarded as a knot in a field of market-based transactions, at best understood as minimization of transaction costs (as postulated by Ronald Coase) but otherwise adding little to the overall efficiency of the system of competitive capitalism.

One of the implications from this disciplinary divergence between, for example, management researchers and economists is that for the latter, the firm is, *ex hypothesi*, no more no less efficient than the surrounding market efficiency and can thus never surpass the market in terms organizing its internal production activities more efficiently than what the market permits. For management researchers, this is an intriguing hypothesis that is not rejected *a priori*, but it is not accepted as a legitimate proposition. Instead, firms and managerial decision-making may be more or less efficient, but the level of performance and accomplishment remains an empirical question, lending itself to investigation. Being essentially insulated against such objections, orthodox neoclassical economists propose that the firm as an economic value generating entity serves the corporate system and competitive capitalism best if the economic value generated is transferred to the shareholders, operating in the finance market and thus, by implication (albeit by no means representing a trivial argument), are in a better position to determine where the economic value should be reinvested. If the dividends issued derive from a high-growth industry, shareholders purchase more stocks in in the industry (thus representing a hope to make further yields), but if the dividends derive from stagnant industries, the finance capital is transferred to other industries with higher growth potential, the neoclassicist argument goes. Leaving a series of objection and conditional assumptions aside, this shareholder-dominated corporate system is justified on basis of market-pricing efficiency arguments and a free-market ideology that grant shareholders rights and privileges that were never intended by corporate law. Therefore, the externalities that the legislators anticipated—that is, a tipping of the power balance in the favour of finance capital owners, always a concern in the governance of competitive capitalism—are either ignored in the economists' argument or are simply dismissed as standing in the way for the maximization of efficiency in the use of aggregated resources in the corporate system. Either way, the externalities of shareholder welfare governance are overlooked by economists.

Unfortunately, to assume that these externalities are trivial or marginal is to turn a blind eye to significant empirical evidence. It is outside of the scope of this introductory chapter to cover all of this literature, but a few examples are presented to substantiate the claim that corporate law cannot be bypassed at low or negligible costs. Tomaskovic-Devey et al. (2015: 542) argue that the new shareholder welfare governance model served to leverage risk to increase the return-on-equity (ROE) measure by replacing equity with debt, which in turn, over time, served to erode the substantial economic value of non-financial firms: "Our results suggest that financial investment strategies, in concert with the shareholder value movement and CEO compensation strategies reduced the long-term value of the non-finance corporate sector and transferred income to financial service firms and rentier capital in general." One indication of the emphasis on ROE is the debt ratio of American companies: "The debt ratio increased from about 0.55 in the early 1980s to more than 0.70 in 1993," Lin (2016: 977) writes. "In 2005, the debt ratio for the largest U.S. nonfinancial firms was about 0.67, which indicates that these firms still heavily depend on debt to fund their operations" (Lin, 2016: 977). Higher levels of debt imply that companies are more vulnerable to economic downturns, which executives handle by layoffs to maintain stock market evaluations (Coffee, 2006: 83), i.e., higher debt ratio translates into weakened employment growth (Lin, 2016: 975): "[W]henever there is an economic downturn or cash flow problems, firms with more debt face greater pressure to reduce labor costs under the threat of bankruptcy" (Lin, 2016: 977). This is largely consistent with the shareholder welfare governance model, dominating since the early 1980s:

> [Between 1982 and 2005] there was a 10% increase in the concentration of revenue but a 15% decrease in the concentration of domestic employment in the largest U.S. firms. In absolute terms, in 2005 the largest U.S. firms increased their gross revenue by more than $780 billion but hired 2.8 million fewer workers.
>
> (Lin, 2016: 972)

Lin (2016) thus aligns shareholder welfare governance, the loss of blue-collar work, and growing economic inequality:

> Firms' investment in financial markets increase the demand for professional/supervisory and service labor, while the dependence on debt and the pursuit of shareholder value, respectively, undermine production-related and service workers' job security. All these developments contribute to the polarization of the labor market and growing inequality.
>
> (Lin, 2016: 985)

Guillén and Capron (2015: 153) argue that shareholder welfare governance has served to destabilize the economy and to erode the business ethics standards being developed over decades of corporate leadership:

> The rise of shareholder capitalism during the late twentieth century created the conditions for the various financial crises and corporate scandals of the first decade of the twenty-first century. The fact that so many countries around the world continue to experience severe economic and financial distress, corporate scandals, and rogue behavior by managers and traders is paradoxical because all of these problems have proliferated at a time when corporate governance rules, including shareholder rights protection, have presumably been 'improved' around the world
>
> (Guillén and Capron, 2015: 153)

Lazonick (2013: 508) address these issues in a foreboding tone, proposing that "as long as US-based corporations are permitted to be governed by [shareholder value] ideology, the US economy will remain incapable to restore sustainable prosperity."

In addition, shareholder welfare governance has served to justify the extraction of economic value from firms at the expense of, for example, employees, thus tipping the power-balance in the favour of finance capital owners. In the U.S., this shift is indicated in the decline of benefits accruing to employees: "[T]he share who receive health benefits from their employers fell from almost 42% to just over 26% between 1979 and 1998," Hacker (2004: 253) writes. Moreover, Hacker (2004: 253) continues, "there has also been a basic decline in employers' support for retirement benefits and, in tandem, a major privatization of risk." This "privatization of risk" is closely bound up with shareholder welfare governance, whose protagonists tend to portray such benefits and retirement funds as a "waste" of the shareholders' money, needless to say, a statement that aims to modify the institution of the corporate system to better serve owners of financial capital. Under all conditions, the advocates of shareholder welfare governance have been most successful in making such claims:

> Between the early 1980s and the mid-1990s, the value of pension benefits to current workers dropped in every income group, but by far most rapidly among the lowest paid workers, who already had the lowest coverage levels . . . In addition, tax breaks for private pensions and other retirement savings options heavily favor better-paid employees: Two-thirds of the nearly $100 billion in federal tax breaks for subsidized retirement savings options accrue to the top 20% of the population.
>
> (Hacker, 2004: 255)

In the retail sector, a sector of the economy particularly exposed to the swings of the economic cycle and receding demand, health care insurance coverage is disappearing:

> Analyses of 2006 CPS [Current Population Survey, published by the U.S. Bureau of Labor Statistics] data indicate that, among workers in the retail sector, only 52 percent of full-time workers and 16.4 percent of part-time workers had health insurance coverage through their employer; across industries, only 18.6 percent of part-time hourly workers were covered by health insurance through their employer.
>
> (Lambert, 2008: 1206)

In a more recent paper, Cobb (2015: 1332) examines the reduction of benefits and concludes that "U.S. corporations have largely abandoned their role as a primary risk bearer." Not only do salaried employees to a lesser degree benefit from corporate-funded welfare provisions, but a larger proportions of the workforce also suffer from "[d]eclining job tenure, increased long-term unemployment, and the use of nonstandard work arrangements" (Cobb, 2015: 1332)—factual evidence that supports the idea that "market uncertainty" is increasingly borne by workers, not by the employers, now being increasingly committed to enrich their shareholders. As Cappelli (1999: 146) noticed in the late 1990s, "career jobs" (meaning "full-time jobs that last reasonably long, pay reasonably well, and offer benefits") are gradually disappearing. For hardcore free-market protagonists, the decline of "career jobs" is worthy of little concerns as they are understood as being indicative of the market efficiency that they enthusiastically endorsed in the first place. If employees suffer from the loss of such safe and reasonably well-compensated jobs, it is they who are to blame, not the employers and certainly not the markets, being the unforgiving but allegedly fair price-setting mechanism (market "mispricing" is a theoretical absurdity within this framework). Cobb (2015: 1340) argues that the "financial volatility" motivates firms to "shift retirement risks and costs onto workers," which means that the most vulnerable actors are now expected to carry the highest proportions of the risk, in turn amplifying systemic risks (measured as financial volatility) in the economic system.

To summarize, the new shareholder welfare governance model, established over six decades of free-market advocacy (and covered in Chapters 1 through 6 in this volume), established the new doctrine that the corporate system would maximize its efficiency if, and only if, shareholder received the so-called *residual cash flow* (the money that remains when all other costs are covered). As this governance model was implemented, managers were incentivized and disciplined to pursue no other goals than shareholder interests, and therefore all costs were now considered—even the benefits and retirement funds allocated to the employees. However, this new governance policy, representing a disruptive shift from the legislator's intensions with corporate law, discredited by followers of orthodox neoclassical economic theory as an efficiency-reducing and thus questionable legislation, rest on its own tragedy, pointed out by, for example, the economist Michał Kalecki: a downward push in salaries and benefits may generate positive effects for the holders of stock in *one isolated* company as long as not *all the other* companies act in accordance with the same beliefs, but if this downward shift in compensation is implemented on broad basis—as it is very likely to have been the case when shareholder welfare governance became *à la mode* by the early 1980s—the decline in demand that follows from lower degrees of compensation for the work conducted leads to downward spiral of the economic activity (Kalecki, 1971: 26). In this scenario, the short-term profit of the finance capital owner (i.e., the owner of stock) preys on his or her long-term profit.[1] More specifically, the distribution of economic value from one stakeholder or team production partner, for example, employees (in the form of lower real wage growth, reduced benefits, and smaller retirement funds) to another stakeholder (i.e., the shareholders), the economic inequality in the economy grows, with implications for aggregated demand. As wealthy groups dedicate a smaller proportion of their income and wealth to consumption, economic inequality, all things equal, further reduce aggregated demand. The excessive capital accumulating in the top income groups, by now an undisputed fact (Stockhammer, 2015; Weeden and Grusky, 2014; Van Arnum and Naples, 2013; Atkinson, Piketty, and Saez, 2010; Kelly and Enns, 2010; Piketty and Saez, 2003; Alderson and Nielsen, 2002; Rueda and Pontusson, 2000), is claimed to be reinvested in emerging and high growth businesses according to orthodox neoclassical economic theory.

Unfortunately, also rich individuals, despite not having to worrying about their subsistence, tend to be risk averse and the accumulation of finance capital has thus primarily benefitted the expansion of the finance industry per se, capable of providing lucrative investment opportunities. Today, the finance industry holdings outnumber the total aggregated global gross domestic product (GDP) by at least a factor of ten (Sassen, 2014).

To not take this line of argument further into the dwindling pathways of the global finance industry, the principal idea is that the shift towards shareholder welfare governance represents a decisive moment and a significant accomplishment of the free-market protagonist community. As is argued in this volume, this success is not so much a matter of presenting theoretically robust models and empirically substantiated facts supporting such models—in fact, free-market protagonists have systematically failed to do so—but the success is based on the support from wealthy financiers who saw the shareholder welfare governance model as a pathway to a rehabilitation of the autonomy of the business community vis-à-vis the sovereign state, the legal system, the trade unions, and basically any social actors who demonstrated an interests in having a say about how the economic value generated in the corporate system was reinvested and distributed. That is, *The Making of Shareholder Society* is not a traditional heroic story of the triumph of reason over inherited but essentially corrupt social practices; instead, it is a study of how certain interest groups can mobilize resources and turn the world to their advantage, regardless of even the presence of powerful and widely endorsed and respected constitutional law, discrediting many of the claims made by these activists. By the end of the day, policy-making, legislation, theoretical frameworks, and enterprising activities, rooted in both public and private interests, constitute a brew from which novel corporate governance practices were formulated and established. In this process, also small wins and originally preposterous claims can gain a foothold if there are tenacious institutional and moral entrepreneurs in place, capable of keeping their eyes on the prize over significant periods, and financiers willing to fund their activities. The case of the making of shareholder welfare society is one such story of how constant dropping wears away a stone and how long-term commitment to a cause can eventually pay off greatly when the tide change and novel ideas suddenly become the new conventional wisdom.

Principal Argument and the Outline of the Book

The shift from managerial capitalism, an economic regime based on managerial discretion, state regulation, oligarchies, and a mass production/mass consumption system, to investor capitalism, the more recent economic regime based on "the market for managerial control" and the idea of the firm as a bundle of financial assets that is most effectively managed in unregulated free markets, did not happen overnight. Instead, the change from the managerial capitalist regime that came to prominence during the New Deal capitalism recovery programs to the finance market-driven economy that scholars today try to understand and to better monitor is rooted in extensive institutional, political, social, and not the least cultural changes since, say, the 1950s. This volume seeks to outline the gradual shift from a corporate system based on corporate legislation (e.g., corporate law, antitrust legislation, and a variety of accompanying legislative framework determining more detailed issues) and managerial discretion—salaried managers and directors' authority to independently conduct business decisions—to today's finance market-based control of, for example, public firms.

Managerial capitalism was by and large a heterogeneous framework of legislation, practices, doctrines, norms and beliefs and conventional wisdom, serving to entangle the corporations and the state and its regulatory control in various ways. The investor capitalism regime, in turn, is based on an entirely different analytical model; this model is based on neoclassical economic theory, based on the propositions of price theory (assuming that prices reflect and accommodate all available market information) and the assumption that free, unregulated markets is the superior mechanism—in fact, it has few, possibly none, contestants—for organizing economic transactions and allocating resources. Based on these premises, the leitmotif for the institutionalization of investor capitalism has been to advocate increased *efficiency* in economic activities. Per se being a notoriously complicated term, including various types of efficiencies (e.g., *production efficiency* and *allocative efficiency*) and being self-referential in orthodox neoclassical economic theory, the efficiency criteria is a tenuous basis for broad-ranging institutional changes, especially on a global scale. However, what the term *efficiency* lack in terms of conceptual coherence and empirical grounding is well compensated in terms of its communicative possibilities and its normative and even aesthetic content. In short, ideas about efficiency are easily communicated and fit nicely in the rift that occurs between formal theoretical frameworks and the messy and confusing world of policy-making, a borderland that, for example, lobbyists (Choi, Jia, and Lu, 2015; Vidal, Draca, and Fons-Rosen, 2010) and think-tank economists (McLevey, 2015; Medvetz, 2012; Leeson, Ryan, and Williamson, 2012; Lowry, 1999; James, 1993) are skilled at navigating within. In addition, the normative, even moral connotations of the term efficiency should not be underrated: Everybody tends to want things to be "efficient," even in the case where we do not yet know what efficiency would mean, what the alternatives would be, or what sacrifice such efficiencies would demand. Being loaded with positive connotations, the efficiency criteria are quite likely to mute any criticism as soon as it is introduced. Yet, at the same time, the term efficiency cannot be separated from the wider politico-theoretical framework that brought it forward in the first place.

In neoclassical economic theory, the term *efficiency* is not some kind of value-neutral that can be advanced without other competing economic and social objectives being affected. For instance, efficiency is widely understood to be accomplished on basis of the retrenchment of state interventions and regulatory practices to enable markets to "operate more freely." That is, governmental interventions and oversight of necessity—regardless of the benefits they bring—reduce the efficiency of market operations; they impose costs, demand additional activities, create possibilities for opportunistic behavior, and so on (e.g., Stigler, 1971). In free-market advocacy, the term *efficiency* is thus like a mantra repeated to shield off any interventions orchestrated by the sovereign state and its defined regulatory agencies. In order to understand how this efficiency ideal have been established and entrenched in the regime competitive capitalism, a medium to long-term perspective needs to be taken on corporate governance practices. The earliest laws for the incorporation of businesses date from the eighteenth century in the English common-law tradition (Bryer, 1997), and business charters were originally granted towns, monasteries, and similar social associations to enable, for example, economic venturing (Djelic and Bothello, 2013; Djelic, 2013; Kaufman, 2008; Handlin, Oscar, and Handlin, 1945). Over the course of decades, business promoters were granted business charters to support venturing and business creation, but the business charter was still a contract between the individual, or a team of individuals, and the state. That is, from the very outset, the firm was embedded in the state and was responsive to its interests and priorities. When competitive capitalism "took off" (as economic historians say) by the mid-nineteenth century, characterized by a swift urbanization, the geographical expansion of telegraph systems, the growth of railway mileage and shipping industry tonnage (Braudel, 1992; Hobsbawm, 1975), in short the development of the advanced and differentiated capitalist economic system that we benefit from and maintain still today, firms tended to grow in size on basis of economies of scale and the capital accumulation that followed (Chandler, 1977; Yates, 1989; Perrow, 2002). By the last decades of the nineteenth century there was a widespread concern in both political circles and in the wider public that what was once quite limited businesses have now become gargantuan conglomerates and enterprises, dwarfing even national economies in size and geographical outreach, could now dominate the economy. As a response to such concerns, the antitrust legislation (e.g., the Sherman Act of 1890) sought to limit the size of conglomerates and firms to "protect competition" and small and medium-sized firms from monopolists.

In the following, the content of the two parts and six chapters of the book are briefly summarized:

- In the 1950s (Chapter 1), a group of economists and legal scholars were united in a joint criticism of antitrust policy, advancing the efficiency criteria to discredit the state's ambition to secure competition through legislation. While competition is by and large a condition that is not only praised by free-market advocators but is regarded as the *primus motor* and a *sine qua non* of efficient markets (and, more widely, so-called economic freedom[2]), in the case of antitrust legislation, this stated objective was not accomplished within the existing legislation, this critique made clear. Instead, the state's intervention into supposedly self-regulating and efficient markets harmed the efficiency of the aggregated operations to the level where the competition that was enabled on basis of the legislation could never justify the initial efficiency losses. This early critique of antitrust legislation served a key role in establishing two fundamental principles in the forthcoming critique of state interventions into markets. First, the *efficiency criteria* per se was made manifest as the measure of all things in the new neoclassical economic theory model, serving as a vehicle to criticize the ban on trusts and monopolies. Second, the idea of *efficient markets* (i.e., unregulated markets) as being the superior mechanism and arbiter of market transactions was advanced as an axiomatic principle, closely entangled with the price theory model that was introduced to operationalize the concept of efficiency. Once these two fundamental principles were established, the door was open for a long-term and persistent critique of market interventions that would last for the remainder of the twentieth century and that would ultimately transform into the institutionalization of investor capitalism. The critique of antitrust policy and legislation in the 1950s (and continuing well into the 1980s) would thus be followed by a series of specific themes in the following decades.

- In the 1960s (Chapter 2), the legal scholar Henry Manne (1965, 1967) introduced the concept of "the market for managerial control," based on the voting rights that comes with the ownership of shares and the role of the finance market in assessing managerial decision making quality, either directly through voting or indirectly by selling off stock in companies with perceived low managerial decision making quality. Representing one step closer to a finance market-based control of managers, and no longer taking managerial discretion, rooted in the legal idea of the managers' fiduciary duties vis-à-vis stakeholders, for granted, the market for managerial control was yet another corporate governance mechanisms that celebrated the concept of efficiency and free markets as indisputable components of competitive capitalism.
- In the 1970s (Chapter 3), the idea of a market for managerial control, centred on the key role of the finance markets, at this stage still in its infancy and being highly regulated, local, and essentially still by and large unaccompanied by academic finance theory, and devoid of many of the highly sophisticated yet convoluted practices and assets—think of robot trading and Collateralized Debt Obligations (CDOs), for instance—that is part of the market today, was further advanced under the label of *contract theory.* The contractual theory of the firm or, shorter, contract theory, was based on the idea that the relationship between the managers and directors, located inside the firm and responsible for the day-to-day operation and business practice decision making and the outside investors (i.e., primarily the shareholders but also creditors such as bond-holders), and the shareholders should be

understood in contractual terms. Encouraged by the antitrust critique and is efficiency criterion, and free-market advocacy and the principal idea that managers (or more accurately, their decision-making quality) located inside firms were most effectively monitored on basis of the market valuation of financial assets—stocks and bonds—being issued on the market, contractual theory discredited extant corporate legislation and court rulings granting discretion to managers and directors and its legal statute that enacts the firm *sui juris*, as a free-standing, sovereign legal entity "that owns itself." Instead, proponents of contractual theory claim that there is an (implicit) contract between managers and directors and their investors (i.e., the owners of stock) that *de facto* (albeit not *de jure*, but that is disputed too) makes the managers and directors the investors' agents. Advocates of contract theory thus boldly declares that existing corporate legislation and court rulings are mistaken as they undermine of the allegedly efficient markets for corporate control, and therefore, they call for legal reform. However, just like in the case of antitrust critique, proponents of contract theory articulate their criticism of the present legislation on basis of the one-dimensional efficiency criterion, and turn a blind eye to the wider issues and concerns that policy makers and legislators handle. The antitrust critique, the advancement of the market for managerial control as an efficient mechanism for monitoring and disciplining managers and for assessing managerial decision quality, and the contract theory advocacy thus share a belief in the virtues of the one-dimensional efficiency criterion and in the efficacy of free-market pricing. Still, these three theoretical developments addressed primarily legislation and regulatory control on an aggregated level but did not explicitly address (even though there were certainly practical implications derived therefrom) corporate governance practices. In the early 1980s, agency theory would take that final step towards new boardroom practices that followed consistently from the critique developed in the 1950s, 1960s, and 1970s.

- The agency theory model (discussed in Chapter 4) served to bring together the previous critique of interventions into supposedly efficient markets and rehabilitated the work of Adolf A. Berle and Gardiner C. Means, published in 1934 at the height of the Great Depression and the New Deal project to restore competitive capitalism in America. Agency theory followed closely the idea of efficiency as the only legitimate criterion for economic pursuits on various levels and the belief in free markets, and adopted Berle and Means's (1934) vocabulary to portray the investors of the firm (primarily the shareholders) as being the firm's *principals* and therefore assigned the manager and directors the role as the shareholders' *agents*. Contract theory advanced the idea that the shareholders were *not* the owners of the firm but its "investors." This argument was an attempt to disarm corporate legislation and to bury court ruling cases granting discretion to primarily directors but also, by implications, to the managers whom directors bestow with operative jurisdiction in the firm, enshrined by the so-called business judgement rule being referred to in court cases. If shareholders were not *de jure* the owners—a proposition that legal scholars forcefully dispute on basis of corporate law strictures—they were at least *de facto* the firms' investors. The most important and decisive practical implication following from this re-enactment of managers and directors as agents, no longer being endowed with discretion and autonomy in making business decisions, is that shareholders are entitled to the so-called *residual cash flow* or *free cash flow*. Corporate governance practices should thus be oriented towards shareholder welfare, that is, to maximize the economic value the shareholders can extract from the firm.

- This four-stage efficiency and free-market campaign, evolving over the period from the 1950s to the 1980s gradually advanced and successfully enforced the idea that efficiency is the sole and only legitimate criterion for assessing economic activities, and argued that free markets (characterized by the absence of governmental interventions or other forms of regulatory control), based on the right to contract, are the superior mechanism in the dynamic economic system of competitive capitalism. In the 1990s and 2000s (Chapters 5 and 6), these basic theoretical propositions and declarations were effectively translated into new policy and legislation, regardless of the persistent critique from, for example, legal and management scholars at every stage of the free-market advocacy. Seen in this light, the institutional changes deconstructing managerial capitalism include the abandoning of a multidimensional and heterogeneous regulatory and legal framework, dominated by legislation, regulatory control, and well-defined managerial responsibilities and privileges rooted in the idea that managers are trustees with fiduciary duties as prescribed by corporate law (Smith, 2002; Howard, 1991; DeMott, 1988; Frankel, 1983), and led to the establishment of a more linear and one-dimensional model, rooted in orthodox neoclassical economic theory framework being advocated successfully by economists, lobbyists, and think tankers, sharing the commitment to free markets and its alleged virtues.

In the new era of investor capitalism, corporate governance practices are heavily geared towards the production of shareholder wealth, and the rapid and relentless growth of economic equality in advanced economies reveals that the strategy to promote, justify, and legitimize shareholder interests at the expense of other stakeholders (most notably labour) have been most influential. The question still remains, though, whether these institutional changes and novel legislation, orchestrated over the last six decades and developed on basis of the persistent claim that the efficiency criterion are beneficial *for all social actors*, thus sharing the fruits of increased efficiency gains (the normative and justificatory claim made by, for example, contractarians and agency theorists), and conducive to a sustainable and resilient economic system. The intuitive view among scholars taking neither the efficiency criteria nor free-market virtues as axiomatic and fundamental principles is that the reforms may have benefitted productive efficiency (but still more evidence is needed) but that the allocative efficiency is yet limited. On the other hand, much of the free-market advocacy has been sponsored, founded, financially supported, and otherwise entrenched on basis of neoliberal, neoconservative, and libertarian interests, and financiers have been anxious to support theoretical development and academic arguments in favour of theories that have greatly benefitted their interests and justified their privileges and economic benefits. The lasting conflict and disputes between, on one hand, orthodox neoclassical economic theory, advancing the efficiency criterion and free-market efficacy as foundational principles, and, on the other hand, legal scholars, management scholars, and economic sociologists, not of necessity being opposed to neither efficiency nor free markets per se, but not taking them for granted but making them hypotheses or propositions amenable for empirical testing, indicate that economists have been able to spread their message and to have their tenuous propositions and statements turned into policies and legal reforms (as occurred in the 1990s, "the decade of deregulation" in the U.S.). Advancing policies and legal reforms is thus a matter of proposing bold, yet easily understood statement and to recruit and enroll wealthy financiers to pay for the academic work that serves to substantiate (or, perhaps better, legitimize) these statements. That is, economists have not been successful because they have been right—in fact, evidence suggests otherwise, compromising the much-repeated promise of "efficiency" in considerable ways—but because they have been able to overlook, ignore, and otherwise mute and neutralize the critique of legal scholars, management researchers, and economic sociologists, and many others who have discredited the hyper-simplistic orthodox neoclassical models and its preference for reducing, for example, the realities that a legislators and policy makers need to apprehend in meaningful ways, to one-dimensional and parsimonious constructs and propositions.

However, as we learn from history, in real life and in the messy world of policy-making and legislative practice, being right is not worth so much because there are substantial difficulties involved in proving the accuracy of one's statements (especially in non-experimental sciences such as economics, operating in social worlds that are characterized by emergence, self-referentiality, and recursivity), but telling engaging and intriguing stories about e.g., how markets can do the job for us and how there are significant amounts of money left on the table (i.e., efficiency gains) that we are free to claim if we only want to, is a narrative that is more appealing for many social actors than, as other advisors may insist on, to delve into boring and complex details of, for example, legal strictures and court ruling cases. Therefore, when all is said and done, the story of the de-institutionalization of managerial capitalism and the establishment of its successor, investor capitalism is essentially a narrative about how competing analytical frameworks and storytelling have played a key role in making the world converge with theoretical propositions, in many cases theoretically inconsistent or unsubstantiated by data, and yet have provided attractive blueprints for reform, at least for those financing the neoclassical economic theory policy advocacy over the course of the second half of the last century.

Summary and Conclusion

In the economic regime of competitive capitalism, structured around the corporate system and the limited liability of the business charter, the question of corporate governance is a key issue when explaining the vitality and resilience of this economic system. Writing a sort of "history of the present" (with Michel Foucault's handy phrase) of corporate governance is one way to examine how institutional changes do not occur randomly but is the outcome of the strategic and tactic work conducted by certain groups to shape economic practices into what suits their interest or convictions. To accomplish such reforms and changes, a fair share of storytelling and rhetoric are included in the work. The question of corporate governance matters because is addresses how the corporate system compensate various stakeholders for the work they contribute with to the team-production efforts. Historically, many stakeholders have benefitted from this joint work and risk taking, which in turn has rendered the corporate system and therefore also the economic regime of corporate capitalism legitimate and thus institutionally embedded, rooted in the relations between various participants and interest groups. Today, the situation looks different, with the finance industry coming out as the winner of the institutional and legal changes occurring over the period since the early 1980s.

In addition, corporate governance theory addresses questions about long versus short-term horizons in corporate investment and venturing, wherein the term *efficiency* has been proposed as a euphemism for a short-term, liquidity focus at the expense of long-term investment.[3] Competitive capitalism is essentially based on the idea that risk can be discounted and the adage that money in the hand today is more secure than a little bit more money in the hand tomorrow. Yet, this preference for liquidity and the flight from long-term commitment, propelled by the finance market trading logic where the financial yield can be liquidized at virtually any point of time during the trading day, short-term "efficiency" preferences dominates corporate governance decisions. Therefore, corporate governance is the domain of expertise and professional decision-making where the present and the future are negotiated. In the end, corporate governance is of wider societal and economic interest because it denotes the professional practice to determine the worth of the contributions of various participants in existing operations and within the temporal horizon of existing and perceived investment opportunities.

Notes

1. Another option is to increase the level of debt to compensate for lower economic compensation for work. The supply of credit has grown substantially over the last decades, and the level of global debt is today (in 2015) 286 per cent of world GDP. (Fernandez and Wigger, 2016: 423).

2. The British liberalism tradition is heavily indebted to John Locke's *Two Treatises of Government* (first published in 1690). Here, Locke declares in a much-cited passage that property rights derive from the very embodied work of the subject: "The *labour* of his body, and the *work* of his hands, we may say, are properly his" (John Locke, *Two Treatises of Government*, Book II, Chapter 5). For Locke, individual property is thus original and therefore by definition independent of and regardless of the individual's social relations, both in the hypothetical "state of nature" of classic contract theory (as in Hobbes's *Leviathan* and Rousseau's *The Social Contract and Discourses*) and in civil and political society. Therefore, the role of the state is to preserve the person's property right and this objective becomes "a constant and unchanging goal for citizens and for political society" (Stillman, 1988: 1041). In contrast, one of Locke's true contestants within the philosophy of rights, liberties, and freedom is George Wilhelm Friedrich Hegel's *The Philosophy of Right* (published in 1820). Hegel also makes property and property rights the basis for his legal philosophy, but while Locke's subject is "socially and psychologically somewhat static and protective" (Stillman, 1988: 1040), simply because he has already everything he needs, Hegel's subject is dynamic and developmental. The subject's property and property rights are for Hegel not the end point and the foremost social and political objective but are, on the contrary, the starting point from which the subject can appropriate and apprehend him- or herself: "Since property is the embodiment of personality, my inward idea and will that something is to be mine is not enough to make it my property; to secure this end occupancy is requisite," Hegel ([1820] 1952: 45, §51) writes. This appropriation of the self in turn presupposes a social context and a society that actively encourages further development of social relations:

 > [T]he social context adequate to persons with property does not, for Hegel, define and determine the ultimate social context for fully developed individuals. The social and political world Hegel envisions must grow progressively richer, more complex and more various, after abstract right, in order to generate the values and relations that can enrich the developing individuality that citizens pursue and that politics encourages.
 >
 > (Stillman, 1988: 1041)

 From these different views of the role of property and property rights, Locke and Hegel's ideal society deviates considerably. In the tradition of British liberalism, soon to be complemented by the path-breaking work of Adam Smith that orthodox neoclassical economists venerate, the state should protect property rights in order to secure an essentially negative freedom (with Isaiah Berlin's, 1958, term)—the freedom from the oppression of the sovereign. In the Hegelian tradition of thinking, society and its foremost institution the state is given a more active and enabling role, and consequently Hegel is sceptical of both the metaphor of the contract and other market-based metaphors to describe and apprehend the role of the state: "If contract is understood in its specifically modem sense as 'the exchange of equivalents' in the market place, then it cannot be used as a norm to define the grounds of political authority in the modem state," Hegel writes (cited in Stillman, 1988: 1052). In addition, Hegel rejects any utilitarian consideration (say, the wealth of the nation, value, economic efficiency, or gross national product [GNP]) as what would justify or legitimize neither jurisprudence nor market exchanges (Stillman, 1988: 1052). Moreover, and being of importance for the idea of economic freedom of orthodox neoclassical economists in the Chicago School tradition, to consider freedom solely on basis of being a matter of free choice on basis of market offerings is inadequate as this model ignores the "[c]onstrained alternatives available to be chosen, the ways in which the individual is dependent on forces beyond his control, and the coercion of the institutional setting, the market in which choice occurs," Hegel argues (Stillman, 1988: 1053).

This claim is rooted in two conditions. First, Hegel argues, the competitive-contractual system of market choice "imposes on individuals limited and unappealing ways of thinking and acting"; "[h]uman relations are reified and instrumentalized, mediated by money in calculated and utilitarian contracts. Men are thrown into positions of subservience and dependence" (Stillman, 1988: 1054). That tendency undermines and counteracts the role of private property as a means to further develop the subject's social relations and his ability to apprehend himself. Second, market choice and market transactions tend to, as a matter of fact, to result in contracts that are shaped by the inequality of power. If market are to function smoothly and fairly, that is, they do not demand any governmental intervention, there must be what Hegel calls "double competition"—competition among both buyers and sellers (Stillman, 1988: 1056). In oligopolistic and monopolistic markets (i.e., markets favoured by free-market protagonists, opposing e.g., antitrust enforcement under the auspices of efficiency maximization), this conditions remains unfulfilled, and therefore such markets may only poorly support the subject's own choosing in order to become independent and self-determining (Stillman, 1988: 1053). Therefore, Hegel does not wish to "impose images, metaphors, or models of private property and free contract throughout all social life" (Stillman, 1988: 1054).

The Lockean version of the minimal state that primarily protect property and property rights derived from the subjects embodies capacities and skills, and the Hegelian view of the state that further develops and realizes the potentiality of the individual already endowed with property rights thus leads, despite starting from the juridical statutes of property rights as being elementary rights, to entirely different ideas about what is here referred to as economic freedom. In the British Locke–Smith version, the state is subservient to the market (and should thus be minimized), while in the Hegelian version, the market demonstrates structural incompleteness and/or inequalities in power, and cannot therefore fulfil the role of the state. Sen (1988: 271) remarks that "[i]t is fair to say that in the general tradition of economics the instrumental role of freedom [i.e., negative freedom] is much more prominent than its intrinsic relevance [i.e., positive freedom]." Moreover, Sen 1988: 293) continues: "[T]here is a deep divide between seeing freedom in primarily 'negative' terms—in terms of the absence of constraints imposed by others or the state—and viewing it in a 'positive' form, reflecting what a person is actually free to do, taking everything into account."

The harsh antistatism stance taken by many free market protagonists time and again (e.g., Fisher Black, Milton Friedman, Gary Becker) and their followers are therefore rooted in political philosophy. However, the New Deal policy markets of the Roosevelt administration, whose work the free-market protagonists actively worked to undermine, were "strongly influenced" by continental social reformers and political philosophers such as Auguste Comte and Henri de Saint-Simon and the "the idealistic statism" of George W.F. Hegel and German historicists (Adelstein, 1991: 165). For the New Dealers, the democratic state was "the voice and active agent of the social being in the world of affairs," Adelstein (1991: 165) says.

3. Laverty (1996: 826. Emphasis in the original) defines *economic short termism* accordingly: "I characterize economic short termism as *representing decisions and outcomes that pursue a course of action that is best for the short term but suboptimal over the long run.*" *Efficiency* as an analytical and normative term is thus contingent on stable preference among various stakeholders for liquidity over fixed production capital, and *efficiency* cannot therefore be assumed to be a value-neutral economic term.

Part I

The Making of Shareholder Value Ideology, 1950–1980

1 The 1950s' Antitrust Legislation and Enforcement Critique and Its Response

Introduction

In the early 1950s, the America economy was burgeoning and the U.S. was indisputably the leading economic, political, and cultural power of the world, making an excellent example of the virtues of competitive capitalism that was brought by the bourgeoisie revolution in Europe in the seventeenth and eighteenth centuries in Europe. At the same time, the New Deal policy was now in place, and it generated a series of changes in competitive capitalism, wherein state regulation and oversight and trade unionism were part of the new socio-economic model. For free-market protagonists, the New Deal policy—regardless of its ability to restore and stabilize the capitalist regime of production after one of its major crises—was a lingering concern that needed to be approached from a variety of angles. Conservatives, libertarians, and the pro-business community were critical of the new "collectivism" and the "post-entrepreneurial" American economy, but they also realized that the upsurge of economic well-being among millions of Americans in the new mass-production economy, couched in a Keynesian welfare state model, could not be ignored. In order to advocate their free-market argument, this heterogeneous group of activists identified antitrust policy, having its roots in the last decades of the nineteenth century but being strongly accentuated in the New Deal era, as a legitimate domain of scholarly critique and policy advocacy.

In the mid-1950s, the emerging so-called second Chicago School of Economics, engaging free-market activists and scholars since the 1930s, started to criticize antitrust policy as a political means that was claimed to reduce overall efficiency and that otherwise imposed limitations on market pricing. In this new line of scholarship, both legislation and regulation were now examined on basis of the proposition that "the burden of proof lies on the regulator to show market misconduct and that antitrust regulation should be limited to clear violations of the law and cases of market domination (i.e., some restraints of trade and a few mergers)" (Wood and Anderson, 1993: 26). In addition to this new assumption, many followers of the Chicago school were explicitly sceptical regarding government intervention *in any case* being able to provide greater efficiency than available market solutions, testifying to a systemic scepticism towards the role of the state. Eventually, conservative financiers such as the John M. Olin Foundation targeted America's law school to finance a new approach to legal studies known as Law and Economics: "[C]onservatives in business were desperate to find more legal leverage. Law and Economics became their tool," Mayer (2016: 107) writes.

While orthodox neoclassical economic theory by and large ignores management theory, which explore the inside of the firm qua a team production function—for neoclassicists, the firm is little more than market transactions bundled in ways to minimize transaction costs—and inscribe little value in, for example, managerial decision making, neoclassicists have a harder time ignoring and surpassing legal theory as, for example, corporate law is a so-called constitutional law in the American common law tradition. Furthermore, legislative practices are constitutionally speaking a matter of congressional decision making, and economists, regardless of potential concerns regarding the efficacy of democratic politics among, for example, free-market protagonists, cannot explicitly eschew democracy altogether. In order to bypass rather than to confront legal scholars head-on, free-market protagonists advocated the idea that legislation should prioritize efficiency enhancing criteria, an objective that was claimed to be socially beneficial as it came at the advantage *for all* citizens, the argument proposed. Unfortunately, when neoclassicists speak about *efficiency*, is it something entirely different than it is in the eyes of politicians, policy-makers, legislators, law enforcers (e.g., the courts), legal scholars, and the social scientists more broadly, as, for example, economic inequality is excluded on basis of a loose definition of what is called *allocative efficiency*, one of two efficiency criteria (*productive efficiency* being the other). Therefore, what orthodox neoclassical economists regard as a natural state of free markets, devoid of regulatory control and with minimal legislation in place, is not of necessity a desirable state for legislators. Still, the law and economics school was advanced on the basis that the orthodox neoclassical efficiency criterion is the only legitimate contestant for determining the degree of antitrust enforcement and other comparable market legislation enforcement activities.

This proposition has been contested from the earliest days of law and economics scholarship, and this chapter reviews the literature to demonstrate how free-market advocacy was based on an extensive critique of the legislative centrepiece of the regulation of the corporate system—the antitrust legislation and its enforcement. This critique served as the basis for the forthcoming and gradually expanding scholarship examining constitutional law, for example, corporate law, which eventually formed into the shareholder primacy governance model that today serve as the new conventional wisdom in corporate governance theory and practice. However, between the mid-1950s and the consolidation of shareholder primacy governance in the last decade of the century, much free-market advocacy water has passed under the bridges, and the scene and its actors and their arguments changed considerably over the course of the coming decades. Yet, the law and economics critique of antitrust enforcement served a key role in making economic measures of efficiency a legitimate contestant for the assessment of legislative efficacy.

The U.S. Legal System and the Antitrust Legislation and Enforcement

It is commonplace to remark that in the common-law tradition in e.g., the U.K. and the U.S., there is a difference between the written law and its interpretation made in the courts: "Two courts can interpret and apply the same law in markedly different ways and with very different consequences" (Christophers, 2015: 13). In the case of antitrust enforcement, the legislator (i.e., Congress in the U.S.) regards efficient competition between market participants as a primary social objective as it is assumed to provide societal benefits:

> Economic competition limits excessive concentration of power, dispersing benefits broadly along the contours of a market. It provides a mechanism for upward mobility as new market entrants challenge the primacy of old competitors. Economic competition also promotes individualism, innovation, resourcefulness, wider choice, and greater efficiency as participants try to succeed in a competitive environment.
>
> (Wood and Anderson, 1993: 1)

However, the legislator needs to balance the positive and negative consequences of competition. The same forces that drive competitors toward "[i]nnovation, resourcefulness, and efficiency may also push them toward efforts to reduce competition," Wood and Anderson (1993: 1) say. When being freed from "outside interference," competitors often "collude or resort to unfair practices to restrict competition" (Wood and Anderson, 1993: 1) suggest. In order to maximize the beneficial effects of competition while curbing regressive activities, leading to the reduction of competition, antitrust enforcement includes a variety of activities and resources including legislation, investigations and litigations (i.e., court rulings), and regulatory control.

The U.S. antitrust legislation rest on two major acts, the Sherman Act of 1890 and the Clayton Act of 1914, and various amendments to these laws have been enacted over the years. The Sherman Act makes illegal "all contracts, combinations, or conspiracies that would result in 'restraint of trade' in interstate or foreign commerce, and all monopolization or attempts to monopolize" (Wood and Anderson, 1993: 2). In practice, that means that the legislation has been constructed to proscribe such collusive behaviors as "price fixing, bid rigging, territorial allocation agreements, and resale price maintenance" (Wood and Anderson, 1993: 2). In addition, what Wood and Anderson (1993: 2) refer to as "structural arrangements" that would "tend toward monopolistic practice" are outlawed. The Sherman Act was based on a "pervasive hatred of monopoly and concentrated economic power" and served to demonstrate the political ambition to counteract the advancement of large-scale organization, causing "widespread uneasiness," Adelstein (1991: 166) argues. Practically speaking, the Sherman Act had originally focused on "illegalizing restraints on trade as committed by the large railroad trusts towards small businesses" (Davies, 2010: 74), but once the legislation was in place, it took on a wider significance as being opposed to monopolies and oligopolies.

The Clayton Antitrust Law of 1914 was a continuation of this policy and proscribed "price discrimination, exclusive dealing contracts, and other predatory tactics that the trusts had used to boost their profits" (Cassidy, 2009: 128). The act served to strengthened the Sherman Act and prohibited "price discrimination" (Section 2), "exclusive dealing and tying contracts" (Section 3), and "corporate mergers" (Section 7)—a key target for the critics of antitrust legislation—when their effect would be 'substantially to lessen competition'" (Wood and Anderson, 1993: 2–3). In addition, the Clayton Act bans "interlocking directorates" (Section 8) that would restrict competition. (Wood and Anderson, 1993: 2–3). In 1950, the U.S. Congress passed the Celler-Kefauver Act which closed "certain loopholes" in the Clayton Act by "[p]rohibiting mergers accomplished by either stock or asset acquisitions that would substantially lessen competition or 'tend to create a monopoly in any line of commerce in any section of the country'" (Wood and Anderson, 1993: 3). Therefore, Section 7 of the Clayton Act "became the basis for government challenges of corporate mergers," regardless whether the mergers were horizontal, vertical, or conglomerate "in style" (Wood and Anderson, 1993: 3).

Many commentators regard these pieces of legislation as being a strictly juridical matter, but the law and economic scholars who started to criticize the antitrust enforcement in the 1950s introduced economic theory to examine whether the antitrust legislation actually played the role it purported to play: to uphold competition for the benefit of consumer welfare. In addition, Wood and Anderson (1993: 2) argue that political factors play a key role in the advancement of antitrust enforcement, but add that much antitrust scholarship tends to underrate the influence of "institutional factors." In contrast, Wood and Anderson (1993: 2) suggest that politics, not "economics or bureaucracy," is the best explanation for the "changing vigor and substance of U.S. antitrust regulation through time." As a consequence, legislative activities and the financial resources committed to antitrust enforcement changes, when either Democratic or Republican presidents hold office, making antitrust enforcement a foremost political matter. The fact that "competition" is one of the key objectives of antitrust legislation and enforcement underline the political nature of antitrust ideology. As

Christophers (2015: 54) remarks, "competition" is "[a]n enormously slippery and elusive concept" that has been used in "different ways by different commentators, and for different reasons." Questions regarding what competition means, how it is to be measured, and how much of it is desirable and needed are thus questions that both legal scholars, economists, political scientists, and management scholars are actively discussing. However, regardless of these legal and econometric intricacies, "the halcyon days of vigorous and effective U.S. competition law enforcement had begun [in the late 1950s], and they were to last until the mid-1970s," Christophers (2015: 179) summarizes.

The Sherman Act of 1890 and Beyond

After the Wall Street crash of 1929 and the Great Depression that followed, the Roosevelt administration launched a series of programs and reforms aimed to stabilize and rehabilitate the capitalist economy. Among conservatives, this initiative was widely rejected as a form of collectivism kindred to the socialism that had spread in parts of Europe after World War I. The remarkable success of Keynesian economics and the emergence of the mass-production/mass-consumption economy and the accompanying expansion of welfare state provisions, did little to silence such criticism. One particular concern, targeted by the so-called law and economics school developed at the law school at University of Chicago in the 1950s, was the antitrust legislation that was part of the New Deal reforms.

After the Wall Street crash of 1929, foreboded by excessive speculative activity, also involving a novel class of investors, the proverbial man on the street, and the U.S. economy was cast into its most pervasive crisis to date. The policy-makers saw few other possibilities than to pursue an antitrust policy that inevitably led to an "oligopolization" of the American industry, capable of reaping economics of scale while maintaining at least a minimal level of competition, Rowe (1984: 1518) argues that "[i]n the euphoria of the 1920s that sank into the Great Depression of the 1930s, antitrust fervor faded and ultimately died. The alliance of government and business for World War I's industrial mobilization created a climate of collaboration that lasted for years" (Rowe, 1984: 1518). However, at the end of the 1930s, when some recovery had been made while unemployment and economic hardship was widespread in the U.S., the issue of "economic concentration" reemerged on the Roosevelt administration's policy agenda:

> The Oligopoly Model matched that era's mood to perfection. The Second New Deal had declared war on 'business monopoly' and the 'concentration of private power.' In the day's rhetoric, economic recovery was sabotaged by greedy industrialists, 'fat cats,' and 'economic royalists.' Big Business was in disrepute; faith in government regulators ran high.
> (Rowe, 1984: 1544–1545)

This "revival of antitrust" came from the failure to establish economic growth and prosperity. In the 1937–38 recession, which "pushed production and employment down to distressing levels" (Rowe, 1984: 1520), including strikes, unrest, and even the killing of unarmed laid-off demonstrators at the Ford plant in Dearborn, Michigan (known as the "Dearborn Massacre"), the Roosevelt administration "[s]witched course and turned on Big Business as the culprit of the intractable malaise" (Rowe, 1984: 1520).

As the post–World War II economy started to take off, much of the sentiments of the late nineteenth century vanished, and novel concerns emerged, for example, the widespread presence of oligopolies in a number of industries, potentially indicating that antitrust legislation did not work as intended. In practical terms, the restrictive enforcement of antitrust laws incentivized managers to "consider acquisitions only in unrelated businesses," where the firm's core skills add little economic value," Kaufman and Englander (1993: 54) remark. As a consequence, the cash flow generated in the post-war era of economic boom led to the creation of conglomerates including heterogeneous industries exploiting few synergies. In the 1950s, the critique of antitrust legislation and enforcement were articulated in scholarly communities (addressed shortly). By the 1960s, the antitrust enforcement had regressed to become a kind of lawyers' game in court cases dealing with mergers (made legally suspect or illegal within the present legislation) to define markets at the advantage of their paying clients; that is, the antitrust legislation became more of a legal services industry matter than a factor that promoted economic growth and that secured market competition:

> As enforcement of the new anti-merger law gained stride, oligopoly-based legal norms promised clear rules and quick results. Streamlining the tasks of lawyers and judges, presumptions predicted the prospects of mergers from market shares and market structures, and obviated proof of anti-competitive purpose or effect. In concept, then, the law could stop all mergers that combined high market shares of the leading producers, and thus stem the 'tide of concentration' or roll it back. But . . . this bright promise proved delusive, as anti-merger policy became a Procrustean regimen that fostered large conglomerations while hounding trivial acquisitions in 'numbers games.'
>
> (Rowe, 1984: 1524)

In the period, the antitrust legislation led to an "antitrust craze" and the Federal Trade Commission initiated antitrust enforcement activities "[a]gainst mergers threatening to raise concentration in markets for frozen pizza, for carburetor kits, for urological catheters, and for 'knockdown casket parts,' and attacked local acquisitions of eleven grocery stores and three credit-reporting bureaus" (Rowe, 1984: 1528). Again, it was the lawyers that benefitted the most from being able to participate in "market creation activities" on basis of juridical reasoning and calculative practices that served to define markets on basis of interests rather than factual and indisputable conditions:

> In concept, counting market shares seemed quick and easy, but the market itself became mirage . . . Opposing lawyers fought to make the market look smaller or bigger, in order to bloat or to shrink the defendant's percentage share within. Thus, du Pont escaped breakup by convincing the Supreme Court that it held not a monopolistic seventy-five percent share of the cellophane market, but a modest twenty percent of a broader 'flexible packaging materials' market including other 'reasonably interchangeable' products.
>
> (Rowe, 1984: 1536)

In terms of the legal practice of court rulings, the legal procedures that aimed to uphold the competitive nature of markets could not catch up with the swiftly changing nature of the markets. Like in Aesop's fable, the tortoises of the legal practitioners had a hard time competing with the hares of the market participants and market makers in industry, but unlike in the fable, it was not the tortoises that were ultimately successful (and, needless to say, the fable's morals regarding the virtues of persistency and self-discipline were lost). As the market "invites manipulation," market structure becomes a "delusive norm," Rowe (1984: 1537) says. The tragedy of the antitrust legislation and its ambition to optimize market competition to both enable economies of scale and secure the interests of smaller market participants, not controlling funds sizeable enough to hire lawyers to define markets at their advantage, is that "[a]mid shifting technology and global contests, markets move faster than antitrust suits for their reorganization"—"Antitrust's Big Case is doomed to a tragic cycle: by the time the barbecue is fit for carving, the pig is gone" (Rowe, 1984: 1537).

In summary, as suggested by Rowe (1984), antitrust policy may have served a role in the 1890 to the Great Depression era, but thereafter, oligopolies and conglomerates became the dominant organization form in the American economy, and antitrust enforcement became increasingly difficult to maintain but also to justify. The criticism of the antitrust legislation beginning in the 1950s, discussed in the following, coincided with a series of institutional, macroeconomic, political, and theoretical changes in the 1970s, in particular, including the collapse of the Bretton Woods system in the early 1970s, the first and second oil crises in 1973 and 1978, both caused by geopolitical and military conflicts in the Middle East and political turbulence following from the Watergate scandal (Stein, 2011). In fact, the stock index fell more in the mid-1970s than it did during the Depression (Stout, 2013, 2007), and inflation was soaring and coinciding with economic stagnation more widely, a puzzling phenomenon defying the conventional wisdom of mainstream Keynesian economic theory. The decline of the American economy and the global economy more largely served to benefit a new generation of free-market advocators who had been biding their time in the era of hegemonic Keynesianism, now being ready to take office and to inform policy (Jones, 2012; High, 2009).

The Law and Economics School and the Quest for Efficiency

The Intellectual Basis for the Law and Economics School: Aaron Director and the Concept of Economic Freedom

In the 1950s, Aaron Director initiated research activities that should wed economic and legal theory at the law school at University of Chicago. When Friedrich von Hayek was touring America after the publication of *The Road to Serfdom*, he was approached by a conservative businessman who was willing to fund an "American version" of the book, but Hayek proposed that funds could serve free-market interests better if being used to study "the legal foundation of capitalism in order to plan for competition" (Nik-Khah, 2011: 138). As this project materialized in the summer of 1946 under the label the "Free Market Study" (FMS), it was Aaron Director who was entrusted with the assignment to lead the research project. In the spirit of *The Road to Serfdom*, Director's outline listed "a number of legal and policy areas to investigate in order to move toward a competitive market" (Nik-Khah and Van Horn, 2012: 264). Somewhat surprisingly given the recognition of the Chicago school, the economics department was considered too conventional to be the best location for the research program that Director anticipated, and consequently, the law and economics program was originally seated outside of the university's soon to be famous department of economics. "[I]t important to bear in mind that Director's organized efforts to reconstitute liberalism to countervail collectivism and thereby exert political pressure departed from the tradition of Chicago economics of the 1930s," Nik-Khah and Van Horn (2012: 264) argue. Edward Levi, the dean of the Chicago Law School, assisted Director's project, and the conservative Volker foundation invested in what became known as the "Antitrust Project" (Nik-Khah and Van Horn, 2012: 265).

Director followed the work of Frank Knight, one of the most prominent economists of the first generation of Chicago scholars, in making the *economic system* the scholarly objective of economic analysis. At the same time, Van Horn and Emmett (2015: 1447) argue, unlike Knight, who "followed progressive thinkers in more clearly aligning freedom with democracy," Director treated democracy as a necessary evil, always posing a threat to the economic freedom he held in esteem, an idea that he shared with other Mont Pèlerin Society members such as Friedrich von Hayek and Milton Friedman. More specifically, Director mistrusted liberal intellectuals whom he thought stifled individual freedom because they failed to see the inextricable connection between "economic freedom" and "political freedom," and therefore advocated economic equality as a political objective. This "spirit of equality" was potentially a threat to economic freedom as it rested on polity and legislative procedures that departed from what Director regarded as the only true warrant for economic freedom: free-market pricing and unregulated transactions. In Director's view, political reformers and liberal intellectuals "neglected to appreciate that only under a system of voluntary exchange would freedom be maximised" (Van Horn and Emmett, 2015: 1451). As a consequence, Director deduced, the division of labour between "political and economic institutions had to be preserved" (Van Horn and Emmett, 2015: 1451). For Director, just as for Hayek and Friedman, economic freedom was more highly valued than was political freedom, and economic freedom would, as one of the many auxiliary benefits of free-market pricing advocated, by default, provide political freedom. "Put differently," Van Horn and Emmett (2015: 1447) argues, "whereas classical liberals had seen democracy largely as a check on the abuse of political coercion, post-war liberals often saw it as expanding the potential for political coercion." Directors' antagonists, liberal reformer, and welfare economists (working in a program developed by the Cambridge economist Arthur Pigou), thus tended to refer to the constitution when they advocated political reform and/or legislation and regulatory practices, whereas Director advocated a clearer separation between politics and economic matters. As a consequence, Director was not of necessity opposed to all legislation, but the term *free market* was introduced to denote markets where the presence of "a well-crafted legal framework" preserved "effective competition," and thereby promoted "individual freedom" (Van Horn and Emmett, 2015: 1452).

Already from its outset, the Antitrust Project that further consolidated into the law and economics school was viewed "an attempt to oppose collectivism" (Nik-Khah and Van Horn, 2012: 266), a project that pledged allegiance to the mission "to create and advocate the competitive order" (Nik-Khah and Van Horn, 2012: 266). That is, legal reform, for most part being derived from political agendas and processes, should never be able to intervene into supposedly free markets (or, at least, only do so to a minimal extent) as free markets per se is the warrant of individual freedom, in turn operationalized as "economic freedom," characterized—seemingly recursively or circulatory—by the absence of governmental influence. For Director, "freedom was ultimately the freedom of choice, expressed most completely in a market economy" (Van Horn and Emmett, 2015: 1453).

Based on these principles, Director initiated the law and economics scholarship at the law school at University of Chicago in the 1950s, aimed at targeting legislation—and more specifically, the seemingly poorly functioning antitrust enforcement and its ban on e.g., mergers—and regulations in order to protect economic freedom from liberals, pursuing harmful economic equality initiatives. Writing in hindsight, Gary Becker and George Stigler (1974: 1), two of the most renowned Chicago economists sharing Director's commitment to economic freedom, argue that the "new economic approach" to political behaviour was to develop a so-called positive theory of legislation—a "positive theory of economics" was one of Milton Friedman's favourite slogans—that is, a theory that was not explicitly "normative" (as in the case of welfare economics, the foremost enemy of the Chicago orthodoxy beside Keynesianism) and yet instructing policy-makers how to handle various economic issues and concerns. As Medema (2011: 163) remarks, writing three-and-a-half decades after Becker and Stigler (1974), and more than half a century after Director embarked on his analysis of law and economics, "a distinctive Chicago approach to antitrust analysis" is today "inescapable in both scholarship and jurisprudence." This account testifies to the successful advancement of an economic theory view of law in both scholarly communities and in judiciary practice.

Price Theory and Efficient Markets

By and large, the law and economics school relied on two basic tenets: (1) *price theory*, suggesting that market pricing is the superior mechanism for accommodating and signalling most, if not all, of the public information, and (2) a scepticism towards governmental regulation derived from the statutes of price theory.

To address the former tenet, the very idea of prices as being indubitable vehicles for information and thus for market-making, forming whenever a number of actors are given the ability to individually determine what price they are willing to pay for e.g., a commodity, serve as the basis for the free-market advocacy of the law and economics school. For instance, what is referred to as the Efficient Market Hypothesis (EMH), for decades the cornerstone of the free-market advocacy of Chicagoans and other free-market theorists but today widely treated as what fails to comply with existing empirical data and what is locally inconsistent (Greenwald and Stiglitz, 1986; Grossman and Stiglitz, 1980), is a direct consequence of price theory. Also the second tenet, that governmental regulation by and large undermines the postulated efficiency of unregulated and allegedly self-correcting markets, is derived from price theory. As no centrally located agency, *ex hypothesi*, can determine prices more effectively than comparative market pricing processes, governmental interventions into efficient markets are, by definition, detrimental to overall aggregated efficiency. "It is my belief that economists, and policy-makers generally, have tended to over-estimate the advantages which come from governmental regulation," Coase (1960: 18) writes in a seminal paper. Therefore, when the law and economics school under the leadership of Aaron Director, Milton Friedman's bother-in-law, started to articulate criticism on antitrust legislation and policy, the arguments were based on price theory and the belief in free-market efficiency in combination with the discrediting of any governmental regulation (Van Horn and Emmett, 2015). "I believe Director's conclusions resulted simply from viewing antitrust policy through the lens of price theory," Richard Posner (1979: 928), one of the foremost law and economics scholars, says.

The efficacy of, for example, price theory should be examined in detail as it constitutes the very foundation for the critique of both antitrust legislation and governmental innovations more widely. Bain (1952) says that "normative price theory" is based on the assumptions that, (1) markets are characterized by pure competition, and (2) that such markets are *laissez-faire* economies devoid of regulatory activities:

> [T]he price behavior and results which emerge from pure competitive markets serve as a convenient measuring rod or standard for appraising the price result in other (and more common) sorts of markets, The price results associated theoretically with pure competition are often held to possess certain *normative* properties or to represent a sort of ideas in capitalist pricing behavior. In any event, many of the traditional justifications for a *laissez-faire* economy, which argue that a capitalist economy is through its price system automatically self-regulating toward ideal results, refer explicitly or implicitly to a world of purely competitive markets or, at any rate, of markets not *significantly* different in their operation from markets in pure competition.
>
> (Bain, 1952: 129. Emphasis in the original)

Furthermore, price theory is, Davies (2010: 66) adds, "founded on a core assumption that, faced with a range of comparable options, individuals will rationally select the one that pays them the greatest utility, over and above its cost." The same idea as expressed by Ronald Coase (1960: 40):

> The main advantage of a pricing system is that it leads to the employment of factors in places where the value of the product yielded is greatest and does so at less cost than alternative systems (I leave aside that a pricing system also eases the problem of the redistribution of income).
>
> (Coase, 1960: 40)

There is one unsubstantiated assumption made and one elimination of an important, real-world economy condition being made. First, Coase just assumes out of hand that the pricing system of necessity (and without any accompanying evidence) lead to the highest possible efficiency. That statement can per se be disputed on both theoretical (as information economics theorists do) and empirical grounds (as a fair share of empirical studies of market deregulation have done). Second, Coase generously "leave aside" the question of economic extraction and redistribution, perhaps two of the most pressing concerns in real-world economic policy. That is, Coase is more interested in establishing price theory as a neoclassical convention or heuristic than to address actual problems and the outcomes from prescribed policies.

As Davies (2010) demonstrates, in advancing price theory as a both universally valid model and a theoretical convention within policy advocacy, Coase pursues a methodological dogmatism and what Davies calls "ontological agnosticism." By committing to price theory, Coase and his followers are remarkably self-confidently endorsing an economic empiricism that once and for all renounce all ontological or *a priori* claims about individuals, the economy, and society. Instead, they advocate a "minimal theory" of economic behaviour that strictly and consistently assumes that "individuals act rationally to maximize utility" and nothing else. The study of such practices of utility-maximization should thus, as the recursive argument goes, be based on the very same theory that stipulates this behaviour, that is, price theory. The methodological dogmatism lies precisely in this disqualification of any other methodologies that would deviate from these minimal theoretical structures. The "ontological agnosticism," in turn, consists of the denial of any meaningful and sustainable distinction between, for example, the "economy and society"—a staple argument in neoconservative, neoliberal, and libertarian political statements for decades to come: "Chicago price theory does not view markets as any 'more economic' than, say, a family" (Davies, 2010: 68). Therefore, taken together, the establishment of price theory as the convention for the critique of, for example, antitrust legislation and the critique of any attempts to regulate or monitor supposedly self-regulating markets enables Coase and his followers to impose an authoritative, and for some, trustworthy general theory that purports to explain a variety of economic phenomena and behaviours. Ultimately, Coase and his followers claim to present a theory that in decisive ways diverge from their targeted competing economic model and theory, that of welfare economics, inasmuch as price theory, Coase (1960: 43) says, eschews "aesthetics and morals" as meaningful economic categories. In Coase's view and for other followers of price theory (and, more specifically, the law and economics school), the theory of efficient pricing and market transaction constitute a *positive* and, more important, *final* theory from which numerous policies and de-regulatory initiatives can be derived.

Medema (2011) argues persuasively that Chicago price theory has been used along two alternative routes on basis what definition of economics that have been endorsed. For the second generation of Chicagoans (including Aaron Director, Ronald Coase, George Stigler, and Milton Friedman), it was essentially Frank Knight's definition of economics as the study of an economic system under the influence of scarcity of resources that was adhered to. In addition, Stigler added that "self-interested behavior" (Medema, 2011: 158) was at the centre of economic analysis. However, Gary Becker, a student of Stigler and Friedman, argued in the 1960s that the "economic approach" was of necessity a "rational choice approach" (as Gary Becker's stated in his Nobel address, cited in Medema, 2011: 158). This rational choice approach thus abandoned the study of economic systems and instead rehabilitated an idea first credited to the London School of Economics economist Lionel Robbins, that economics should study "any kind of human behaviour" (Robbins, cited in Medema, 2011: 173). By implication, the program initiated by Director at the Law School of the University of Chicago, originally aimed at understanding how legal rights influence the economic organization and its performance, was overturned to pave the way for the analysis of how rights "[i]mpact the behavior of rational individuals with respect to law" (Medema, 2011: 172). In Becker's (1968) treatment, for example, criminality is understood as a "rational choice," based on calculative practices taking into account the costs and the benefits of pursuing a criminal career rather than to participate in legal activities (see, e.g., Becker, 1968). Law therefore becomes a matter of how individuals recognize and understand legislation and regulation as one input variable within their calculation of individual utility maximization:

> Law is unambiguously about rights, and rights by their very nature exist because of the problem of scarcity, and under the Robbins definition, phenomenon with a scarcity components are, prima facie, amenable to analysis using price theory.
>
> (Medema, 2011: 173)

Following Robbins's definition of economics as the study of "any kind of human behaviour" and equipped with price theory, the third generation of Chicago economists under the leadership of Gary Becker managed to impose an economics imperialism on a variety of human behaviours. In short, this change examined by Medema (2011) led to what Mirowski (2013: 23) refers to as a "Theory of Everything at the End of History"—an economic theory to end all economic theories, yet strangely being based on conventions, as indicated by the conscious elimination of certain economic conditions for the benefit of coherence and convenient simplicity. Needless to say, for its critics, the Beckerian advancement of rational choice theory into virtually all spheres of human lives represents one of the moments where reason "almost lost its mind" (Erickson et al., 2013), turning economic analysis into a mind-boggling orthodoxy, gladly ignoring or discrediting all other competing or alternative views of, for example, human behavior.

However, this new application of economic theory and methods was something entirely different from what Aaron Director advocated in the 1950s, who primarily included the concept of law to make the analysis of the economic system more complete. But the law and economics scholarship forked into a series of domains of study (as is examined in the forthcoming chapters), with Becker's rational choice colonialism being one of its most comprehensive but also most widely disputed scholarly programs (Amadae, 2016, 2003).

The Question at Hand: The Law and Economics Critique of Antitrust Enforcement

The legal scholar Robert H. Bork was Aaron Director's student in 1953–1954 and eventually celebrated Director a "genius" for rendering antitrust an economic concern (Bork, 1978: xiii). For Bork (1978: xiii), price theory is not only a useful theoretical model but is also "[a] powerful form of rhetoric." In contrast, Bork (1978: 3) suggests, "antitrust is a subcategory to ideology," and its "jumble of half-digested notions and mythologies" (Bork, 1978:54). Comfortably seated within the Chicago School tradition (Robert H. Bork was a Yale Law School professor), Bork was deemed eligible for research grants from the conservative American Enterprise Institute (which Bork, 1966: 7, acknowledges financial support from).

Bork and Bowman, 1965: 364), share the Chicagoans' concern regarding the legitimacy and efficacy of antitrust enforcement. Following the Chicagoan lead, Bork and Bowman (1965: 364) are concerned that antitrust laws cannot serve as the "guarantors of a competitive economy." Instead, antitrust enforcement leads to dysfunctional effects where less efficient market actors are protected against competition, paradoxically in basis of a legislation that purports to secure competition per se. The critique of antitrust legislation puts its antagonists in an awkward position: on one hand, they pledge their allegiance to competitive markets as a means to increase the overall efficiency of the economy; on the other hand, the antitrust legislation is declared to be designed precisely on such grounds, and yet its critics reject such claims on basis of a variety of arguments. Ultimately, efficiency triumphs over competition in their advocacy, even though competition per se is always praised by these critics just the same. Thus, it is somewhat confusing when Bork and Bowman (1965: 364) claim that "anti-free-market forces now have the upper hand and are steadily broadening and consolidating their victory," when they speak about antitrust protagonists who explicitly endorse antitrust enforcement because it is conducive to competition. Apparently, in Bork and Bowman's (1965) understanding, the "free market" is something different than the securing of competition. Such opaque and convoluted argumentation characterizes the critique of antitrust enforcement, making the critics balance on the razor's edge. The concern among free marketeers is that antitrust policy is an effect of polity, policymaking, and legislative practice, and therefore, by default, Bork and Bowman (1965: 364) claim, antitrust policy "[i]s also an expression of a social philosophy, an educative force, and a political symbol of extraordinary potency." The critique of legislation and court rulings that secure the otherwise sacred competitive games in markets is thus compromised on basis of a general suspicion vis-à-vis the state intervening into markets:

> The danger arises from a fundamental and widespread misconception of the nature and virtues of the competitive process. This misconception, coupled occasionally with real hostility toward the free market, exists in varying degrees in the courts, in the governmental enforcement agencies, and in the Congress, with the result that in crucial areas the doctrines of antitrust are performing a 180-degree turn away from competition.
> (Bork and Bowman, 1965: 364)

At the same time as Bork and Bowman (1965) express their concern regarding antitrust enforcement, they strongly emphasize competition as the principal mechanism conducive to economic efficiency; in Bork and Bowman's (1965) argument, the virtues of competition cannot be disputed:

> Why should we want to preserve competition anyway? The answer is simply that competition provides society with the maximum output that can be achieved at any given time with the resources at its command. Under a competitive regime, productive resources are combined and separated, shuffled and reshuffled in search for greater profits through greater efficiency.
>
> (Bork and Bowman, 1965: 365)

In addition, and as an unsubstantiated correlate to the virtues of competition, individual freedom to choose is directly dependent on competition, and by implication, free markets: "Competition is desirable . . . because it assists in achieving a prosperous society and permits individual consumers to determine by their actions what goods and services they want most" (Bork and Bowman, 1965: 365). This is the standard Chicago *modus tollens* line of argument: (1) Free markets enable competition and as competition (2) maximize the freedom to choose; (3) free markets are the cornerstone of economic freedom. This in turn disqualifies any attempt to regulate markets, even in cases where the ambition to secure competition is the principal objective of legislation and/or regulatory reform. It is noteworthy that the term *efficiency* is not included above, already implied in the terms "free markets" and "competition"; since antitrust enforcement explicitly secures competition, its critics need to introduce yet another factor in their arguments, and that is the idea that antitrust laws, regardless of its benefits, is harmful for competition and therefore reduces the aggregated efficiency. This rhetoric that first speaks about the virtues of competition while gradually ends up defending efficiency is not a negligible *faux pas* of the antitrust enforcement critique. In fact, the efficiency criterion is the central concerns in the law and economics critique.

Bork and Bowman (1965: 366) explicitly references Aaron Director's claim that so-called *exclusionary practices*, that is, "price discrimination, vertical mergers, exclusive dealing contracts," and so on, in fact "are not means of injuring the competitive process." This claim seems intuitively incorrect and simplistic as the antitrust legislation bans cartels, price-fixing, and similar opportunistic behavior that undermine or reduce fair competition. For Bork and Bowman (1965), however, Director's statements are taken as factual evidence justifying a critique of antitrust enforcement. In this view, antitrust enforcement is treated as a war on the competitive advantages created by companies that actively pursue strategies that differentiate them from their competitors. That is, to reduce a complex matter to a slogan, antitrust enforcement is "the punishment of the strong to defend the weak":

> A conglomerate merger is one between parties that are neither competitors nor related as supplier and customer, an example being the

> acquisition by a locomotive manufacturer of an underwear maker. It neither increases any firm's share of a market nor forecloses anybody from a market or source of supply. The government's attack on such mergers, therefore, has had to be on the theory that they create a 'competitive advantage' which may enable the new firm to injure rivals. The competitive advantage, upon inspection, turns out to be efficiency.
>
> (Bork and Bowman, 1965: 373)

As, for example, economies of scale are substantial, especially in the 1950s' and 1960s' mass-production economies dominated by oligopolies, conglomerates developed through mergers and acquisitions are conducive to increased aggregated efficiency in the economy, yet the antitrust legislation prohibits such efficiency-inducing strategies. "One of the court's explicit fears was that the merger would create 'economies of scale' (efficiencies due to size) which would put other companies at a competitive disadvantage," Bork and Bowman (1965: 373) stress that

> the Court has with increasing frequency taken extreme anticompetitive positions . . . This means that the Court is making major social policy, and the policy it chooses to make today is predominantly anticompetitive.
>
> (Bork and Bowman, 1965: 375)

This is bad policy in Bork and Bowman's (1965: 373) view, wherein the legislator makes "'the vigor of competition' an end in itself," even at the expense of "societal wealth" and to *de jure* impose a ban on the strategic creation of competitive advantage:

> The result is simply to label efficiency as anticompetitive whenever it may cause injury to competitors or make it more difficult for new firms to enter the market. All efficiency, however, is likely to have just such effects. [The Federal Trade] Commission's rationale, consistently applied, would thus favor inefficient producers at the expense of the consuming public over enormous ranges of economic activity.
>
> (Bork and Bowman, 1965: 373)

In their concluding remarks, Bork and Bowman (1965: 374) do not hesitate to make a straightforward connection between the alleged ban on much-desired efficiency and economic decline as its foremost consequence: "[L]aw that makes the creation of efficiency the touchstone of illegality can only tend to impoverish us as a nation."

The same arguments are advanced by Bork (1966), casting doubt on the relevance of "legislative intent" of the Sherman Act (Bork, 1966: 7, n. 4). Bork (1966: 8) here cites judge Billings Learned Hand's court decision in antitrust cases, saying that as a legal matter, "great industrial consolidations are inherently undesirable, *regardless of their economic results.*" Moreover, Judge Learned Hand claimed that Congress "did not condone 'good trusts' and condemn 'bad' ones; it forbade all." (Judge Learned Hand, cited in Bork, 1966: 9). However, in Bork's (1966: 12) view, a principal issue in, for example, the Sherman Act is that Congress was very concerned that the law "should not interfere with business efficiency, while in fact this is precisely what is does as e.g., all kinds of mergers, aimed at exploiting economies of scale, are illegal within in the present legislation. Not the least Senator John Sherman (R-OH) himself, "took great pains to stress that his bill would in no way interfere with efficiency," and proposed that his bill would "outlaw only those mergers which created great market power" (Bork, 1966: 26). In Bork's (1966: 30) view, the legislation does not effectively distinguish between efficiency-enhancing monopolies and "monopoly by predation in driving smaller rivals from an industry." As consumer benefit is, Bork argues time and again, the *only* legitimate legal objective in the antitrust legislation, this prohibiting of efficiency-enhancing business decisions that leads to competitive advantage is therefore inconsistently counteracting the legal intentions of the legislator:

> Monopoly by efficiency, however, is probably beneficial to consumers and to small business suppliers and customers of the monopolists—at least by comparison with the policy alternative. Breaking up monopoly gained by efficiency is likely to impose higher costs at that level of the distributive or productive chain to the detriment of consumers and all vertically related firms.
>
> (Bork, 1966: 30)

More specifically, as a piece of legislation, the Sherman Act "tells judges very little," Bork (1966: 48) claims. In another article, Bork (1967: 252) proposes that the Sherman Act, "seems to mean the prohibition of certain commercial conduct on moral or ethical grounds." Bork here introduces price theory model as a key resource in assessing the efficiency of, for example, mergers, and deplores that decisions are not sufficiently taking into account such economic factors. Faithful to his Chicago school training, Bork (1967: 243) suggests that "economics may be a science best confined to analysis and shunning the normative." Bork here sees a problematic blending of polity, jurisprudence, and economic thinking, where the term *efficiency*—Bork's guiding lights and measure of all things—is never properly defined, nor examined within a wider socioeconomic context:

> In constitutional law, for example, courts are sometimes forced to engage in unstructured political decisions precisely because they are dealing with values and principles which are by definition to be kept out of the hands of the legislature.
>
> (Bork, 1967: 250)

More important, Bork (1967: 242) is concerned with how "antitrust policy is determined, far more than most people realize, by the Supreme Court." Worse still, Bork (1967: 243) argues that "the existence of an unelected, somewhat elitist, and undemocratic judicial institution thus makes theory more important than it might otherwise be in our governing processes." Being a quite curious statement from a legal scholar who may be expected to respect constitutional democratic institutions and its legislative practices and routines, Bork (1967) is arguably inspired by Aaron Director's sceptical attitude towards democracy as what arguably tend to subordinate economic issues under broader and thus more imprecise political objectives. Therefore, Bork (1978: 54), contradicting his own stipulated "consumer benefit" criterion, suggests that the Supreme Court's "uncritical sentimentality about the 'little guy'" should be scrutinized. Given that Bork (1966, 1967) himself is sceptical regarding the Sherman Act's capacity to enhance consumer benefits, this critique of the Supreme Court ruling is surprising and inconsistent with Bork's overarching critique of the antitrust legislation. Still, the ultimate objective of Bork's antitrust enforcement critique remains overall efficiency, defined on basis of price theory:

> The [antitrust] jurisprudence . . . consists of the notion that under existing antitrust statutes the courts may properly implement a variety of mutually inconsistent goals, most notably the goals of consumer welfare and small business welfare. Together, these ideas are creating a broad trend of policy directed less to the interest of consumers in free markets than to the interest of inefficient producers in safe markets.
>
> (Bork, 1967: 242)

If law is to be declared an "anachronism" (Bork, 1966: 31) and the ruling of the Supreme Court and other legal institutions are disqualified, it needs to be done on basis of economic theory, Bork (1966, 1967) suggests. In Bork's law and economics critique of antitrust enforcement, the seven decades of legislative practice and court rulings are conspicuously ignorant of elementary orthodox neoclassical economic theory, an original claim to make for a legal scholar who is otherwise informed about the intricacies of constitutional law such as corporate legislation. For Bork, legislative practice and court rulings should not confuse social and political agendas and allegedly objectively determined economic conditions.

The Legal Theory Views of the Chicago Antitrust Critique

For critics of the law and economics literature, legal phenomena (say, corporate law and the granting of business charters to business promoters) are not primarily understood as empirical phenomena but are instead examined on basis of "the logic of neoclassical economics" (Swedberg, 2003: 1). Not only are the analytical framework (i.e., price theory and the efficient market hypothesis) assumed to be correct and therefore qualify as what can be used to determine the validity of certain claims or conditions, but this analytical framework is also "[e]xplicitly normative in nature and advocates how judges *should* behave and how legislation *should* be conducted—usually so that wealth is maximized" (Swedberg, 2003: 1). That is, even before the underlying analytical framework have been critically examined and corroborated against empirical data, it is already qualified, its proponents believe, to instruct, for example, lawyers and judges on how to think and how to rule in court cases. "The achievement of the Law and Economics school was to convince judges and lawyers, not to mention other economists, that competition policy should be exclusively concerned with the goal of maximizing efficiency," Davies (2010: 63) remarks. For the critics, both regarding the theoretical consistency of the analytical framework and its ability to stand the test of empirical data and in terms of its alleged legal implications, are questionable to the extreme.

The critique of the law and economics school and the work of legal scholars such as Robert H. Bork was carefully responded to by a series of legal scholars, advancing a number of arguments that justify antitrust enforcement. Elzinga (1977) argues that in all legislative practice, there are tradeoffs between efficiency and "equity" (i.e., wider social benefits) that needs to be recognized. This is the case also in antitrust legislation where the issue of efficiency is certainly not ignored while it is recognized within the wider horizon of the legislator's interests and concerns. The efficiency criteria is based on the virtue of "the maximization of the value of total output," but such efficiency maximization can only be accomplished "[i]f firms are supplying goods and services in accord with consumer preferences and minimizing production costs in so doing" (Elzinga, 1977: 1192); that is, efficiency is a fairly complex parameter to measure, not strictly concerned with internal operations but also dependent on market demand. For instance, if a garment company maximizes its efficiency in producing a certain type of socks, but the socks are not appealing to very many consumers, forcing the company to retail their product at a discount price, the internal efficiency gains are not compensating the low market demand, making the overall efficiency lower. This remark makes the efficiency criteria complicated to serve as the measure of legislation. In addition, if the one-dimensional criterion of efficiency is complemented by equity considerations, as it is in the antitrust legislation, the critique of antitrust enforcement become even more complicated.

Elzinga (1977: 1194) argues that "the conventional wisdom" among economists is that there is "a tradeoff between efficiency and income equality." Income inequality is an economic issue commonly being subject to policy-making, Elzinga (1977: 1194) argues; that is, "antitrust enforcement generally serves to help those at the low end of the income distribution range without decreasing efficiency." Moreover, antitrust enforcement is "consistent with the equity preference for small business and a reduction in aggregate concentration," thus making "antimerger enforcement" a policy that ensures competition "with minimal diseconomy" (Elzinga, 1977: 1198–1199). However, this claim of "minimal diseconomy," i.e., minimal loss of efficiency, is precisely what, for example, Robert H. Bork (1966) disputes. In contrast, Elzinga (1977) argues that it is possible to both pursue "equity goals" and efficiency goals within the present legislation: "Economic policy normally is a matter of tradeoffs, hard choices where benefits come only with significant costs attached. Conceptually at least, antitrust policy represents an exception to this general rule" (Elzinga, 1977: 1199–1203). In addition, Elzinga (1977) claims that the antitrust legislation was never intended to maximize efficiency, simply because the legislators in the late 1880s and thereafter recognized more significant social challenges than a declining or suboptimal efficiency. As series of statements from court ruling decisions testify to the wider socio-economic significance of the legislation, stretching beyond the strict efficiency concern that certain economists and legal scholars are persistently referencing. One such case is judge Billings Learned Hand decision in *United States v. Aluminum Co. of America*, emphasizing diversity in the market and competition:

> [Congress in passing the Sherman Act] was not necessarily actuated by economic motives alone. It is possible, because of its indirect social or moral effect, to prefer a system of small producers, each dependent for his success upon his own skill and character, to one in which the great mass of those engaged must accept the direction of a few.
>
> (Judge Billings Learned Hand, *United States v. Aluminum Co. of America*, Cited in Elzinga, 1977: 1204)

Another exemplary case is Chief Justice Warren's statement in *Brown Shoe Co. v. United States*:

> It is competition, not competitors, which the Act protects. But we cannot fail to recognize Congress' desire to promote competition through the protection of viable, small, locally owned businesses. Congress appreciated that occasional higher costs and prices might result from the maintenance of fragmented industries and markets.
>
> (Chief Justice Warren, *Brown Shoe Co. v. United States*, Cited in Elzinga, 1977: 1204)

In addition, *even if* efficiency would have been the overruling objective of antitrust legislation—which it isn't, Elzinga (1977) concurs—the very term efficiency per se is too complex to measure and is composed of too many factors to be a qualified candidate for how economic performance and resilience should be ensured on basis of legislative practices. As economics is not "a laboratory science" (Elzinga, 1977: 1212), it cannot provide neutral and empirically substantiated measures that are qualified to inform legislative practice. Nor does economic theory attempts to reconcile, for example, efficiency and equity objectives within the domain of legislation. As efficiency is the measure being easier to reach an agreement about and to normatively endorse, "[i]t is more likely that two economists will agree that a policy is efficient than that it is socially desirable on equity grounds" (Elzinga, 1977: 1212). The parsimonious nature of economic theory thus always already undermines any equity criterion simply on basis of its indeterminacy and the complicated relations between different criteria. Elzinga (1977: 1212) thus concludes that efficiency may be a relevant concept within economic theory, being at the very core of the economics discipline, while it is less useful in legislative practice:

> Efficiency is the scientific linchpin of economics. It is closer to the concept of the atom in chemistry or energy in physics than to the political theorist's 'state' or the theologian's 'grace.' Efficiency is itself valueless but, because it so directly promotes or prevents many social objectives, it is capable of securing normative admiration or disdain.
>
> (Elzinga, 1977: 1212)

This brings us to Elzinga (1977: 1212) principal objection to the antitrust enforcement critique on basis of economic theory, that it exclusively advocates the efficiency criterion as the basis for legal reform: "Efficiency . . . is not to be pursued as the goal of goals. Quite the contrary; from the perspective of political economy, a viable competitive market system, appropriately seasoned with antitrust, is only a means, not an end" (Elzinga, 1977: 1212). The legislator's "efficiency as mean" model versus the economist and law and economics scholars' "efficiency as goals" model thus represent two irreconcilable and, as Kuhn (1962) would say, incommensurable models, whereof Elzinga (1977) disqualifies the latter view as a legitimate contestant as it ignore all wider social and economic issues that the antitrust legislation considers. This critique of the efficiency criterion per se is a persistent theme in the critique of the law and economics antitrust re-entrenchment argument.

Pitofsky (1979: 1051) remarks that "antitrust economists and lawyers" have had "[s]uch success in persuading the courts to adopt an *exclusively* economic approach to antitrust questions," but claims that it is "[b]ad history, bad policy, and bad law to exclude certain political values in interpreting the antitrust laws." Consistent with Elzinga (1977) argumentation, Pitofsky (1979: 1051) questions the idea that antitrust legislation should be "blind to all but economic concerns," as this legislation would lead to the dominance of "a few corporate giants," potentially being in the position to be able to eliminate market competition altogether. Speaking about the important difference between "productive efficiency" and "allocative efficiency" (see Rowe, 1984, and Hovenkamp, 1985, discussed in detail later), Pitofsky (1979) suggests that factual monopolies generate "allocative inefficiencies" that are yet socially undesirable. For instance, one of the key concerns for the legislators who prepared the Sherman Act was how to improve the free market and competitive capitalism at large to "head off direct regulation or Marxist solutions" (Pitofsky, 1979: 1057). That is, the Sherman Act protagonists were not the wrongheaded centralists that sought to regulate free markets on basis their own interest, nor to self-servingly reinforce agencies and regulatory bodies in, for example, Washington D.C., but they were social reformers that regarded, for example, the radicalization of the blue-collar worker community as a real threat to competitive capitalism and political stability. These historical conditions are by and large overlooked by the antitrust critics. Therefore, Pitofsky (1979: 1058) argues, it is true that "an antitrust system that occasionally disregards claims of efficiency" is now in operation but primarily because efficiency and nothing but efficiency was never a candidate for being the sole and indisputable objective of antitrust legislation. To claim this should be the case *ex post facto*, when the antitrust legislation per se has provided the ground for such a critique to be formulated as there are now in fact competitive and reasonably efficient markets in place, represent a backward mode of reasoning that overlooks the very basis of its argument: "Although economic concerns would remain paramount, to ignore these non-economic factors would be to ignore the bases of antitrust legislation and the political consensus by which antitrust has been supported," Pitofsky (1979: 1079) summarizes.

Rowe (1984) articulates a similar concern regarding what he refers to as "the Efficiency Model" advanced as part of the critique of the antitrust legislation. Rowe argues that law and economics scholars advocate a theoretical model—that of market efficiency—that is non-dynamic and that assumes "certainty where none exists" (Rowe, 1984: 1513). Relying on orthodox equilibrium economics (see, e.g., Kaldor, 1972), where efficiency is accomplished on basis of market prices' ability to accommodate public information, the antitrust critique "posits a timeless universe in balance, with ideal resource use for all. Such harmony, however, can never exist in the real world" (Rowe, 1984: 1549). More specifically, law and economics scholars fail to develop a meaningful theory of the firm including how the directors and top managers' strategic decisions create economic value not only on basis of price competition (see also Williamson, 1981: 1539):

> Modern organizations integrate production with finance, distribution, and promotion, catering to buyers with inducements and accommodations aside from price. As enterprise becomes multi-dimensional and protean, it strokes, seduces, and satisfies buyers not by price alone but in myriad ways. Indeed, when enterprises offer packaged product/services in shifting arrays, while competition becomes a contest among organizations, capabilities, and systems, the model's product/price concepts catch less and less of the essence of enterprise rivalry.
>
> (Rowe, 1984: 1543–1544)

As the level of the firm is not properly examined within orthodox economic theory, the strategies of individual firm competing within the existing price system is excluded from the analysis and argument proper. For instance, in transaction costs theory, a theoretical framework derived from price theory, the firm is little more than a bundle of transactions, generating minimal aggregated transaction costs (see Coase, 1937), but the internal operations of the firm nevertheless and seemingly inconsistently remain outside of the interest of the orthodox neoclassical model, preoccupied with making the market the origin and privileged source for all economic activities. The consequence is, Rowe (1984) argues, that the diversity and heterogeneity of industries and markets are never incorporated in the Efficiency Model and that, in turn, seriously undermine the credibility of the antitrust argument. That is, if markets are *made*, rather than *presupposed* and deemed to precede the actual behaviour of market participants, then, for example, "business behaviour" should be integrated into the Efficiency Model:

> Most critically, if business behavior defines market structure, not vice versa, what becomes of the market itself as a premise for antitrust norms? Above all, if oligopoly's essence—the suspect syndrome of a few producers in concentrated markets—is no longer presumptively evil, the grand synthesis that gave antitrust law coherence for a generation has fallen apart.
>
> (Rowe, 1984: 1547)

Instead of presenting a coherent and solid model of antitrust legislation, which would recognize the diversity and heterogeneity of industry, Rowe proposes that the law and economics antitrust legislation critique floats on the 1970s' disenchantment with government intervention and is satisfied with simply asserting that market-based pricing is the solution to a long series of efficiency and governance problems. This makes the free, unregulated market, devoid of meaningful antitrust legislation, the answer to all economic policy questions:

> With bold strokes, the Efficiency Model shifts antitrust norms into reverse . . . Producers' vertical integration or constraints on distributors are efficient, for they save transaction costs. Mergers are efficient, for they allow economies of scale. Conglomeration is efficient, since rational competitors strive to cut costs and maximize profits, else why would they conglomerate? To economic libertarians, even price fixing among competitors is efficient, because it coordinates fragmented information in rational ways. So, in somersaults of doctrine, what was once legally suspect becomes a manifestation of efficiency.
>
> (Rowe, 1984: 1548–1549)

That is, "[p]er the truisms of axioms and circular logic, the market ensures efficiency and cures inefficiency if meddling governments keep out," Rowe (1984: 1549) writes. By drawing on price theory and advancing EMH, proponents of what Rowe (1984) calls the Efficiency Model offers "easy answers to antitrust law's hardest questions." For Rowe (1984), a legal scholar, the law and economics critique of antitrust legislation is unsubstantiated and provides no robust basis for the legal reform it proposes: the questions of "allocative efficiency" and "productive efficiency" are never fully examined and properly understood at the level the firm, and many other institutional factors are simply ignored, and therefore, the Efficiency Model advanced by law and economics scholars, Rowe (1984: 1550) stresses, "cannot reveal antitrust policy choices." On the contrary, despite presenting theoretically incredible models, ignoring empirical data and not the least the legal issues at hand that corporate law and antitrust legislation address—potentially in an inadequate and only partially efficient manner, but nevertheless still consider—"[t]he rising logic of efficiency-based norms compels headlong, unending antitrust retreat" (Rowe, 1984: 1567). Law and economics scholars thus essentially want to reform the extant law on basis of the sheer rhetorical force of their theories, price theory and EMH, and in advocating such legal reform, Rowe (1984: 1569) says, "the servant becomes the master, first abetting, then usurping, antitrust law."

In Rowe's (1984) account of the antitrust legislation retrenchment literature, law and economics scholars roll out their theoretical arguments to make the legislation and court rulings comply with yet-to-be-corroborated theoretical propositions. Not being overtly concerned with or embarrassed by the incomplete data, proponents of antitrust legislation retrenchment are eager to instruct legal scholars and practitioners on how to think about economic matters of joint concern and happily impose efficiency criteria as the *only* justifiable and credible measure for economic pursuits (Easterbrook and Fischel, 1996: 38). This "crusade" (with Rowe's polemical term) against antitrust legislation (and virtually any regulatory practice that are deemed to undermine the alleged efficiency of markets) is thus a consequence of the neoclassical economic theory doctrine upon which the antitrust critique rests, making the praise of efficiency, the belief in the virtues of free markets, a scepticism towards centrally located agencies, and a disregard for firm-specific activities and competencies its distinguishing marks.

While Rowe (1984) discredits the efficiency criteria not so much on basis of its disregard for equity concerns (as addressed by Elzinga, 1977), but because the "market efficiency" is not a static condition but the outcome from the strategic, tactic, and operational activities on firm and industry level, Hovenkamp (1985) examines the very term *efficiency* per se and how, for example, consumer behaviour inform the efficiency criteria and thus makes it a weak contestant for being the driver of legal reform. As Hovenkamp (1985) presents a non-trivial argument, the following sections examine his line of reasoning in some detail. First of all, Hovenkamp (1985: 218) questions the law and economics school claim that antitrust legislation has been passed without any decisive economic theory influences. Even if the 1950s and 1960s antitrust critique pursued such arguments, "[f]ederal antitrust policy contained a strong economic element much earlier," Hovenkamp

(1985: 218) argues. "In fact," he continues, "one must go all the way back to the first thirty years of antitrust enforcement to find a policy that can reasonably be characterized as having little or no economic content." Therefore, the claim that antitrust enforcement has been developed without recognizing economic interests is unsubstantiated and invalid. Nevertheless, in the 1950s' law and economic critique of antitrust enforcement, the efficiency criteria is brought forwards as the sole legitimate contestant on basis of well-entrenched neoclassical economic theory doctrines, Hovenkamp (1985: 223) proposes that "[e]conomists have long stated that theoretical economic models cannot evaluate a state of affairs on the basis of how its wealth is distributed. These models are capable only of distinguishing the efficient from the inefficient." More specifically, the "Chicago School Model" that Hovenkamp (1985: 223) examines is "an approach concerned exclusively with efficiency." The Chicago School Model is rests on two basic assumptions, Hovenkamp (1985: 226) proposes:

> Orthodox Chicago School antitrust policy is predicated on two assumptions about the goals of the federal antitrust laws: (1) the best policy tool currently available for maximizing economic efficiency in the real world is the neoclassical price theory model; and (2) the pursuit of economic efficiency should be the exclusive goal of antitrust enforcement policy.
> (Hovenkamp, 1985: 226)

Moreover, both these assumptions are controversial and disputed: the first assumption "[r]aises several economic questions about the internal integrity of the neoclassical price theory model, as well as questions about the ability of *any* economic model to identify efficient policies in the real world" (Hovenkamp, 1985: 226). Analysts and commentators not committed to price theory do not accept the claim that an economic model relying on market prices only, and nothing else is capable of ensuring the highest possible efficiency. In addition, if that proposition would be accepted, the distinction between economic theory and policy making and legislation would nevertheless impose an additional barrier for the implementation of liberal antitrust reform. The second statement, in turn, carries legal and hence political connotations that the first assumption per se cannot mediate or bury: "The second statement is probably contrary to the intent of the Congresses that drafted the various antitrust laws" (Hovenkamp, 1985: 226). Hovenkamp (1985) thus proposes, in line with several other legal scholars' work, that the legislation, the legal intent, existing court rulings, and the underlying political objectives of antitrust enforcement cannot be reduced to and examined on the one-dimensional level of efficiency, even if economists and legal scholars inspired by economic theory believe this is a both convenient and socio-economically relevant approach to legal critique and reform.

This favouring of supposedly straightforward economic parameters at the expense of any other factors worthy of consideration is a direct consequence of what has been referred to as "economics imperialism" (Medema, 2011), one of the distinguishing mark of the latter Chicago price theory school, dominated by Gary Becker's gradual expansion of rational choice theory into all corners of human life, as well as into the intimate sphere of, for example, marriage and procreation. "Within the Chicago School model humankind's economic motives 'trump' any noneconomic motives or else these noneconomic motives are irrelevant to the working of the model" (Hovenkamp, 1985: 230). This "gravity" of rational economic decision making, keeping the world in place through the uncoordinated decisions of thousands and millions of market participants, all seeking to "maximize their utility" leads, *ex hypothesi*, to a form of economic punishment whenever an actor deviate from the conventional wisdom of efficiency maximization:

> [T]he Chicago School model may allow that occasionally firms or actors in them make decisions not motivated by profit-maximization. However, these decisions are either random and incapable of being fit into the profit-maximization model, or else they are of no consequence to antitrust policy because they are self-deterring. A firm that does not make profit maximizing decisions will, other things being equal, lose market share to one that does.
>
> (Hovenkamp, 1985: 230, note 86)

Curiously, the "economic freedom" cherished by free-market protagonists such as Friedrich von Hayek and Milton Friedman thus imposes a form of hyper-conformism wherever markets are established, voluntarily or by the force of market-makers such as the state and transnational agencies such as the World Bank or the International Monetary Fund. This compromises the very concept of freedom to primarily denote "the ability to act on one's own calculations" (Gershon, 2011: 540), a calculative practice that ultimately aim to create individual advantages that are also someone else's disadvantage. By implication, derived from its belief in prices and rational calculative practices, the Chicago school price theory "adheres closely to the classical school's strong preference for a 'free' market—that is, a market left alone by the State and its agencies unless a powerful reason exists for interfering" (Hovenkamp, 1985: 231). Only when markets remain unregulated can the virtues of maximized efficiency be fulfilled and therefore regulatory attempts are disqualified, even in the case where the objective is to secure competition.

These two propositions, stipulating that prices accommodate all market information and markets should be unregulated for the benefit of efficiency maximization, provide the Chicago school with a fairly straightforward model for how to assess, for example, legislation and policy: "If a policy produces bigger gains to businesses than it does losses to consumers, the Chicago School would approve the policy as efficient" (Hovenkamp, 1985: 231). This is, in turn, based on a utilitarian credo wherein the objective to create the biggest possible gain can tolerate individual losses. Taking such a credo and its derived ethics aside, there are several concerns regarding the accuracy of the Chicago model and its antitrust critique. First, Hovenkamp (1985: 234) proposes that there is a distinction between the Efficiency Model's definition of efficiency, which serves the "model's own purposes very well," and "any concept of 'efficiency' that realistically can be applied to policymaking in the real world—more particularly, in a real world democracy." Second, it can be maintained that that "'efficiency' cannot be the only relevant factor in real world policymaking; or alternatively, that any argument to that effect rests on premises that can be neither verified nor falsified" (Hovenkamp, 1985: 234). In the first case, the concept of efficiency used in the theoretical model has low validity when it comes to actual policy-making. In the second case, the claim that "efficiency," no matter how it is measured, has never been a legitimate contestant for being the sole measure of economic policy-making, and even if that would be the case, there is no robust evidence supporting the claim that efficiency is best accomplished on basis of de-regulatory policies.

Furthermore, critics of the Efficiency Model claim that the concept of efficiency must be separated into *productive efficiency* and *allocative efficiency*. Productive efficiency denotes how the efficiency of existing assets and resources can be maximized within a present production system, complicated to modify on short-term notice. Allocative efficiency, in turn, includes the overall economic activity, including how the benefits and gains accomplished on basis of increased productive efficiency are distributed and shared in society. Unfortunately, the literature suggests that these two types of efficiency are not independent variables, and "occasionally practices that increase a firm's productive efficiency reduce the market's allocative efficiency" (Hovenkamp, 1985: 226). As a consequence, a meaningful efficiency concept, which in turn can play a role in, for example, antitrust policy-making, should attempt to maximize *net* efficiency gains, not only the productive efficiency. The Chicago school model dictates that allocative efficiency is exclusively defined by market activities—the market prices assets and resources more effectively, and therefore, each market participants earn precisely what they deserve in terms of their contribution to the productive efficiency—and therefore even the "the legislative history of the antitrust laws is unimportant," unless it shows that the legislative history "supports or undermines the model" (Hovenkamp, 1985: 215–216); in brief, legislation is justified only in the case where it supports the theoretical proposition, which is a *non sequitur* argument, a "let the tail wag the dog" position. Still, the legislation at hand was factually not implemented in the first place to prove some theoretical proposition but to maximize net-efficiency on basis of perceived trade-offs and competing objectives and interests, articulated by various participants. As a consequence, Hovenkamp (1985: 239) summarizes, "[t]he more serious difficulty with Chicago School policy concerning efficiency is its insistence that the *exclusive* goals of the antitrust laws should be to maximize net *allocative* efficiency, and that the classical price theory model can define the circumstances under which this will occur."

One factor that complicates the market-based allocative efficiency maximization argument is that, for example, "consumer statements" frequently "seem to be inconsistent with consumer exercises of preferences in the marketplace" (Hovenkamp, 1985: 242). Consumers express certain beliefs and expectations, but their actions demonstrate a significant deviation from such stated beliefs and expectations (see, e.g., Rizzo and Whitman, 2009: 920). For instance, people may claim they prefer small, local shops while they still take advantage from the economies of scale of large chains and their local store to optimize their grocery budgets. This behaviour is not observed because the consumer dislikes the small, local shop or because he or she is not wary of the risks of economic concentration but because the consumers' "own unilateral purchase decision is not enough to change the economic structure of society" (Hovenkamp, 1985: 242). Uncoordinated market behavior does not, as postulated by the Chicago school model, lead to maximized efficiency given these beliefs and expectations. Instead, if "the world containing the small shops" is more "efficient" (based on the proposition that small shops are what consumers wants, consistent with the economic freedom doctrine and the freedom of choice ideology) than the world without them, then the antitrust policy (or legislative frameworks and other regulatory practices) that protect them would be "efficient" as well (Hovenkamp, 1985: 242–243). The Chicago school model disqualify this line of reasoning on basis of the market efficiency criterion, but that criterion does not recognize the uncoordinated nature of consumer choice, which ultimately leads to a social dilemma where everyone hopes that someone else would be willing to pay the higher per unit price to maintain the local stores and that such consumer behaviour would keep local neighbourhoods and inner-city centres vibrant and attractive (another, more recent case would be, e.g., Internet shopping, where, e.g., bookstores have a hard time to compete with web-based retailers on basis of lower price levels).

In Hovenkamp's (1985: 243) view, this example is indicative of the pervasive "externalities" of almost every market transaction. For instance, it has proved complicated to rely on individual consumer behaviour to control air and water pollution, "even though the great majority of consumers presumably prefer unpolluted air and water" (Hovenkamp, 1985: 243). Therefore, to return to the distinction between classes of efficiency, "in the real world," Hovenkamp (1985: 243) argues, "efficiency and distributional *effects* generally cannot be separated from one another." Nor can allocative efficiency be subsumed under productive efficiency, based on the standard argument in orthodox neoclassical economic theory that economists should only study and provide recommendations regarding how efficiency is maximized—a credo that ignores allocative efficiency. On basis of the concern for net efficiency gains, antitrust enforcement can be justified, Hovenkamp (1985: 243) summarizes.

In a more recent article, Hovenkamp (1995: 332) stresses that orthodox neoclassical economic theory provides a cursory theory of welfare. Using only "a narrow and idiosyncratic" measure of welfare, economists do not even purport to "consider how happy or generally well off people are" but are satisfied with identifying welfare with "willingness to pay." As this willingness to pay is, in turn, defined in Coase's price theory terms, where "efficiency" is, again, the ulterior objective, welfare means by deduction nothing more than "joint maximizing" (Hovenkamp, 1995: 338). Moreover, this association of efficiency maximizing (conceptualized as productive and allocative efficiency, whereof the latter is the more complicated measure) and welfare in orthodox neoclassical economic theory disqualifies or ignores the "distributional concerns that arise in legal policy" as such issues "are considered outside the boundaries of neoclassical economic inquiry" (Hovenkamp, 1995: 332). In addition, the guidelines for so-called *Pareto optimality* in measuring allocative efficiency in orthodox neoclassical economic theory are so loosely defined that "Law and Economics [theory] has little or nothing to say about the optimal distribution of wealth, even though legal policy might be heavily involved with such questions," Hovenkamp (1995: 332) claims (see also Demsetz, 1969: 20; Kaldor, 1939: 551–552). In other words, the complex and multidimensional concept of "welfare" in legal theory and practice cannot be contained by, for example, price theory, and allocative efficiency is therefore defined in terms that justifies further relaxation of the law (i.e., economic inequality is excluded from the analysis as Pareto optimality does not recognize this term). In contrast, Hovenkamp (1995: 332) continues, "the legal policy maker may use more catholic measures for determining economic well-being." As a consequence, the law and economics scholarship uses two distinct rationalities in its critique of antitrust legislation on basis of its cursory definition of (consumer) welfare:

> [T]he efficiency of legal outcomes cannot be studied apart from distributive consequences . . . Chicago style Law and Economics uses two different, inconsistent conceptions of rationality—an optimistic robust concept in its discussion of market efficiency, and a much weaker and more pessimistic concept in its discussion of rational democratic decision making. These inconsistent conceptions of rationality, not the substantive proofs, drive the conclusion that decision making in private markets is more efficient than decision making in deliberative governmental bodies.
>
> (Hovenkamp, 1995: 347)

The ability to maintain these two rationalities within the allegedly conclusive and exhaustive price theory model is, in turn, based on a disciplinary ignorance of other social sciences, including, for example, psychology, Hovenkamp (1995: 346) argues. If welfare were not self-referentially defined as the willingness to pay under optional free-market conditions, the law and economics literature would perhaps better apprehend the role of law and legislators in seeking to accomplish allocative efficiency that is more robust than the minimal demands of Pareto optimality that ignore, just like orthodox neoclassicists do for the benefit of parsimonious but potentially invalid theoretical frameworks, the question of economic inequality. A theory of welfare that exclude the question of economic inequality is thus a curiosity at the fringes of polity and jurisprudence, satisficing only the interest of the community of orthodox neoclassicists.

Summary of the Critique of Antitrust Re-Entrenchment Argument

Critics of the Efficiency Model claim that the market-based solution to antitrust problems, in Rowe's (1984: 1564) formulation, "yields no answers for any but the blackletter textbook case." More specifically, in Rowe's (1984: 1564) account, a concept of the market "without empirical referents—as it is used in the Efficiency Model—becomes "perforce arbitrary, a facade for decisions elsewhere derived." In a real economy setting and in actual economic venturing and regulatory practices, inevitably, "the market entails a mix of intuition, judgement, and choice, relative for each case and every question at hand" (Rowe, 1984: 1564). That is, the market is no transcendental concept or what precedes actual human activities but is precisely what is made and remade on basis of innumerable everyday transactions and negotiations that enables, not by definition but through its operations, efficiency. This distinction between the "market as theorem" (defended from empirical verification or falsification) and "market as practice" play a key role in the antitrust enforcement argument:

> As a basis of antitrust norms, then, *the* market is an illusion reminiscent of the quest for the philosophers' stone . . . The market itself cannot be the predictive premise, the analytic constant for inferring positive or negative prospects of particular enterprise events in any actual case . . . [W]hen reified 'from metaphor to algorithm,' the market feeds the naive delusion that one omnibus principle can define competition and reveal sound policies for steel, finance, health care, or beer.
>
> (Rowe, 1984: 1564–1565)

While Rowe is instrumental in pointing out the difficulties and analytical fallacies derived from the late nineteenth-century legislation and its various amendments over the course of the last century, he still insists that an abstract market concept and alleged benefits derived therefrom is a weak basis for legal reform:

> Used with candor and caution, not touted as truth or revelation, economic models can provide superior insights to improve antitrust administration.

> But misused as norms, they make antitrust law doctrinaire and brittle, cut off from its historical roots, culture heritage, and legal traditions, unable to grow as conditions change.
>
> (Rowe, 1984: 1565)

For Elzinga (1977), Pitofsky (1979), Rowe (1984), and Hovenkamp (1985, 1995), the Efficiency Model, grounded in the Chicago school of economics, advocating de-regulatory reform on basis of price theory and the efficient market hypothesis, therefore cannot provide a theoretically consistent and empirically substantiated argument that justify legal reform. Free markets certainly have their merits and many markets can be kept essentially unregulated for the benefit of consumers, but these virtues are accomplished on basis of actual practices of market participants rather than on the basis of timeless and universal economic theorems and principles, articulated to render theoretical propositions coherent and mutually reinforcing. That is, whether markets are efficient (or at least efficient enough so further regulatory control and/or legislation would not be called for) is a matter of real-world outcomes, not dry logical reasoning and mathematized proofs, derived from fictive cases, expressed in propositions and lemmas. For legal scholars, laws are a thing of this world, not part of some efficiency nirvana that we can only apprehend as through a mirror dimly (e.g., orthodox neoclassical economic theory), and therefore, arguments need to be consistent and hopefully also empirically substantiated.

The Reagan Era Antitrust Reform

With the triumph of the neoconservative political movement, enshrined by Ronald Reagan's winning of the presidential election in 1980, the antitrust legislation was deconstructed to increase the alleged "efficiency" of the free market. A new laissez-faire ideology swept over Washington, D.C., in the 1980s:

> By promulgating a strong laissez-faire ideology, the state signaled to the business community that it intended to limit its role in the economy. By changing how antitrust laws would be enforced, it specifically disturbed the institutional arrangements set up to monitor and limit mergers. In such a normative vacuum innovations are likely to occur.
>
> (Stearns and Allan, 1996: 706)

In 1982, Reagan appointed Attorney General William Baxter, "a notably zealous" and influential proponent of free markets (Wood and Anderson, 1993: 27), and instructed him to liberalize U.S. antitrust policy on basis of the principles of the Chicago school. Baxter's work was dedicated exclusively to "efficiency maximization" as prescribed by the antitrust theorists in Chicago (Davies, 2010: 77). In addition, the Reagan administration initiated draconian cuts in the financial support for the institutions that were accountable for the antitrust enforcement (Wood and Anderson, 1993: 22):

> Fiscal year 1982 saw an abrupt decline of $13.6 million in the Antitrust Division budget with no change in trend. Total personnel fell immediately by about 53 employees, continuing to decline for the remainder of the Reagan administration by about 33 employees annually. By 1988 the total number of Antitrust Division personnel was only about 85% of what it had been during the Nixon administration.
>
> (Wood and Anderson, 1993: 22)

The effects were straightforward in terms of antitrust enforcement: "[T]he Reagan administration produced about 42 fewer investigations annually (about 10% of the series mean level)" (Wood and Anderson, 1993: 24). As the the Reagan administration's four assistant attorneys general (AAGs) "were all zealous advocates of Chicago School economics" (Wood and Anderson, 1993: 31), they placed "[m]uch less emphasis on merger and monopoly cases and more emphasis on restraint of trade cases." Moreover, the courts, given much legislative freedom in the American common-law jurisprudence, were increasingly receptive to these ideas, "which is evidenced by various decisions consistent with Chicago School thinking and subtle changes in judicial philosophy through time" (Wood and Anderson, 1993: 27). In summary, Wood and Anderson's (1993) analysis of novel legal practice supports a "private interest theory of regulation" (as opposed to a *public interest theory* of regulation; Levine and Forrence, 1990) after 1980; the new political climate strongly favoured free-market activities over legal and regulatory oversight, despite the 1980s being the "deal decade" *par excellence*:

> After 1980 the division's primary emphasis was on comparatively minor criminal restraint of trade cases, not large-scale merger and monopoly complaints. This occurred in spite of the fact that the annual number of premerger notifications jumped nearly 300% between 1981 and 1989.
>
> (Wood and Anderson, 1993: 36)

Therefore, Wood and Anderson (1993: 36) continues, antitrust enforcement (or the lack thereof) "can benefit a president because of the economics of antitrust regulation." For example, as in the case of a conservative president like Ronald Reagan, the president can "choose an enforcement strategy that would reward political supporters by enabling them to enjoy the benefits of larger market shares, higher prices, or restricted market entry by potential competitors" (Wood and Anderson, 1993: 36). However, as being political scientists, Wood and Anderson (1993: 36) "question the efficacy of a regulatory process in which the president, appointees, and bureaucrats have so much administrative discretion that they can simply choose not to enforce some provisions of the laws." It should here be noticed that, for example, the Reagan era antitrust re-entrenchment and its underlying political agenda describe exactly the same kind of "politicization of law" that Chicago school law and economics scholars criticize the antitrust enforcement activities for—to make law a political tool in the hands of actors operating outside of jurisprudence. As in some other cases of free-market advocacy, the critique of not adhering closely to orthodox neoclassical economic theory leads to even more significant deviations from such guidelines, but when such deviations are implemented to benefit, for example, finance capital owners, free marketeers are more lenient in their assessment than they are if other social and political objectives on the agenda are considered. Thus, the Reagan administration's political uses of antitrust enforcement would easily fit within the law and economics analysis as a textbook case of the political appropriation of law.

Summary and Conclusion

Being increasingly concerned with the New Deal reforms and their taming of free-market efficiency by the means of regulatory oversight and institutional build-up, the law and economics school, making the antitrust legislation their favoured topic of analysis, proposed the efficiency criteria as a standard for the assessment of economic activities. Based on scholarly reasoning and advocacy, the free market, part fiction or theoretical construct, part an actual, attainable state of minimized transaction costs and maximum information transparency in the free-market protagonist's mind and rhetoric (and almost effortlessly oscillating between these two images of the free market without fully distinguishing the two to lay audiences and interlocutors), the free market was portrayed as the superior mechanism for economic transactions. The free-market model unfortunately demanded a rollback of regulatory control and a muting of the "specific interests" of, for example, trade unions, but if only these deep-seated institutional changes could be ensured, free marketeers promised economic benefits accruing to all participants.

Legal scholars were both sceptical of the antitrust legislation critique and the more general implications deduced from this critique, and suggested that the free-market advocacy was little more than a series of assumptions about a world that could possibly be if all conditions were favourable and underlying agreements would never be disputed. In addition, the tendency in the law and economics school theory to simply overlook extant legislation, carefully established over time on state and federal level on basis of legal-political reasoning, bargaining, and lawmaking, and to favour economic theories that seemed unconvincing or counter-intuitive, was rejected out of hand by legal scholar. Legal reform needs to be justified by robust and credible arguments and theoretical propositions, supported by unobtrusive empirical evidence, legal scholars claim. Despite such unfavourable assessment, the argument that that the corporate system should be "efficient" apparently struck a chord in a wider community and thus became the leitmotif of free-market advocacy in the coming decades.

2 1960s and the Market for Management Control Argument

Introduction

The law and economics scholarship initiated at the law school of University of Chicago was based on the premise that markets are capable of efficiently pricing commodities and to regulate themselves, and therefore, the interventions of the sovereign state merely serve to reduce efficiency. Even in the case where the state actively promotes competition by ruling out, for example, monopolies and business decisions that generate monopoly positions (e.g., price-fixing and cartels), the law and economics scholars, otherwise considering competitive games as the *primus motor* of economic performance and well-being, rejects such a role for the state. The law and economics scholars not only argued persistently that legal matters should be understood on basis of orthodox neoclassical economic theory (as such a theoretical framework was claimed to embody the elementary components of "rational behaviour") but also insisted that legal statutes should be subject to reform and modification whenever economic theory revealed inconsistencies in the extant legislation. In other words, the law and economics school advocated and promoted a new form of economic imperialism wherein the scholarly discipline of neoclassical economic theory for various reasons were considered a more robust basis for judiciary practices that the predominant elite rule of the legal-political procedure dominating to date. In this new worldview, law and regulation are no longer rooted in a broader concern for a variety of interests represented by a number of stakeholders, and thus unfolding as a balancing act intended to maximize the societal benefit of the legislation. Instead, "efficiency maximization," a notoriously complex measure to advocate in normative terms when being devoid of a meaningful context that would serve to define what "efficiency" mean at all in the first place, was advanced as the favoured model for legislative reform. As economists and law and economics scholars could not provide a universal and indisputably robust model for what "efficiency maximization" actually means, they invoke theoretical propositions to justify this claim. By implication and through reasoning on basis of fundamental assumptions, market pricing devoid of regulatory control and other forms of interventions was defined as the model that purported to come closest to the efficiency maximization objective, defined more formally as the maximization of *productive efficiency* and *allocative efficiency*. The former concept denoted that the output was maximized given a defined amount of input, and the latter concept denotes the so-called Pareto optimality, wherein an actor is better off without any other actor losing positions. The latter criterion is a loosely defined efficiency criterion that in no meaningful way make, for example, economic inequality a theoretical concern; if the richest person in the world continues to accumulate wealth, as long as nobody else is losing positions, this is still allocatively efficient. This ignorance of distribution of the gains from the efficiency maximization derives from the orthodox neoclassical doctrine that economic theory can only be concerned with the maximization of output, not its distribution. As questions of distribution is one of the primary concerns of legislators, the economic theory model that is presented as what should, in the neoclassicist's best of possible world, overrule the extant legislation seems poorly fit to carry such a burden.

In the 1960s, the two principal ideas of the law and economics scholarship that criticized the New Deal–era antitrust enforcement—that formal economic theory is the best wager for determining the efficacy of legislation and that efficiency maximization is the measure of all economic activity—was further developed to present the bold thesis that finance markets were a useful and reliable mechanism for determining managerial performance, here defined as "decision-making quality." The idea is that public firms issue stocks and securities, such as bonds, and that the market actors' pricing of such assets can be treated as proxy for managerial decision quality. This idea appears to be counterintuitively wrong and circular in argumentation. First, it seems unlikely that "decision-making quality" can be separated from all other exogenous factors—for example, political decisions, macroeconomic conditions, speculative activities in the market, and so on—that affect stock prices in meaningful ways, thus representing an overtly sanguine view of how finance market operates. Second, if managers are incentivized—as they were from the early 1980s—to make decisions that market actors would appreciate and thus raise their valuation of the stock by buying more stock, the control mechanism is undermined as managers now *only act* in accordance with certain short-term goals and neglect other issues that would be conductive to medium- to long-term efficiency maximization. This ultimately makes "efficiency maximization" a matter of raising stock prices (as decision-making quality is, by definition, measured as what leads to higher market evaluations of the firm's stock, the definition is circulatory and self-referential), which, in turn, is inviting speculative activities that appear to have little to do with efficiency maximization. That is, it cannot be assumed out of hand that all buyers of stock operate under the rationale that fundamental value is mirrored in the stock prices, which thus makes the stock market an unreliable and fickle basis for determining managerial decision-making quality.

Despite such knee-jerk reactions from legal scholars and other economists, the basic idea advanced in the 1960s was that "the market for management control" could actively serve to discipline and monitor managers, who were now made suspicious of being self-serving and/or indolent (and possibly both). As always in shareholder welfare advocacy, it was the market that stood out as the venerated centrepiece within a quite extensive line of arguments, leading to the idea that managers should not be given fiduciary duties as prescribed by corporate law when the market could do the job for the legislators, shareholders, and anyone else benefitting from qualified managerial decision-making. However, in the 1960s, the time was not yet ripe for head-on accusations of escalating managerial malfeasance, so free marketeers had to bide their time and await the 1970s and its economic and political turbulence to better promote their governance model—the market-based control of the corporate system.

The Managerial Capitalism Regime of the 1950s and 1960s: Economic Growth, Oligopoly, and Mass Production

By the early 1960s, the American competitive capitalism was running at high speed, based on a mass production and mass consumption model that managed to make the average American considerably wealthier than citizens in most other comparable industrialized countries. The American economy had naturally benefitted greatly from the two world wars, where the European economies lost much of its competitive edge as vast parts of the continent lay in ruins. Marris (1964) refers to the new corporate system dominating in this regime of competitive capitalism as *managerial capitalism*. Managerial capitalism was characterized by an oligopolistic economy wherein large-scale divisionalized organizations (an organization model developed by Du Pont and General Motors in the interwar period) and the executive suites in these behemoth organizations and the political bodies in Washington, D.C., maintained tight connections. "The 1960s: the heyday of managerial capitalism," Dore, Lazonick, and O'Sullivan (1999: 109) argue. Keller and Block (2013: 635) speak of the entire post–World War II period until the early 1970s as "the golden age of managerial capitalism."

In this economic system based on large-scale production units, with manufacturing companies and not the least the American automotive industry leading the way, salaried managers played a key role in allocating resources and making decisions that affected millions of Americans, either being directly employed in the firms this new managerial caste was overseeing or relying more indirectly on the new oligarchic corporate system. "We define 'the management' as the particular in-group, consisting of directors and others, which effectively carries out the functions legally vested in the board," Marris (1964: 15) writes. For example, for orthodox neoclassical economists, the influence of the management profession was problematic as managers tended to favour large-scale production units rather than relying on market transactions, thus re-creating a market within the divisionalized organizations the managers themselves had created. Managerial capitalism was thus in many ways the anathema of the proponents of free-market capitalism, primarily relying on market transactions and individual one-on-one contracting, Chandler (1977) argues:

> In many sectors of the economy the visible hand of management replaced what Adam Smith referred to as the invisible hand of the market forces . . . The rise of modern business enterprise in the United States, therefore, brought with it managerial capitalism.
>
> (Chandler, 1977: 1)

In addition, professional managers threatened another favoured figure, *the entrepreneur*, the critics of managerial capitalism claimed. The entrepreneur creates of new business *ex nihilo* and *de novo* on basis of an enterprising spirit or an entrepreneurial drive and not the least finance capital being raised from business investors, and is therefore widely understood as a more "pure" and venturesome actor than the professional managers, presiding in the executive suites and boardrooms of the large-scale conglomerates that were consolidated in the post-war period. John Kenneth Galbraith (1971: 59) noticed early on that, for example, economists venerated the entrepreneur while salaried managers were never held in esteem in the same manner: "The entrepreneur—individualistic, restless, with vision, guile and courage—has been the economists' only hero. The great business organization arouses no similar admiration." Also Marris (1964: 1), otherwise affirmative of managerial work despite being an economist by training, stresses that the entrepreneur easily is understood as an endangered species in managerial capitalism:

> In many sectors of the economic activity the classical entrepreneur has virtually disappeared . . . [As a result] entrepreneurship has been taken over by transcendent management, whose function differs in kind from those of the traditional subordinate or 'mere managers.' These people, it is argued, can wield considerable power without necessarily holding equity, sharing profits or carrying risks.
>
> (Marris, 1964: 1)

In short, Marris (1964: 6) continues, "a manager is a different type of person from an entrepreneur, with different ideals and different personal values." Furthermore, employment data collected for the 1940–1973 period reveal that the entrepreneurial stock (at least in terms of measured the degree of self-employment) was in decline in the entire period:

> [It] appears that between 1940 and 1973 there was a virtually monotonic annual decline in the rate of self-employment in the United States, from around 20% to under 10%; from 1973 to 1976 the self-employment rate was basically stable, but since then there has been a slight but steady increase in the rate of self-employment.
>
> (Steinmetz and Wright, 1989: 9745–9976)

According to Steinmetz and Wright's (1989: 1002) data, "[t]he 1960s in particular were the high point of an intensive within-sector proletarianization process: the total class shift effect was 16.1%, much higher than in any other decade, and the sectorial contributions to this decline were fairly evenly distributed across the economy." However, for the anti-management crusaders who wanted to restore entrepreneurship and self-employment to secure free markets, the 1970s fortunately represented "[a] sharp break in the pattern of the previous two decades" (Steinmetz and Wright, 1989: 1002), leading to fewer employees in large-scale corporations. In the 1970s, managerial capitalism was re-structured under banner of shareholder welfare.

More important than merely pushing self-employment to the periphery of the economy and making it exceptional rather than the rule, while the entrepreneur has little choice than to optimize the use of the resources he or she has raised, the salaried professional managers were made suspicious of not really being concerned with efficiency maximization; instead, the sheer growth of the conglomerates they managed indicated that they favoured stability and "a quiet life" (Bertrand and Mullainathan, 2003) over efficiency maximization, a preference that conspicuously violated the efficiency criteria enacted in orthodox neoclassical economic theory. That, in turn, Marris (1964) argued, indicated that managers pursued agendas diverging from, for example, the shareholders' interests: "[I]t is by no means obvious that action intended to maximize the utility of a company's stockholders is consistent with maximizing the utility of the action-takers, i.e., of management" (Marris, 1964: 5). In a highly influential volume published in 1959, William Baumol (1959: 31–32) had noticed that "[p]rofits do not constitute the prime objective of the large modern business enterprise." Baumol (1959: 43) continues: "[T]he businessman's desire to increase his profits lends itself to translation into a desire to expand his firm." Unlike many other economists, Baumol was not critical of this managerial preference but recognized that the sheer complexity of decision-making work conducted by managers demanded some "rule of thumb" (with Baumol's term) that could guide and coordinate decision-making across organizational tiers and divisions. In Baumol's (1959) account, managers responded to cognitive limitations and perceived complexities by buffering resources that would secure the long-term viability of the corporation: "So long as profits are high enough to keep stakeholders satisfied and contribute adequately to the financing of company growth, management will bend its efforts to the augmentation of sales revenues rather than to further increase its profits," Baumol (1959: 50) argued. This view was also consistent with the work of Herbert Simon and his followers, formulating "a behavioural theory of the firm" outside of the rational choice doctrine that dominated in economics (Simon, 1957; March and Simon, 1958; Cyert and March, 1963). Unfortunately, not all economists took an equally sanguine view of such managerial decision-making, and orthodox neoclassicists instead started to make the claim in the 1970s that salaried managers were "wasting" the shareholder's money and used it to fortify and protect their own interests and careers against the cleansing fire of free-market competition and market pricing. Still, in the 1960s, such rhetoric was a thing to come—more precisely with the first oil crisis of 1973 and the soaring energy costs that made managerial capitalism and the Keynesian economic policy it relied on start to crack—and throughout the 1960s, the oligarchic corporate system ran relatively smooth.

However, despite its merits and the ability to leverage the living standard for millions of Americans, even liberal economists and commentators were concerned that the oligarchic managerial capitalism led to, in Marris's (1964: 1) formulation, "[a] system in which production is concentrated in the hands of large joint-stock companies." Galbraith (1971) even compared this economic system with the planned economies of the Soviet bloc and pointed at consumers as being the foremost victims of a less-than-efficient corporate system:

> [W]e have an economic system which, whatever its formal ideological billing, is in substantial part a planned economy. The initiative in deciding what is to be produced comes not from the sovereign consumer who, through the market, issues, the instructions that bend the productive mechanism to his ultimate will. Rather it comes from the great producing organizations which reaches forward to control the markets that it is presumed to serve and, beyond, to bend the consumer to its needs.
> (Galbraith, 1971: 6)

What one economist justifies (i.e., growth of conglomerates to resist the volatility of the economic cycle) the other brands as "a waste" or a "squandering" of economic resources at the expense of societal efficiency and above all the shareholders' loss. Therefore, both economic theory and legal theory address the managerial discretion instituted by corporate law and the court rulings relying on the so-called *business judgement* principle. In contrast to this model, the market for management control, was advanced as what maximized the efficiency of the corporate system. Rather than granting salaried executives full discretion to make decisions as it suited their own interest (as critics proposed), executives need to better respond to market expectations. Therefore, the market for management control was advanced as a mechanism that solves both the efficiency and accountability problems that followed from the managerial capitalism model. Unfortunately, as will be demonstrated, the market for management control is based on several logically inconsistent propositions and assumptions and that are not empirically supported, and consequently, the new model for management control displays some serious flaws.

Advocating the Market for Management Control

The legal scholar Henry Manne (1965) formulated the concept of "the market for management control" to denote how finance markets serve the role to monitor the quality of managerial decision-making on basis of the pricing of the assets (e.g., stocks, securities such as bonds) the focal firm issue on the market. This idea is central to a long series of theoretical arguments and legal reforms implemented since the mid-1960s, and it is an argument that serve the key role to align a finance theory view of the market as a pricing mechanism and legal theory, not of necessity assuming that markets are efficient in pricing heterogeneous assets, especially when information scarcity is a factor to consider. While Manne did not teach in the most prestigious law schools in America, he was, Mayer (2016: 108) says, "an acolyte of the Chicago School of free-market economics" and was thus sponsored by the conservative Olin Foundation to develop and promote his arguments. In the eyes of his financiers, Manne was "brilliant, impolitic, and an ideological purist," but unfortunately he "'was considered a marginal, even eccentric character in the legal academy,' according to [political scientist Steven M.] Teles" (cited in Mayer, 2016: 108).

In 1962, Manne had received some attention when a highly polemical paper in a law journal enticed Adolf A. Berle to respond to his allegations. With seemingly limited effort, Berle (1962) rejects most of Manne's central propositions regarding, for example, the value of proxy fights as an efficient corporate governance mechanism (proxy fights are "extremely rare," Berle, 1962: 440, says), that firms are dependent on capital markets for their financing ("there is some truth in this but not much," Berle, 1962: 440, ripostes), that monopolies are "inefficient" (public utilities firms, essentially enjoying monopoly positions, do attract considerable private investors; i.e., they are attractive investments in the eyes of the finance traders, Berle, 1962: 440, remarks), the stock owners being the firm's "investors" (a claim rooted in "folklore habit" or being "pure fiction," in Berle's, 1962: 463, view), and that managers should not assume corporate responsibilities or tailor "business statesmanship" roles for themselves (as a legal matter, corporate law, and court rulings—*A. P. Smith Mfg. Co. v. Barlow* in the New Jersey Supreme Court, being one example, never overruled by the Supreme Court—permits such beliefs and attitudes, Berle, 1962: 443, shows). Despite these responses, in his summary, Berle (1962: 437) admitted that what he referred to as the "the American industrial system," was "eons from perfection," and yet, this system being "under guidance and control" of professional managers and federal and state-level agencies and regulators,

> has done more for more people, has made possible a higher standard of living for the vast majority of a huge population in a huge country, has preserved more liberty for individual self-development, and now affords more tools (however unused or badly used) from which a good society can be forged so far as economics can do so, than any system in recorded history.

Despite Manne's failure to bypass or marginalize Adolf A. Berle on basis of his free-market model, the accomplishments to get Berle into the ring and

Manne's demonstration of a commitment to the free-market cause secured his financing from the Olin Foundations. Manne appeared to be, regardless of his peripheral position in legal scholarship, a viable opportunity to promote the law and economics agenda for the time being.

As Manne remarks (1965), the idea of the market for managerial control assumes a strong correlation between "managerial efficiency" and the market price of the stocks and bonds that the firm issues. Needless to say, this is a non-trivial assumption being made:

> A fundamental premise underlying the market for corporate control is the existence of a high positive correlation between corporate managerial efficiency and the market price of shares of that company. As an existing company is poorly managed—in the sense of not making as great a return for the shareholders as could be accomplished—the market price of the shares declines relative to the shares of other companies in the same industry or relative to the market as a whole.
>
> (Manne, 1965: 112)

Manne (1967) explicates the concept of the market for managerial control, and despite being a legal scholar, Manne is critical of the idea that the corporate system, including, for example, business charters, limited liability, and dispersed ownership as in the case of the public firm, developed within competitive capitalism, can be attributed specifically "to law and lawyers" (Manne, 1967: 260). Instead, the corporate system is entangled with a series of policies, reforms, and activities aimed to create a dynamic capitalist economic system. Seen in this view, the nature of the firm (in Coase's, 1937, formulation) is not primarily a *legal construct* but a "vehicle" or "device" for the raising of capital to finance a business venture: "The fundamental fact about the development of American corporations in the 19th century is that they came into existence because entrepreneurs, or promoters, needed some device to raise capital from a relatively large number of investors," Manne (1967: 260) says. In addition, the idea of "centralized management" is a direct consequence of the concept of large corporations as being "a capital-raising device" (Manne, 1967: 260). This, in turn, Manne (1967) argues, locates the *business promoter* as the central actor, being responsible for the raising of capital and for hiring and monitoring managers. The shareholders only come in second, after the business promoter have already incorporated the business and offers the possibility of co-ownership in the new venture. Expressed differently, the business promoter performs "an entrepreneurial function" in raising capital and issuing shares in the business venture. Centralized management is part of the differentiation of the business venture, wherein different specialized functions add to the aggregated efficiency and thus "allow the system to operate more efficiently" (Manne, 1967: 260). Furthermore, just as in the case of the critique of antitrust enforcement, it is *efficiency* that is brought forward as the sole legitimate contestant as the measure of managerial performance.

In order to maximize the efficiency of managerial decision-making and to support the business charter as a capital-raising device, there needs to be "liquidity for investment," Manne (1967: 263) says. That means that there should be a market for the buying and selling of, for example, corporate stocks and that the costs for liquidizing financial assets should be fairly modest; that is, market liquidity is assumed. If individual minority investors are unsatisfied with the performance of the managers and the firm more broadly, they need to be able to sell off stock to release finance capital to be re-invested elsewhere. Unless there are markets for the buying and selling of stocks, individual minority investors would need to divest the entire corporation at considerable effort and costs, thus minimizing their incentives to liquidize their capital holdings:

> Another aspect of market liquidity relates not to changes in investment needs but to the investor's freedom to dissociate himself from a particular corporation if for any reason he becomes dissatisfied with its management. There is only one alternative to market liquidity as a way out for corporate investors. That alternative is dissolution of the corporation and the sale of its assets, with subsequent distribution to the shareholders of the proceeds. But the market allows discrete decisions to be made by individual investors, whereas the dissolution alternative requires some level of general agreement among the share-holders before it can be utilized. A system in which a minority shareholder is given the power to force dissolution of a large corporation because of his own dissatisfaction or a change in his own investment needs would not be workable.
>
> (Manne, 1967: 264)

Moreover, in order to effectively monitor the managerial decision-making, the ownership of each stock needs to be accompanied by voting rights, that is, the owner of the stock's legal right to influence the operative work in the firm. Based on these premises, Manne (1967) argues that there are basically three markets that the corporation has to respond to: first, the "market for investment capital," being the market where promoters "search for new funds" (Manne, 1967: 264); second, the market for "the buying and selling of existing securities" (Manne, 1967: 264); and third, "the market for corporate control," bundling economic rights and voting rights in ways that helps the corporation to raise capital but also become monitored by the investors, that is, the shareholders (creditor, e.g., bondholders are not given voting rights):

> The market for corporate control can function only because shares carrying votes can be bought and sold. Thus, given the concept of majority determination of corporate control, it is possible to buy control of the corporation directly by buying fifty-one per cent of the voting shares.
>
> (Manne, 1967: 264)

Once these mechanism are in place—ownership rights, voting rights, and managers endowed with business judgement discretion—the market for managerial control operates on basis of the market pricing of the stock and, by default, the securities issues by the firm, Manne (1967: 264) argues: "Unless a publicly traded company is efficiently managed, the price of its shares on the open market will decline, thus lowering the price at which an outsider can take over control of the corporation." The functioning of the market for managerial control is thus based on a series of assumptions. First, there need to be a straightforward and uncomplicated relationship between managerial decision-making quality and market pricing. That condition is not easily proved on basis of empirical evidence as there are numerous intermediary layers between, for example, the executive suite and the boardroom and stock market pricing (including, e.g., speculation and more recently firm-specific stock repurchase announcements). Second, and being the critical argument for most corporate governance theory relying on free-market advocacy since the 1960s, the managers and the directors are understood to be directly accountable to the shareholders only and nobody else. This assumption does not rely on any empirical evidence but only on the assertion that a corporate system that relies on the market of managerial control—in turn, being dependent on the proposition that only shareholders are the "residual risk bearers" that the theory simultaneously seeks to justify—is more efficient than any other comparable system, not the least the corporate law system based on the principles of the business judgement rule and the fiduciary duties of managers and directors (two legal doctrines examined in detail in Chapter 3).

While the former assumption has been heavily criticized for simply being unable to harbour sufficient factual evidence to be sustainable, the latter assumption is so closely bound up with a series of claims and propositions derived from orthodox neoclassical economic theory that it becomes complicated to separate what parts that can be tested empirically and what are simply assumptions based on theoretical propositions or normative beliefs. Under all conditions, the claim that the shareholders are the residual risk bearers and thus have invested their finance capital to be able to receive their share of the residual cash flow—the money that remains when all other costs are covered—interfere in considerable ways with corporate law and court rulings. First, the so-called business judgement rule is a legal doctrine that grant considerable decision-making discretion to directors and managers to be able to operate within a competitive, free enterprise, essentially devoid of government regulation and monitoring. In a court ruling, where, for example, disputes between, say, the board of directors and a minority shareholder who believes he or she has suffered from the negligence of the board, the business judgement rule is frequently invoked to justify the board and their defined as an autonomous decision-making entity within the firm. In Manne's (1967: 270) view, the business judgement rule is "one of the most important doctrines of corporation law" but also one of "the least understood concepts in the entire corporate field." In addition, Manne (1967: 270) asserts, in corporate law, directors—and *a fortiori* managers—"owe no special fiduciary duty to individual shareholders." That is, corporate law, as it is written, interpreted, and enforced in a court ruling, grant the shareholders no particular privilege vis-à-vis other stakeholders. Despite the presence of two legal doctrines, Manne (1967) argues that the market for managerial control overrules these doctrines by the sheer force of the efficiency of market pricing, a theoretically derived proposition rather than a fact grounded in empirical evidence. Following the law and economics scholars in their critique of the efficacy of market regulation and oversight (including extant corporation law as such), Manne presents a Chicago school argument in favour of an entrenchment of legal enforcement to give more free play to the market for managerial control:

> [L]arge corporations function in a largely permissive framework and that market forces rather than legal ones have dictated their organization and structure . . . One is almost tempted to suggest that the large corporation system could and would function substantially as it does if there were almost no state corporation statutes beyond provisions for incorporation. This may not be so far-fetched, for the effect of most modern amendment programs dealing with basic provisions of the corporation acts has been to modify them in the interest of the close[ly held] corporation. Our general corporation laws seem to be in the process of becoming general close corporation laws with only incidental relevance to large companies.
>
> (Manne, 1967: 270)

Corporate law stipulates the mechanism of fiduciary duties, prescribing that directors and their managers have responsibilities vis-à-vis their various stakeholders, and the business judgement rule to fortify their discretion in the day-to-day work. For Manne (1967) and his followers, corporate law therefore provide a far-too-weak protection against managerial opportunism and managerial malfeasance as, for example, managerial incompetence or tardy responses to changing market conditions would not be ruled out on basis of the extant corporate legislation. That is, Manne concurs, corporate law tolerates inefficiencies within the existing corporate system.

Against this legal framework, Manne (1967) and his followers advocate the market for managerial control, where stocks carry voting rights, and thus enable certain shareholders and investors to acquire the control over the firm. By implication, the pricing of firm-specific assets serve to assess the "quality" of the managerial decision-making; when poor decisions are made in the eyes of the market participants, either holding the stock already or being potential buyers, the price of the assets (ideally both stocks and securities such as bonds) fall, and managers are incentivized to make decisions that better satisfy market participants' interests, or they are at risk to receive a tender offer when the firm's stock is at a low price. If a tender offer bid is successfully made, the managers may lose their jobs and accompanying privileges and benefits.

In Manne's (1967) argument, the market for management control is a superior control mechanism for public firms as it provides a ceaseless monitoring of managers, as opposed to corporate law that merely grants managers discretion and thus, by implication, reduces the overall efficiency of the corporate system. As demonstrated in the following, this theory stipulating fair and unbiased assessment of managerial performance is compromised in considerable ways, making the smooth and close to cost-free monitoring of managers on basis of market pricing as conceived by Manne (1965, 1967) much more complicated to establish in real markets. Especially when considering the claim that shareholders are the only legitimate residual risk bearers is disputed, the market for management control model becomes more clunky and convoluted. In addition, economists (e.g., Garvey and Swan, 1994) and legal scholars (e.g., Coffee, 1986, 1984, discussed in the following) reject the idea that shareholder are the legitimate residual risk bearers, the cornerstone of the shareholder welfare argument. Garvey and Swan (1994: 154) argue (as also Goldberg, 2013, 1976a, b, does, discussed in the next chapter) that the assumption made regarding a zero-transaction-cost world and thus the presence of "complete contracts," that is, contracts that demand no additional monitoring to terminate, an unrealistic assumption to make from a real-world economy perspective, undermines and disqualifies the status of the shareholders as the sole residual claimants. In addition, the product factor market and the market that the focal firm serves (what Garvey and Swan, 1994: 156, refer to as "input and output markets") are not perfectly competitive (i.e., they are not perfectly efficient in terms of its information processing capacities): "[S]hareholders are not identical to the Marshallian entrepreneur, a 100 per cent residual claimant surrounded by competitive input and output markets and completely specified contracts," Garvey and Swan (1994: 156) contend. The normative claim that shareholders are entitled to the residual cash flow is problematic, not least because this claim may entice this group of market actors to act in ways that arguably undermine the straightforward connection between market price and managerial performance (see, e.g., Coffee and Palia, 2016). Before the critique of Manne's model is discussed, some of his followers' work is reviewed.

Extending the Market for Management Control Argument

Fischel (1978) endorses and advocates the theory of the market for management control and justifies the consequences of the model, including the much-disputed use of tender offer bids, a new mechanism that played a significant role in the 1980s "de-conglomerization movement." Like Manne (1965, 1967) and the law and economics scholars who criticized antitrust enforcement, Fischel (1978: 1) puts his faith in the efficient market as the solution to the question of how to monitor managers for the benefit of increased efficiency in the corporate system. Invoking the antitrust enforcement critique literature, Fischel (1978: 1) declares that capital markets are "allocationally efficient," a key point of debate in the antitrust scholarship literature:

> [C]apital markets like those provided by our national stock exchanges are allocationally efficient has gained increasing support. In general terms, a capital market is efficient in this sense if the prices of traded securities accurately and promptly reflect the securities' intrinsic values relative to all publicly available information, or in other words, if the market responds immediately to relevant information that any trader may have and never attaches the wrong evidentiary weight to the information.
>
> (Fischel, 1978: 1)

As have been noticed, there is a series of assumptions being made in Fischel's (1978) claim that capital market have the benefit to maximize overall efficiency, including the claim that prices "accurately and promptly" (i.e., correctly and more or less instantly) reflect "intrinsic values" (i.e., some innate and fundamental value of a tradable asset; see, e.g., Pistor, 2013: 316–317; Gerding, 2005: 397) and thus accommodate "all publicly available information." All these assumptions are disputed and rely on either propositions yet to be proved on basis of empirical evidence or remain theoretical deductions from axiomatic principles. Anyway, on basis of these propositions, Fischel (1978: 1–2) repeats Manne's (1965, 1967) principal argument: "If a firm is poorly managed, the price of its securities will be lower than under more competent management, and the firm and society in general would benefit from a transfer of control to more capable managers." The Efficient Market Hypothesis, being widely endorsed by the late 1970s by orthodox neoclassicists, deserves a proper explanation within Fischel's (1978) free-market argument. Fischel (1978) here closely follows the Hayek/Chicago doctrine wherein it is the uncoordinated yet self-interested search for "mispriced" financial assets that effectively bring out all public information and reflect it in the asset price:

> An efficient capital market is one in which a trader cannot improve his overall chances of speculative gain by obtaining public information about the companies whose securities are in the market and evaluating that information intelligently in determining which stocks to buy and sell. Paradoxically, the efficiency of the market results from the competitive efforts of securities analysts and investors who strive to earn superior returns by identifying mispriced securities-securities that are either overvalued or undervalued.
>
> (Fischel, 1978: 2–3)[1]

Self-interest is beneficial for collective well-being, Adam Smith made clear in *Wealth of Nations*, and close to two centuries later, this proposition was leveraged to the status of a definition of economics in the hands of George Stigler (as was discussed in Chapter 1). The Efficient Market Hypothesis thus enfolds the virtues of self-interest within competitive games and the more tenuous propositions of price theory and the informational content of prices to create an image of the market as a superior information-processing mechanism, capable of handling all kinds of human interests under the auspices of efficiency. So far, Fischel (1978), a legal scholar, follows the Chicago doctrine closely. However, Fischel (1978: 5) adds that simply because markets are capable of sifting out and signaling what managers that underperform—declining stock value is of necessity indicating managerial incompetence and nothing else in this model—it does not follow that there are equally efficient mechanisms "whereby control shifts from less capable managers to others who can manage corporate assets more profitably" (Fischel, 1978: 5). However, this is precisely an analysis that Fischel (1978) will embark on, making, for example, tender offer bids[2] a legitimate and even socially desirable mechanisms for ousting managers failing in the competitive game of finance market pricing.

Within Fischel's analytical framework, poor management is operationalized as unfavourable market pricing of firm-specific assets: "Poor performance of a company's securities in the capital market is a common indication of poor management" (Fischel, 1978: 5). By courtesy of the market for managerial control, incompetent or uncompetitive managers can no longer sit idly as there is now a market for takeover bids, putting the managers' careers and all their privileges and benefits at risk, thus incentivizing managers to perform better and, most critically, to make decisions that one specific form of stakeholders, the actual or presumptive owners of stock, appreciate and value. Unless the managers are capable of performing better, they expose themselves to tender offer bids:

> The market for corporate control and the threat of cash tender offers in particular are of great importance in creating incentives for management to maximize the welfare of shareholders . . . inefficient performance by management is reflected in share price thus making the corporation a likely candidate for a takeover bid. Since a successful takeover bid often results in the displacement of current management, managers have a strong incentive to operate efficiently and keep share prices high.
>
> (Fischel, 1978: 9)

Fischel (1978) defines tender offer bids accordingly:

> The essence of the cash tender offer is the offeror's public invitation to all shareholders of the target company to tender their shares at a specified price within a specified time. The tender offer price will generally

> be considerably above the market price of the securities at the time of the offer. The tender offeror may seek to acquire all the target company's shares or only a fixed number less than the total amount outstanding.
>
> (Fischel, 1978: 2)

In the model that Fischel (1978: 6) advocates, the tender offer is "the most advantageous means of acquiring control if shares are widely held." When the corporate takeover is now introduced as the means through which managers are disciplined (or incentivized, to put it in less harsh terms), the countermovement of managers is, Fischel (1978: 21) claims, to resist takeover bids and to establish mechanisms that deter or avert takeover bidders. Needless to say, this is where the real debate unfolds, whether managers, endowed with fiduciary duties and the business judgement rule protection, should freely accept or even endorse an alternative, market-based model for the control of the corporation, especially since the market for management control enacts the professional salaried manager as a group that shirk and suboptimize the use of firm resources in predictable ways?

For Fischel (1978), putting his faith in accurate market pricing as the optimal check on managers, there is little doubt that all resistance is both futile and only of benefit to self-serving ends, that is, mortally questionable. What remains to be accomplished, though, it to advocate a liberalization of corporate law and other relevant strictures that delimit or inhibit the market for management control. Of specific interest for Fischel's is the Williams Act of 1968, an amendment of the Securities and Exchange Act of 1934, that regulate tender offer bids, an act that Fischel (1978), consistent with his propositions and theoretical framework, believes reduce the efficiency in the managerial control:

> By increasing the cost of making a tender offer and by reducing the exchange value of privately produced information, the Williams Act limits the effectiveness of cash tender offers and thereby undermines a check against entrenched inefficient management to the detriment of current shareholders.
>
> (Fischel, 1978: 26)

In fact and in consequence, the Williams Act serves a role similar to that of antitrust enforcement in Robert H. Bork's (1966, 1967) analysis, as a piece of legislation that protects allegedly mediocre managers performing below-efficiency maximization. The social costs generated when permitting such indolent behavior, Fischel (1978) says, are significant. As we will see in, for example, John C. Coffee's critique of the concept of the market for management control, not only are the underlying assumptions of this model disputable, but the costs imposed on society in the market-based model of managerial control are also not lower than in the case of legal control of the corporate system. Considering both productive and allocative efficiency, the market-based model and its privileging of the shareholders at the expense of all other stakeholders—a condition that corporate law and other strictures regulating the corporate system takes into account but ignored by the proponents of the market-based model—raise the aggregated costs when it benefits shareholders. Therefore, what may be beneficial for shareholders, making the mangers their agents and nobody else's, comes at a loss for all other stakeholders (say, creditors, now exposed to higher risks that does not entail any additional compensation, employees, exposed to risk including lower levels of economic compensation) that also play a key role in what Blair and Stout (1999) refer to as the "team production" of the corporate system.

The Intermediary View: Williamson's Transaction Cost Economics Theory of the Firm

Before the legal theory critique of the market for management control model is examined, the work of Oliver Williamson, heavily indebted to the work of Ronald Coase and his idea of the firm as being a form of market and what minimizes the aggregated transaction costs on basis of available market offerings, included in the firm's production activities, merit some attention. As opposed to the legal scholars and economist who put their faith in the market as the supreme arbiter of monetized claims, Williamson does recognize that there are, in fact, firm-specific competencies that adds to the overall value of the firm and that contributes to the generation of residual cash.[3] Williamson says that the firm needs to be recognized as both a "production function" and as a "governance structure" to fully apprehend internal and firm-specific processes (Williamson, 1981: 1539). At the same time, Williamson accepts the proposition that the market has the benefit of enabling free contracting, a key process on the theory of the firm that emphasizes minimal transaction costs (i.e., below those of comparable market transactions) as measure of efficiency:

> The first principle of efficient organizational design is this: *the normal presumption that recurring transactions for technologically separable goods and services will be efficiently mediated by autonomous market contracting is progressively weakened as assets specificity increases.*
> (Williamson, 1981: 1548. Emphasis in the original)

However, despite the merits of market-based contracting, the "internal organization" of the firm provides advantages over market contracting for transactions that are "supported by highly specific assets as both contract-writing and contract-execution stages" (Williamson, 1981: 1548–1549); that is, it is more costly to write contract with market participants than it is to develop and maintain "in-house" resources and services. Seen in this view, managers are not of necessity shirking and acting self-interestedly as assumed, either implicitly or explicitly in the market for management control literature and in the literature on contractual theory developed in the 1970s and the 1980s' agency literature, but they do contribute to the solution of actual, real economy organizational problems. Just because managers are granted discretion in the corporate legislation, it does not follow that they, of necessity, take the opportunity to enrich themselves and otherwise act self-servingly, especially at the expense of shareholders, as suggested in these literatures, Williamson (1981: 1559) says.

Williamson's theory of the firm, recognizing the firm's production and governance functions, is of a theoretical framework that relies on the idea of markets without making markets per definition more efficient than any other mechanism, and without ignoring the internal processes of the firm. Nor does Williamson claim that shareholders are the sole residual risk bearers and therefore solely to entitled the residual or free cash flow generated in the firm-specific team-production activities. In short, Williamson (1981) represent a more moderate, yet market-oriented theoretical view of the firm. Above all, Williamson's emphasis on the internal operations of the firm, ignored by economists for doctrinaire reasons (for an dyed-in-the-wool free-market economist, the firm is indicative of market failure, and as market are superior to all other human means to allocate resources and to settle conflicts between opposing goals, firms are treated with utmost scepticism) and by legal scholars for disciplinary reasons (legal scholars tend to examine the economic system from a legal point of view and have limited expertise—as indicated by the business judgement rule—in firm-specific activities), represent a radically different view than that of the proponents of the market for management control. For Williamson, markets do their share of the job, but to assume that market participants would know more and know better than professional managers with perhaps career-long expertise in an industry is a free-market fallacy; it is an unflattering disregard of both managerial skills and the management studies discipline.

The Legal Theory Argument Against the Market for Management Control

Coffee (1986) presents a detailed critique of the concept of the market for management control from a legal theory view. In the mid-1980s, the takeover market had already grown substantially, partially on basis of the encouragement from economists and legal scholars but for most part because of the inflow of overseas savings into the American economy during the Reagan era (Stearns and Allan, 1996; Krippner, 2011), and on basis of the deregulation of financial markets that promoted the junk bond market that supplied the capital for the new financial engineering activities (Coffee, 1986: 3–4). However, unlike the proponents of the hostile takeover movement, Coffee (1986) does not believe that this upsurge in corporate restructuring is indicative of the efficacy of a market of management control; there are too many puzzling empirical phenomena (i.e., why were well-functioning firms targeted if takeover activities were claimed to discipline poorly performing managers?) and unexplained assumptions (i.e., why would outside finance market actors be better informed than insiders with specialized know-how?) in the model to verify its robustness:

> [T]he more controversial disciplinary thesis, which holds that superior managements are displacing inferior ones, cannot explain why even the best operationally managed companies seem to experience such disparities between asset and stock value, and the 'private information' theory, which assumes that the bidder knows something that the market does not, cannot be reconciled with the fact that the existence and size of such discounts are apparently well known to the market.
>
> (Coffee, 1986: 5)

In addition, in the mid-1980s, takeovers frequently led to successful bidders closing down operations and selling off divisions, but the theory of the market for management control does not explain in what way that defensive divesture strategy served to maximize efficiency, especially not for all stakeholders (Coffee, 1986: 5). Coffee (1986: 73) is also sceptical of the unsubstantiated proposition underlying the entire model, the idea that managers are shirking and underperforming in predictable ways—if that would be the case, it is complicated to explain the sharp economic growth, low unemployment, and economic and financial stability in the era of managerial capitalism. For free-market theorists, both salaried managers and the government persistently perform at substandard levels, but this bold claim stands in sharp contrasts against the fact the post–World War II period's economic growth and welfare remains unprecedented to date. For Coffee (1986) and many other commentators, these anti-management, anti-government sentiments fail to recognize elementary factual conditions. Furthermore, Coffee (1986) proposes that managers cannot only be portrayed as villains as they are also the victims—especially middle managers losing their jobs at an alarming rate in the mid-1980s:

> Implicit in much recent commentary about hostile takeovers has been a view of managers as the villain of the story. Their ability to shirk or consume excessive perquisites or otherwise overreach shareholders is seen as providing the rationale for the hostile takeover. True as it is to say that managers sometimes do all of these things, they also can be presented as the victims of the story. Threatened with loss of job security and expected deferred compensation in a volatile stock market in which few companies are not at some point rumored to be takeover targets, managers have been forced as a takeover defense to leverage up and accept a higher level of risk.
>
> (Coffee, 1986: 73)

If there were some tensions between the managers and shareholders from the outset, the takeover movement and the theory of the market for management control has "substantially intensified" these tensions (Coffee, 1986: 11). Under all conditions, Coffee (1986: 11) argues that the theory of the market for management control has assumed, that takeovers exclusively involve shareholders, and that there are "no externalities" involved. This assumption is overly simplistic as the firm is originally granted a business charter to serve society in a variety of ways, not only to benefit the firm's investors, and the assumption that takeovers include no externalities is therefore mistaken or ignorant of economic facts. The "no externalities assumption" also understates the underlying theory of the firm (to be discussed in Chapter 3 of this volume), that the firm is a "a complex web of contracts" (Coffee, 1986: 12). Some critics have also suggested that the takeover market produce diseconomies, that is, serve to reduce overall efficiency while being beneficial for a small group of shareholders who favour liquid assets over illiquid rent-generating holdings. Coffee (1986: 12) remarks that such claims need to be verified on basis of empirical data before the market for management control model can justify legal reform.

Heterogeneity in Incentives: On the Question of One or Many Economic Rationalities

One key concern regarding the takeover activities and the theory of the market for management control is how the rationality of the various actors is ignored in order to make the point that managers underperform and even withhold residual cash flow on purpose to benefit their own interest (so-called empire building). Orthodox neoclassical economic theory otherwise renders self-interested behaviour (operationalized as utility-maximizing calculative practices) a central factor when studying or explaining economic pursuits and activities—in fact, orthodox neoclassical economic theory explicitly disqualify any other explanatory factors including culture, customs, and social beliefs (Amadae, 2003)—but when it comes to the manager–shareholder relations, the "asymmetry in attitudes toward risk held by the typical manager and the typical shareholder" is ignored (Coffee, 1986: 13). While the rational manager "has good reason to be risk averse," the fully diversified shareholder has "every reason to be risk neutral" (Coffee, 1986: 13):

> Modem financial theory assumes that rational shareholders will hold diversified portfolios . . . This generalization certainly fits institutional investors, who today dominate the marketplace. In any event, it seems clear that investors, whether individual or institutional, are better diversified than managers. Managers are inherently overinvested in the firm they serve.
>
> (Coffee, 1986: 17)

Therefore, Coffee (1984: 1190) argues elsewhere, a "[r]ational apathy characterizes the behavior of shareholders": "No single shareholder can fully appropriate the gain that his individual efforts might produce and so none will individually incur the costs that it would be rational for all shareholders collectively to expend. As a result, what is supposedly introduced as a means to leverage efficiency in corporate governance and in managerial decision-making quality leads to a classic 'free rider' problem" (Coffee, 1984: 1190. See Olson, 1965, for an extended argument regarding the free-rider problem).

The claim that managers are "inherently overinvested in the firm they serve" is a statement that merit some explication. In Coffee's (1986: 17) view, proponents of the market for management control turn a blind eye to the fact that the lateral mobility among senior corporate executives is limited and that managers develop firm-specific human capital over time. Therefore, managers cannot therefore assume that there are external labour markets that would price their firm-specific skills as high as the present employer: "[T]he basic contrast is that shareholders own many stocks, but managers have only one job," Coffee (1986: 18) says. In addition, the firm itself oftentimes further reinforces the development of firm-specific managerial skills as the employer awards the manager "stock options and other fringe benefits" to increase the loyalty and to impose barriers for leaving the present employer (Coffee, 1986: 18). Finally, in the regime of managerial capitalism, the internal labour market model developed in conglomerates and divisionalized firms ensures that a considerable proportion of the manager's expected aggregate compensation is deferred to the end of his or her career, economic compensation that is not conferred to the manager until he or she has climbed "an elongated seniority ladder." Moreover, Coffee (1986: 24) says, "such deferral may be in the shareholders' interest because it gives the manager an incentive to compete vigorously for advancement within the firm's internal labor market, but it also exposes the manager to a double risk."

Still, regardless of these different risk-appetite regulation mechanisms, the managers' role within the corporation imply, Coffee (1984: 1196) argues, that managers do not see themselves as the shareholders' agents, but as officers managing "a joint venture with its shareholders in an enterprise that is substantially dependent upon management's skill and judgement for its success." That is, managers think of themselves and the shareholders as partners in a team-production activity and do in many ways share beliefs, norms, and ethical standards with the owners of finance capital; that is, the antagonist relationship that economists and law and economics scholars stipulate between, for example, regulators and shareholders (i.e., between the state and the finance capital owners) is not present—at least not as an endemic condition—in manager–shareholder relations, Coffee argues. At the same time, derived from self-interest, the managers and the shareholder have diverging risk preferences that proponents of takeovers mistakenly, Coffee (1986) argues, regard as evidence of managerial opportunism:

> [T]he less risk-averse shareholder wants a high payout, while the manager wants to hoard cash and assets to protect against future contingencies. Of course, tax motives may also play a role here, because dividends are highly taxed; but if managers were simply conforming their behavior to the incentives that the tax laws held out, they would long ago have increased the firm's degree of leverage. Because they clearly have not, tax effects seem to have only a partial explanatory power. In particular, tax incentives cannot explain the critical empirical finding that management-controlled firms are characterized by lower levels of systematic and unsystematic risk than owner-controlled firms—a finding that dovetails with the managerial risk—aversion hypothesis here expressed.
>
> (Coffee, 1986: 23)

Psychological factors are yet another issue pertaining to managerial decision-making and risk preferences. Orthodox neoclassical economic theory commonly reduces the entire apparatus of psychological inclinations and preferences to the level of rational choice, but certain streams of economic theory have recognized the importance of understanding, for example, decision-making routines. The work of Daniel Kahnemann and Amos Tversky, awarded the Nobel Prize in the Economic Sciences, have proposed that individuals do not seek to maximize the expected value of different alternatives but start to define a reference point (or aspiration level) for themselves that they thereafter seek to achieve (Coffee, 1986: 59). Whenever that reference point or aspiration level is reached, individuals display a "preference reversal," and they consequently cease to appreciate risk-taking and become more risk averse: "[M]anagers, having met their aspiration level, thereafter act in a risk-averse manner and pursue growth over higher profitability," Coffee (1986: 65) says. As opposed to the managers' risk utility function, the diversified shareholder demonstrates a preference for high levels of risk and thus pushes managers in that direction, at times to the level where the future of the firm is jeopardized. According to the theory of the market for management control, excessive risk would, the theory predicts, lead to, for example, creditors (being more risk averse than shareholders) or some shareholders to value the firm's finance assets at a lower level to compensate for the higher levels of risk (and thus of default); in practice, Coffee (1986: 67) argues, empirical evidence suggests that high leverage has imposed "additional and unbargained-for risks onto creditors."

Such evidence is indicative of another implicit assumption made by proponents of shareholder welfare, namely that finance market actors (e.g., institutional investors managing pension funds and mutual funds) behave in ways that are beneficial for *all* stakeholders. Coffee (1991) rejects such claims on basis of both substantial evidence and theoretical deductions:

> Institutional investors should not be mistaken for financial saints. Their representatives on a board will not automatically represent all shareholders; to the extent that conflicts among shareholders exist, board members who are institutional employees or agents may favor the interests of their employers.
>
> (Coffee, 1991: 1334)

The first condition to consider when finance market actors are portrayed as the guardians of economic efficiency is to examine their incentives and temporal investment horizon—an analysis that may reveal a strong preference for liquidity over other qualities: "The first and most obvious problem with institutions as monitors is that they are watchdogs whose every incentive is to flee at the first sign of trouble. This is where the liquidity/control trade-off is the most acute" (Coffee, 1991: 1329). Second, introduced as an empirical question, the issue of opportunistic behaviour among finance market actors needs to considered before this group can be endowed with regulatory licenses. For Coffee (1991: 1335), there is an "overriding danger of market manipulation" if finance market actors execute control over the corporate system. Unlike managers, who tend to favour "steady earnings and stock price growth," for example, institutional investors (and hedge fund managers, in particular) can benefit from "volatile swings in stock price and could manipulate corporate affairs to create profitable trading opportunities"; that is, they can reap the benefit of market instabilities that incur costs for other stakeholders. Therefore, when considering all empirical, legal, and theoretical issues and conditions, and when recognizing what Coffee (1991) names the liquidity/control trade-off, finance market actors should not intervene into the day-to-day control of the corporate system, Coffee (1991) concurs.

Orthodox neoclassical economic theory has long argued that managers lack "true entrepreneurial spirit," and therefore, they are under-compensated, but in fact, it may be that managers are compensated precisely because they are able to maintain risks at a level wherein a variety of constituencies (and not only shareholders) can benefit from the firm activities (Coffee, 1986: 24). Under all conditions, Coffee (1986) argues, it cannot be claimed that managers underperform or withhold residual cash flow simply on basis of making reference to a more moderate risk-utility function than that of the shareholders. There are several good reasons for why managers act as they do, paying attention to a wider array of factors than to maximize shareholder welfare, as prescribed by the business charter granted by the state.[4]

The theory of the market for management control is thus based on the wrong assumption regarding alleged managerial opportunism and substandard performance. Managers act in accordance with the legal role they are assigned, within the incentive system wherein they are operating, and within the horizon of meaning that they have individually and collectively developed and reinforced (i.e., they act rationally). However, the theory of the market for management control can still be defended if its proponent believes in the assumption that the managers are the shareholders' agents, but that is a normative position that deviates considerably from extant corporate legislation and court ruling cases.

The Role of Information Costs

Coffee (1986) point out that the theory of the market for management control ignores information cost in the market—in the price theory framework, prices do accommodate all information, a proposition disputed by elementary information economics theory (see, e.g., Akerlof, 1970)—and suggests that this omission leads to simplistic conclusions that render, for example, all conglomerates inefficient (a recurrent theme in the 1970s' literature), while in fact the efficiency of the conglomerate form is an empirical question that may display considerable variety. That is, for the average financial trader, it is costly to separate "good" and "bad" conglomerates (i.e., it involves information collection and analysis costs), and therefore, *all* conglomerates suffer from being lowly priced in the market, thus making them more attractive targets for takeover bids:

> [I]f investors cannot distinguish 'good' from 'bad' conglomerates (in terms of their likely future behavior), a 'market for lemons' effect could arise along the lines suggested by Professor Akerlof. That is, even if only a minority of all conglomerates exhibited the behavior predicted by the managerialists [e.g., growth and economic stability is prioritized over profit maximization], the market might still penalize the stock prices of all conglomerates by an average discount factor because monitoring by investors could not easily distinguish between these firms.
>
> (Coffee, 1986: 36)

Not least does empirical evidence regarding what firms that are approached by tender offers reveal that it is not primarily poorly functioning firms that are targeted (see, e.g., Davis and Stout, 1992). On the contrary, well-managed and financially sound companies are attracting tender offer bids: "[T]akeovers do not focus on the worst-managed companies, but rather operate only within an intermediate range where the expectation of a short-term turnaround profit exists" (Coffee, 1984: 1200). As the market for management control is *primarily* advocated on the premise that is provides a mechanism that disciplines poorly performing managers, the bidder preferences reject companies in a dire condition undermine the legitimacy of the market-based governance model:

> Financially distressed firms appear relatively immune to takeovers, either because no turnaround seems likely or because the level of risk associated with these companies makes them unattractive candidates for acquisition. Ironically, truly sick companies—or at least those whose problems do not appear to be easily remedied—become indigestible and survive, immune from attack precisely because of their pervasive inefficiency.
>
> (Coffee, 1984: 1204)

Moreover, the market for management control model predicts that substandard managerial decision-making (and, by implication, allegedly soaring and excessive agency costs passed on to shareholders, as agency theorists would argue in the 1970s), but such concerns were not listed by presumptive takeover bidders:

> A 1981 nationwide survey by Touche Ross & Co. asked corporate directors to rate from a list of specified factors the characteristics that made a potential target company attractive. It found that 'excellent management' was listed as either a 'major attraction' or a 'minor attraction' by ninety-eight percent, while the vast majority of responses denied that the perceived inefficiency of the target made it an attractive takeover prospect.
>
> (Coffee, 1984: 1212)

Such data are an embarrassment for proponents of the market for management control as their model fail to predict the correct drivers for takeover bids. Therefore, when considering empirical evidence, "[t]he utility of the hostile takeover is bounded," Coffee (1984: 1200) contends. More explicitly, Coffee (1984: 1157) is concerned that "the likelihood of erroneous business decisions" is significantly pronounced when a bidder, acting on basis of information "relatively inferior to that possessed by the target's management"—remember, this claim runs counter to the price theory and efficient market hypothesis—can obtain control of a corporation and "reverse existing policies." That is, the takeover bid procedure that the proponents of the market for management control hold in esteem and treat as the ultimate check on managerial performance, Coffee regards as a substandard mechanism for governing the corporate system. "Even in an efficient market," Coffee (1984: 1196) claims to substantiate his argument, "abundant empirical evidence shows that insiders can outperform the stock market with respect to investments in their own corporation's stock."

Existing Bailout Protection

Another factor that the theory of the market for management control fails to accommodate in the analysis is how, for example, finance markets are affected by regulations that protect certain market actors from losses, granting them the license to participate in high-risk projects without carrying the full responsibility for the consequences, or being able to transfer the liabilities to other actors. For instance, the swift growth of the junk bond market, being a principal source for the finance capital raised to fund takeover activities, is best explained on basis of the activities of savings and loan associations or pension funds, representing classes of institutions that are largely protected by government insurance (Coffee, 1986: 45). As a result, these investors have "little reason to monitor the level of risk accepted by their financial institutions," leading to a "a classic moral hazard problem" when the high returns paid on junk bonds are not "counterbalanced by high risks to these depositors so long as they can look to government insurance" (Coffee, 1986: 45). In short, the government carries the responsibility for potential losses of the savings and loan associations and pension funds' high-risk projects, which makes certain takeover activities more attractive and lucrative than they would be without such protection, especially if junk bond-financed takeover bids are *à la mode* among fund managers in saving and loans institutes, pension funds, and so on.

More generally, speaking about the higher presence of fully diversified funds in the finance market, the higher the risk appetite, and fund managers will be less willing to pay for diversified conglomerates and instead will search for stocks to fill specific niches in a portfolio (Coffee, 1986: 59). This preferences for stocks in companies with specialized know how—"core competences" as they would be referred to in the 1980s and 1990s (Hamel and Prahalad, 1994)—tend to underprice conglomerates and to portray managers as being overtly risk averse, that is, as a group that underperforms vis-à-vis shareholder risk preferences in predictable ways. At the same time, as Coffee (1986: 67) remarks, "it is not all shareholders who want the corporation to accept a higher risk level than managers prefer, but only diversified ones." Again, the theory of the market for management control is not a *general theory* of corporate governance but a *special theory* of how to maximize the economic benefits for one constituency, the shareholders with a preference for high-risk/high-yield holdings.

The Core Question: What Changes in the Law Can Be Justified on Basis of the Market for Management Control Argument?

In legal theory, in corporate legislation, and in several cases of court rulings in disputes between managers and directors and shareholders, the modern corporation includes a variety of rights, duties, and responsibilities involving different constituencies. In addition, within this legal framework, consisting of legal theory, law, and court decisions, Coffee (1986: 104) argues, "shareholder wealth and social wealth are not synonymous"; "the former can be enhanced in ways that do not increase, and may even decrease, the latter." Therefore, when being viewed optimistically, the theory of the market for management control regards, for example, takeover activities as "a mechanism by which shareholders are at last able to counteract management's inherent bias toward risk aversion and excessive earnings retention" (Coffee, 1986: 104). In contrast, when viewed more pessimistically, there are additional social costs associated with "this newfound shareholder power," simply because the firm serves a wider set of constituencies than merely the firm's most risk-inclined investors and because "society as a whole may share the manager's aversion toward risk or may benefit from his investment in firm-specific human capital" (Coffee, 1986: 104). As Coffee (1984) argues elsewhere, there are at least two major concerns, despite having some merit, regarding the efficacy of the market for managerial control, as explicated by Manne (1965, 1967):

> [T]he capital market can and does perform a socially desirable function in monitoring and deterring managerial inefficiency, it will argue this thesis has been overstated and has not received the critical scrutiny it deserves. Two basic criticisms will be advanced. First, the discipline generated by the market for corporate control is sufficiently limited that it can serve only as a remedy of last resort for massive managerial failures and not as the principal enforcer of corporate accountability. Second, any attempt to significantly increase the frequency of hostile takeovers may lead to serious diseconomies.
>
> (Coffee, 1984: 1153)

That is, the takeover activity is thus not a competitive game wherein alternative management teams present themselves as competing alternatives on basis of their ability to enrich the shareholders (see, e.g., Jensen and Ruback, 1983), but takeover activity is a form of financial engineering that may serve the end held in esteem—to maximize firm efficiency and, by implication, social welfare—but is more likely to benefit certain constituencies at the expense of the others. "If part of the gain [from a successful takeover] can thus be considered a wealth transfer from employees to shareholders, a normative issue surfaces: is it equitable for the law to facilitate such wealth transfers to shareholders from nonshareholder classes?" Coffee (1986: 104–105) asks and responds negatively. That is, Coffee (1986) argues, the theory of market for management control is based on the wrong premises (that shareholders are the only residual risk bearers and are therefore exclusively entitled to the free cash generated) and remains unsubstantiated in terms of the various assumptions made. At the same time, Coffee (1984: 1294) does recognize that hostile takeovers "generate a disciplinary force that constrains managerial behavior" and says that this "cannot seriously be disputed." But to further emphasize the role of market judgement, which is, after all, a "disciplinary mechanism" that is ultimately not the market but "rather the individual bidder who, having imperfect information, is more error-prone than are internal monitoring mechanisms within modern decentralized firms" (Coffee, 1984: 1249), beyond this point is not meaningful as long as there is evidence of internal managers and directors having "superior information" in comparison to market actors. In addition, Coffee (1984: 1294) adds, even "the most zealous proponents of the takeover [bid]" needs to agree that "there can be too much of even a good thing": "Given the currently competitive character of the market for corporate control, there is little evidence that public and private interests diverge significantly at present" (Coffee, 1984: 1295). Therefore, a legal reform that seeks to maximize the frequency of takeovers is likely "fail to minimize agency costs" in the same way as "other techniques of accountability" would but with the undesirable consequence of "significant diseconomies that will adversely affect not only shareholder welfare but also the more important goal of the efficient allocation of economic resources" (Coffee, 1984: 1156). As a consequence, the theory of the market for management control does not merit any legal changes or modifications in court decisions.

Summary and Conclusion

The 1950s' law and economics school critique of antitrust legislation as being detrimental for "efficiency" was expanded by Henry Manne (1962, 1965, 1967) in the 1960s. In Manne's argument, market efficiency (being predicated on basis of the price theory models and the efficient market hypothesis) enables market actors to monitor and reward managerial decision-making taking place inside the firm. The analytical model proposes that firms issue stocks and securities such as bonds, and the price of such stocks and securities should be seen as a measure of the degree of contentment among market actors. As stocks comes with voting rights, substandard and poor decisions in the existing management team may be punished if this team's members are exposed to the risk of a takeover, leading most likely to the loss of their jobs, a scenario they avoid. Based on this line of reasoning, Manne not only faithfully maintains the efficiency criteria inherited from the law and economics theory but also "turns the corporation inside out" by making the claim that, for example, owners of stock are in a better position to know what is a good decision than are insiders, that is, professional managers. Finance market actors can thus monitor and discipline managers, and legislation should therefore favour such a finance market control as that would benefit all constituencies, Manne claims.

Legal scholars avert such a call for reform and point at a series of highly unrealistic assumptions made and inconsistencies in the underlying theoretical model to reach the conclusion that a market for management control is neither possible to construct or render operable, nor is it a desirable arrangement as it would lead to a number of consequences that would impair the corporate system. Despite being portrayed as a daring but ultimately incredible proposition, the idea of a market for managerial control provides two major arguments to free-market advocacy and its shareholder primacy governance model: (1) the evaluation of stocks and securities corresponds to actual conditions and managerial activities inside the firm, normally concealed to outsiders (i.e., the finance market is devoid of speculative activities, rendering prices as what effectively mirror existing public information); (2) finance market actors are therefore capable of monitoring insiders "from afar"; that is, in cases of managerial malfeasance, the risk of a takeover and the recruitment of a new managerial team serve a prophylactic function. Both these propositions are rejected by moderate legal scholars, but the idea of finance market control being more effective than managerial elite rule (as prescribed by legal theory) is the basis for the contractual theory of the firm discussed in the next chapters. In addition, the second proposition, the idea that finance market actors are capable of assessing managerial decision-making quality and know better than insiders is a key assumption of the agency theory, examined in Chapter 4. The work of Henry Manne and others thus brought the law and economics school's critique of regulatory control of markets into the firm and the corporate system. From now on, the corporate system was to be monitored by finance market actors, free-market theorists argued.

Notes

1. Based on such convictions, Fischel (1978: 24) is even critical of the ban on insider trading, otherwise being widely regarded as a form of unjust trading as insiders are very likely to access information that others do not: "It is conceivable that management will possess inside information not reflected in security prices primarily because of prohibitions against insider trading. Efficient capital market theory, however, suggests that this situation is relatively rare." For Fischel (1978), highly speculative efficient capital market theory thus trumps both common-sense thinking and the carefully developed finance market legislation.
2. Tender offer bids are bids on the market stock price with a premium that are accepted by the board of directors, because the bid is beneficial for the shareholders (as prescribed by, for example, Delaware corporate law). In contrast, the term *hostile takeover* is used when tender offers are not gaining approval from the board of directors (Davis and Greve, 1997: 9).
3. The residual cash is transferred to the shareholders either as dividends or, more recently, in the form of stock repurchases, pushing market stock prices upward and therefore indirectly transferring the residual cash to the owners of stock (see, e.g., Grullon and Ikenberry, 2000; Dittmar, 2000).
4. As a legal matter, under Delaware law (the state where the majority of New York Stock Exchange companies are incorporated; Romano, 1985; Levitin, 2014), it is only in cases where "a change of control is anticipated through a sale or merger" that the directors have a "duty to maximize shareholders wealth" (Robé, 2012: 9, Footnote 23). The court case *Revlon v. MacAndrews and Forbes Holding* (506 A.2nd 173; Del. 1986) established this governance principle, but these "Revlon duties" do not apply in the "day-to-day management of the corporation's affairs," Robé (2012: 9) remarks.

3 1970s
The Contractual Theory of the Firm

Introduction

By the mid-1960s, the profit levels of American manufacturing industry started to decline, and in the 1970s the global economy, burdened by the first oil crisis, sank into a severe recession. The 1950s' antitrust enforcement critique and the 1960s' literature on the market for management control had both targeted state regulation and the corporate law as governance mechanisms that did not serve to maximize the efficiency of the corporate system, and in the 1970s, propelled by influential papers by Alchian and Demsetz (1972) and Jensen and Meckling (1976) portraying the firm as a nexus or bundle of contractual relations between business partners, the legal term *contract* was introduced by legal scholars and economists as a useful term fortifying the market-based corporate governance model. Liberal, free-trade economies have a long tradition of contractual freedom, stretching back to the eighteenth century, granting enterprising individuals the right to contract with whom they want to. For Thorstein Veblen ([1919] 1964: 158) for instance, one of the leading institutional economists, "the rights of free contract and security of property" were chief among the specific rights by which the Western civilization, promoting "equal opportunity and self-help," was built; for Veblen, the right to contract and the right to property are "paramount rights of civilized men" that cannot be compromised.

At the same time, the laissez-faire capitalism of the nineteenth century, leading to significant externalities including pauperization and human misery in, for example, the quickly urbanized industrial centres in Europe and North America, needed to be regulated and monitored by the sovereign state, not the least to handle labour rationalization and to secure the corporate system, and thus, the legal mechanism of the contract was a solution to the problem of how to handle a series of competing interests and trade-offs: "The laissez-faire rationalism of the nineteenth century found its juridical expression through the creation and sanctification of freedom of contract" (Urofsky, 1985: 65). Not the least did the legal device of the contract carry the promise of making industrial society sustainable and a better place for a larger proportion of its citizenry, while at the same time encouraging and promoting an enterprising culture; as Richard Hofstadter remarked (cited in Urofsky, 1985: 64), "industrialized society was to be humanized by law."

When proponents of contract theory introduced the idea of the firm as a nexus of contracts, a corollary the market for management control argument, they did not primarily think of the contract as a vehicle for social betterment but as a mechanism that specify the one-on-one relations between the firm's investors (i.e., primarily the shareholders qua allegedly residual risk bearers but also the creditors, who, importantly, do not contract for the residual cash flow) and the managers and directors overseeing the operations inside the firm. As discussed in this chapter, this innovative use of the term *contract*, derived from orthodox neoclassical economic theory and its proposition regarding market efficiency and market pricing, was not accepted by legal scholars who claimed that this represented a distorted and highly ideological use of the legal term *contract*. In addition, as corporate law as a constitutional law already provides a set of mandatory rules that prescribe and specify the relations between business venture participants, the new concept of contract could not surpass or retire the extant legislation. In the end, mainstream legal scholars claimed, the contact theory of the firm represents little more than a thinly veiled attempt to displace jurisprudence by an incomplete economic model resting on a series of assumptions that are either unsupported by empirical evidence or rely on idealized economic conditions (i.e., market efficiency).

Still, by the twist of fate and a fair share of pro-business mobilization and political activism, when the 1970s ended and the 1980s' agency theory argument was advanced on broad front that shareholders were *the only legitimate claimants* of the residual economic value generated by the firm, the institutional conditions and the political climate had undergone significant changes, which, in turn, served the interest of contractarians and agency theorists. Even though they advocated a debased and piecemeal application of contract theory, tailored to suit the interests of the owners of finance capital, after the 1980s' pro-business, and neoconservative and libertarian political takeover in the U.S., the question was no longer so much about "being right" as it was about saying what the financiers of free-market advocacy had paid for; what they paid for was to hear academics and policy-makers saying that regardless of extant corporate law—treating the firm as a team-production entity involving many stakeholders, and therefore being understood as a being carefully managed to balance a variety of interest—the firm's shareholders (in the case of public firms with dispersed ownership) were still the firms investors and thus eligible for the residual cash flow. No matter how much legal scholars, management studies researchers, and economic sociologists objected to this enactment of the firm, by the mid-1980s, this free-market model of the firm, deviating from corporate law's statutes and intensions, was fortified. In other words, the new corporate governance policy was not so much a matter of securing the long-term viability of the corporate system and, by implication, the system of competitive capitalism as it was geared towards maximizing the economic value extraction to benefit short-term-oriented finance capital owners. The long-term consequences of the 1970s' contract theory and the 1980s' agency theory, both equally porous as scholarly theories of the firm, are significant and yet to be determined.

The Neoconservative and Libertarian Pro-Business and Free-Market Mobilization of the 1970s

In comparison to the 1960s, at least its first half—the profit rates started to wane after 1966, being the earliest indications of the decline of managerial capitalism—was characterized by a comfortable consensus regarding how to organize businesses. The exception was a few ultraconservative and libertarian and, on the other side of the political continuum, left-leaning groups who in their own idiosyncratic ways expressed their impatience with the capitalist economic system. In the politically and financially shaky decade of the 1970s, that consensus would quickly wither away, and the sea change did not favour left-wing politics as a pro-business, free-market community including business tycoons and wealthy capital owners were now ready to pour their money where they could earn benefits. In the 1970s and 1980s, the entire regime of managerial capitalism and Keynesian welfare state policy came under fire and was replaced in considerable parts with a neoconservative and libertarian agenda that benefitted the owners of financial capital greatly.

In many ways, 1971 was a key year as president Nixon declared that the U.S. was now abandoning the sinking ship of the Bretton Woods monetary system. Less spectacular but almost equally important in hindsight was the short memorandum that the Judge Lewis F. Powell sent to the U.S. Chamber of Commerce, only weeks before Nixon named him a Supreme Court judge. The so-called *Powell memorandum* (at times even referred to, somewhat misleading, as the *Powell Manifesto* by his followers) expressed Powell's deep concern regarding the standing of private enterprises in American society. "No thoughtful person can question that the American economic system is under broad attack. This varies in scope, intensity, in the techniques employed, and in the level of visibility," Powell (1971: 1) ominously declared. In Powell's (1971: 1) memorandum, "extremists of the left" ("Communists, New Leftists and other revolutionaries") are portrayed as an highly influential group being "far more numerous, better financed, and increasingly are more welcomed and encouraged by other elements of society, than ever before in our history." In addition, Powell (1971: 3) continues, "[t]he assault on the enterprise system was not mounted in a few months. It has gradually evolved over the past two decades." As these groups have advanced their agenda, Powell worries, the "ultimate issue" for the American businessperson is to secure the "survival of what we call the free enterprise system, and all that this means for the strength and prosperity of America and the freedom of our people" (Powell, 1971: 3). In order to preserve the free-enterprise system that built America and is written into the very fabric of the American Republic, "top management" (remember that Judge Powell is addressing the Chamber of Commerce, where managers are paying members, which at least in this setting would secure them from the critique of bypassing market evaluations, as free-market protagonists would persistently claim throughout the 1970s and 1980s), need to take action "to protect and preserve the system itself" (Powell, 1971: 3).

Judge Powell then proceeds to identify the key enemies of the free-enterprise system, unsurprisingly making "intellectuals"—the targeted group *par preférénce* in populist and conservative thinking (see Hofstadter, 1963)—located at university campuses as one key group that needs to be disarmed and muted. Not only do these "intellectuals" (Judge Powell himself uses the citation market to distance himself from this allegedly subversive group) dominate university campuses; "in many instances, these 'intellectuals' end up in regulatory agencies or governmental departments with large authority over the business system they do not believe in," Powell (1971: 4) warns. In addition, the news media, the Supreme Court (somewhat unexpectedly given Judge Powell's successful career in jurisprudence), and Congress and the Senate are areas where Powell sees evidence of anti-enterprise thinking: "Business has been the favorite whipping-boy of many politicians for many years," Powell (1971: 6) claims. Somewhat surprisingly, given the neoconservative and libertarian crusade again the American trade unions, Judge Powell does recognize the role of organized labor, albeit in the passing:

> [M]ost of the essential freedoms remain: private ownership, private profit, labor unions, collective bargaining, consumer choice, and a market economy in which competition largely determines price, quality and variety of the goods and services provided the consumer.
>
> (Powell, 1971: 7)

All these social changes (including e.g., the citizen right movement, women's liberation, and the "sexual revolution" derived from, *inter alia*, the launching of the contraception pill in the early 1960s) that Judge Powell sees as undermining free enterprise are also a threat to "individual freedom" (Powell, 1971: 7). Even more important for the forthcoming problem formulation activities in the quarters with which Powell communicate, he stresses how shareholders are suffering losses when other groups advance their interests:

> [T]he 20 million stockholders—most of whom are of modest means—are the real owners, the real entrepreneurs, the real capitalists under our system. They provide the capital which fuels the economic system which has produced the highest standard of living in all history.
>
> (Powell, 1971: 6)

Judge Powell (1971: 7) closes this memorandum with a most foreboding phrase, declaring that "[b]usiness and the enterprise system are in deep trouble, and the hour is late."

Writing in hindsight, it is easy to think of Judge Powell's memorandum as a foremost treatise within what Thomas Frank (2012: 122) refers to as "the political economy of self-pity," wherein the wealthiest and most influential groups of the American society—certainly not men and women "of modest means"—are campaigning for draconian action to curb any reforms conducive to economic equality. However, Judge Powell's memorandum is, Mayer (2016: 73) suggests, "a virtual anti-*Communist Manifesto*," a tract that "laid out a blueprint for a conservative takeover." It is thus no wonder that neoconservative and libertarian groups regard Powell's short text, virtually unaccompanied by any factual evidence supporting the claims made, a form of free-market manifesto. At the same time, to simply assume that this eminent social servant, just a neat little step from a Supreme Court seat, would recourse to a delirious paranoia is not a flattering scholarly attitude. Instead, the actual changes between say the mid-1960s and the early 1970s, a period of extraordinary, almost unprecedented social changes in the American society, needs to be examined.

Industry Regulation and Governmental Oversights

Vogel (1983: 23) argues that in the 1970s, "[t]he business community found itself fighting its political battles primarily on terrain defined by those who wanted to reduce its prerogatives." In fact, the "mutual distrust and antagonism" that developed between the regulators (i.e., state-based and federal regulatory agencies) and the regulated (industry) in the 1965–1975 period "has no parallel outside the United States," Vogel (1983: 24–25) claims. This sense of losing the foothold in American society was not totally devoid of substance as the rising welfare and living standard accomplished in the post-war era were gradually being taken for granted and leaving room for a more detailed critique of capitalism despite its obvious merits. Just as the New Deal policies had been so successful in restoring and rehabilitating competitive capitalism that its sheer success bred an anti–New Deal culture in, for example, conservative suburban communities (Phillips-Fein, 2011: 731), in the same manner, the success of competitive capitalism gave rise to anti-capitalism sentiments among certain groups. The new generation of intellectuals and left-leaning groups who were fortunate to not have to endure the Great Depression, increasingly claimed that capitalism should be able to perform better and take on the responsibility to not only produce goods and services but also care for the environment, promote gender equality, citizens' rights, and other auxiliary benefits really never being the businessman's (or businesswoman's) foremost priority. This culture of expanding expectations, a form of unexpected by-products from the stability of the well-functioning corporate system, gradually spilled over into policy-making. Vogel (1983: 27) points at the magnitude of this new regulatory frenzy in Washington, D.C.:

> Before the passage of the national Traffic and Motor Vehicle Safety Act in 1966, the automobile industry was completely unregulated by the federal government . . . ford Motor Company did not even have a full-time lobbyist. By the mid-1070s, nearly every aspect of the automobile was regulated, including exhaust levels, fuel efficiency and safety: a major share of the car industry's research and development became devoted to compliance with government directives, while the cumulative impact of eighteen government mandated specifications adopted between 1968 and 1974 was estimated to have increased the retail, price of the average car by $300.
>
> (Vogel, 1983: 27)

As Vogel (1983: 28) recognizes, the American business community continued to "cry wolf" at "every new invasion of its prerogatives," but its complains and grievances appeared to have lost much of their weight as policy-makers were now essentially taking the corporate system of managerial capitalism for granted, seemingly ironically, very much as the orthodox neoclassicists did. The response to the regulatory activities was that Washington, D.C., was now the site for a significant institutional build-up in the power balance between policy-makers and industry; Washington became the home of substantial amounts of industry sponsored lawyers, lobbyists, think tanks, and activist groups, among others, all mobilized in the struggle over industry autonomy in a political climate favouring regulation: "Between 1968 and 1978 the number of corporations with public affairs offices in Washington increased from one hundred to more than five hundred" (Vogel, 1983: 30–31); between 1972 and 1978 alone, the number of lawyers increased from 16,000 to 26,000 in Washington, "in large measure due to the increased corporate demands for legal representation" (Vogel, 1983: 31). "In 1971," Hacker and Pierson (2010: 176) write, "only 1975 firms had registered lobbyists in Washington, but by 1982, 2,445 did."

In this new political climate, where polity and industry interest no longer could be assumed to proceed in lockstep, the very institutional structure of American policy-making was altered. While the U.S. has been, Vogel (1983: 25) proposes, "traditionally considered the most conservative or pro-business capitalist democracy," in the 1970s, industrial relations moved in the direction that Judge Powell had hoped for. During the decade, pro-business activism and scholarship financiers started to pipe money into conservative think tanks such as the American Enterprise Institute (AEI; which sponsored, e.g., the antitrust enforcement critique work conducted by Robert H. Bork) and its "rival conservative think tank in Washington" (Mayer, 2016: 90), the Heritage Foundation. In addition, the neoconservative John M. Olin Foundation, chaired by the former secretary of Treasury of the Nixon and Ford administrations and one of the most persistent and successful pro-business activists, William E. Simon (Asen, 2009), started to fund not only law and economics scholars at the University of Chicago, including George Stigler and Chicago allies located elsewhere such as the legal scholar Henry Manne. Moreover, the Olin Foundation financed American Enterprise Institute, the Manhattan Institute for Policy Research, and the Hoover Institution at Stanford, all neoconservative and pro-business strongholds, and provided generous funding for conservative writers and scholars such as Irving Kristol and Allan Bloom, following Judge Powell's lead. During the 1970s, Washington, D.C., became a battlefield wherein the status of free-market capitalism was fought for, with pro-business and free-enterprise institutes and organizations gaining the upper hand in terms of its financial endowments. Judge Lewis Powell was probably happy to see that his call for immediate and steadfast action led to considerable mobilization in the 1970s.

Unsurprisingly, these efforts translated into a new political climate during the Carter presidency, and the bill reducing capital gains taxation passed in 1978 was one of the first major breakthroughs in the advancement of neoconservative, pro-business policy:

> The bill reducing capital gains taxation enacted in 1978 represents a classic piece of class legislation: it provided direct financial benefits for businesses as a whole and virtually no benefits to middle and lower income taxpayers. The passage of this legislation was an extraordinary political achievement for business: it represented the most important redistributive policy initiated by business in more than a decade.
>
> (Vogel, 1983: 39)

The new political climate was also surfacing in President Carter's announcement in a State of the Union address, that "government could no longer solve people's problems" (cited in Jones, 2012: 254). In 1980, Ronald Reagan won the election on basis of a pro-business agenda that Judge Powell would have heartily approved, and in the 1980s, much of the conventional wisdom of managerial capitalism, established in the American corporate system on basis of New Deal Legislation, was gradually retrenched. During the Reagan presidency, The Heritage Foundation delivered no less than 1,270 policy proposals, of which 61 were adopted by the Reagan administration (Mayer, 2016: 90), one legitimate measure of how well the free-market, pro-business community managed to advance its interests. Judge Powell's memorandum had been translated into a successful political agenda, wherein shareholder welfare was now not only a centrepiece—it was the very guiding principle of economic policy and legislation, either directly or in its consequences.

How to Bypassing Corporate Law: The Contract Theory View

Corporate law relies on the idea of fiduciary duties, giving directors and defined for their managers specific responsibilities vis-à-vis the constituencies affected by the business charter granted by the state, and court rulings have persistently emphasized the business judgement rule to reinforce managerial discretion in cases of disputes. In mainstream legal theory, the rule of law is to maintain the interest of a variety of constituencies and neither *de jure*, nor *de facto* exclusively support efficiency maximizing activities. This was the basis of the antitrust enforcement critique of law and economics scholars in the 1950s and thereafter and equally so for the proponents of the market for management control, first articulated in the 1960s. In the 1970s, strongly supported by the neoconservative and libertarian pro-business mobilization, a new theoretical model was gradually advanced as a contestant for the regulation of the corporate system—the *contractual theory of the firm* or, more shortly, *contract theory*. As demonstrated in the previous chapters, for free-market advocators, any kind of governmental intervention into supposedly self-regulating and market efficient comes at a loss of efficiency and therefore, any legislative or regulatory activity or initiative is met with great scepticism or outright hostility. Also in cases where the state and its legislative procedure were instrumental in establishing easy-to-understand, yet enforceable legal strictures governing the corporate system and thus enabling market creation on wide scale in the last decades of the nineteenth century, the ahistorical view of orthodox neoclassical economic theory turns a blind eye to these efforts and accomplishments and instead assumes that markets are "naturally occurring" (Harcourt, 2011) This idea, which its critics dismiss as a "creation myth," or wishful thinking (Vogel, 1996) as there is always a need for a market-maker and a sovereign that serve as the ultimate guarantor for free markets. Thus over the course of the post–World War II period, corporate law per se, relying on trust and fiduciary duties, Kaufman, Zacharias, and Karson (1995: 61) propose:

> Totalitarianism might thus lurk ominously behind trust, and this treat loomed large in postwar writing on the modern corporation. Few could avoid comparing the concentrated power of large corporations and their 'supporting' regulatory apparatus with that of various Soviet counterparts. This comparison was particularly disturbing in regulated industries like energy, communications m and transportation, in which the distinctions between private and public administration were far from clear.
>
> (Kaufman et al., 1995: 61)

The oligopolistic economy that evolved during the post–World War II economic expansion was thus met with scepticism in pro-business quarters, otherwise favouring business interests. Consistent with its disregard of any elitist—an attitude otherwise affirmed as the idea that an unregulated market tends to bestow great wealth on elites was appealing to the pro-business community, itself commanding considerable wealth—and centralists attempts to regulate markets and business matters, a contractual theory of the firm and a contract theory more widely were advocated.

In the eyes of the pro-business community, contract law was regarded as a better protection of private rights (whether of the propertied or the propertyless, of owners, managers, or workers, etc.) than was corporate legislation that emphasized trust and fiduciary duties that easily justified further government interventions such as additional detailed legislation and new regulatory practices (Kaufman and Zacharias, 1992: 528–529). More specifically, given the antitrust critique and the advocacy of the market for management control, what was especially appealing with contract theory was that it postulated that shareholders were not the owners of the firm theoretically speaking (already affirmed by corporate law and thus a stricture that unfortunately could not be bypassed), but instead they were granted the status as the firm's *investors* (Kaufman and Zacharias, 1992: 554). Moore and Rebérioux (2011: 87) explain the wide-reaching implications from this new proposition:

> The rejection of the concept of ownership, as applied to the business firm, is a standard assumption of this contractarian approach in law and economics . . . By definition, one cannot possess a contract (or contracts) as one can possess a standard asset. Shareholders are therefore not depicted as owners, but rather as 'principals.' The implications, as far as corporate governance is concerned, are basically the same: managers and directors, who are the 'agents,' should be accountable solely to shareholders.
>
> (Moore and Rebérioux, 2011: 87)

In the 1980s, propelled by the previous antitrust critique of law and economics scholars and the theory of the market for management control, the "post-corporate law" view of the firm as a "nexus of contracts" (as prescribed by Alchian and Demsetz, 1972, and Jensen and Meckling, 1976) was widely embraced in orthodox economic theory and legal theory adhering to free-market principles. "The word 'firm' is simply a shorthand description of a way to organize activities under contractual arrangements that differ from those of ordinary product markets," Cheung (1982: 3) asserts, for instance, very much in line with the new conventional wisdom.

Of Contract Theory

In the following, the legal view of contact theory is examined, starting with the proponents of the abandoning of the concept of fiduciary duties and trust to pursue the contractual theory of the firm based on contracts between the various stakeholders participating in or having a stake in the economic value production of the firm. Easterbrook and Fischel (1996) are one example of legal scholars being ardent defenders of contact theory as a legal device that serve to increase the efficiency of the corporate system. Starting with an examination of one of the key legal innovations enshrined by corporate law, the principle of limited liability, prescribing that, for example, shareholders are accountable to only the finance capital they have invested in, for example, a business venture in the unfortunate case of default. The limited liability clause have been controversial and disputed from the beginning as it is claimed to promote opportunistic behaviour and to create moral hazard as, for example, managers are not carrying the whole downside risk of their decisions (Djelic, 2013; Djelic and Bothello, 2013; Ireland, 2010; Bryer, 1997; French, 1990). In response to such critique, Easterbrook and Fischel (1996: 41) lists a number of benefits; first, limited liability "[d]ecreases the need to monitor agents" as there are already clear "rules on the game" that define responsibilities and rights (Easterbrook and Fischel, 1996: 41); second, and by a large a corollary of the first proposition, limited liability "[r]educes the costs of monitoring other shareholders" (Easterbrook and Fischel, 1996: 42); third, and related to the market for voting rights provided by stock markets, the free transfer of shares, limited liability gives managers "incentives to act efficiently" (Easterbrook and Fischel, 1996: 42); fourth, being an implication of the third proposition, limited liability makes it possible for market prices to "reflect additional information about the value of the firm" (Easterbrook and Fischel, 1996: 43), a condition that increases the efficiency of the corporate system. In addition, as the fifth proposition suggests, limited liability allows more "efficient diversification"; and, sixth, it "facilitates optimal investment decisions" (Easterbrook and Fischel, 1996: 43).

Taken together, the ability to grant limited liability on basis of dispersed ownership facilitates firm-specific production of economic value. Still, the limited liability of shareholders, enacted in corporate law, does not solve the problem regarding how the economic value generated inside the firm should be distributed, nor does it prescribe how to minimize the risk of managerial opportunism and poor managerial performance. In Easterbrook and Fischel's (1996: 38) contract theory, the solution to both the distribution and the monitoring problem is simply, following the previous free-market advocacy programs discussed in Chapters 1 and 2, to institute the shareholders as the only legitimate bearers of residual risk and therefore being entitled the right to claim the whole of the residual cash generated. Easterbrook and Fischel (1996: 38) base this argument on the assumption that managers are incapable of following only straightforward instructions whose outcomes are easily assessed on basis of market pricing (an argument being at the core of agency theory, discussed the next chapter):

> Managers told to serve two masters (a little for the equity holders, a little for the community) has been freed of both and is answerable to neither, Faced with a demand from either group, the manager can appeal to the interest of the other. Agency costs [the shareholders' costs to monitor managers] rise and social wealth falls.
>
> (Easterbrook and Fischel, 1996: 38)

How market prices, postulated to have a superior ability to accommodate not only certain information but *all* information, would be unable to effectively price the outcome from a more complex set of managerial objectives and decisions is not explained by Easterbrook and Fischel (1996) but is nevertheless indicative of the varying degree of information effectiveness in contract theory and other theories based on or derived from price theory and the efficient market hypothesis: in some cases, the market "knows all, sees all," while in other cases, when its suits the consistency of the theoretical argument, markets are less fit to accommodate information in its pricing mechanisms.

As have been already addressed in Chapter 1 and 2, the question for more moderate commentators and policy-makers is on what grounds shareholder welfare argument justify legal reform, and Easterbrook and Fischel (1996) answer this question by making the claim that what is good for shareholders is also good or anyone else; that is, they admit no externalities in shareholder primacy governance:

> [M]aximizing profits for equity investors assists other 'constituencies' automatically. The participants in the venture play complementary rather than antagonistic roles, a successful firm provides jobs for workers and goods and services for consumers. The more appealing the goods to consumers, the more profits (and jobs). Prosperity for stockholders, workers, and communities goes hand in glove with better products for consumers.
>
> (Easterbrook and Fischel, 1996: 38)

Needless to say, this is a proposition that demands empirical substantiation and that fortunately it is lending itself to empirical testing. The evidence suggests that a one-sided concern for shareholder welfare is not of necessity beneficial for "other constituencies automatically." This claim is discussed in more detail later.

Still, this definition of the shareholders as the primary benefactors of the firm's production of economic value is advanced as an indubitable proposition in contact theory. Easterbrook and Fischel (1993) therefore examine the differences between contact theory and the corporate law concept of fiduciary duties to examine a principally important distinction between the view of managers as an autonomous actor operating under fiduciary duties prescribed by corporate law and the contract theory view that enact managers as the shareholders' agents (the firm's investors are therefore, *ex hypothesi*, the managers' principals). The legal concept of *fiduciary duty*, based on trust rather than a legally enforceable contractual relation, is one of the cornerstones in much legislation and in corporate law. In order to discredit corporate legislation (despite its status *qua* law and its historical roots and role in institutionalizing competitive capitalism), contract theorists portray fiduciary duties as an inefficient mechanism to monitor managers and to accomplish other desirable outcomes. In Easterbrook and Fischel's (1993) treatment of fiduciary duties, the term is simply re-interpreted in accordance with the contract theory they prescribe, and they propose that fiduciary duty is, in fact, nothing more than a form of contractual relation—a venturesome idea that legal scholars strongly object to (Howard, 1991; DeMott, 1988). Following their stated proposition that managers are capable of responding only to *one* objective, Easterbrook and Fischel (1993: 425) suggest that "many agency relations that fall under the 'fiduciary' banner are so diverse that a single rule could not cover all without wreaking havoc." What "wreaking havoc" means in this setting remains unexplained, but following the efficiency criteria of contract theory, it must be assumed that it denotes to perform below the maximum efficiency and benefit of investors. While Easterbrook and Fischel (1993: 426) generously admit that "no contract can cover all contingencies," they still claim that parties are able to handle the major issues on basis of contracts. In contrast, any legislation and regulatory practice that rely on fiduciary duties on part of the so-called agent (i.e., a manager) impose unnecessarily high costs on the venture:

> [A] 'fiduciary' relation is a contractual one characterized by unusually high costs of specification and monitoring. The duty of loyalty replaces detailed contractual terms, and courts flesh out the duty of loyalty by prescribing the actions the parties themselves would have preferred if bargaining were cheap and all promises fully enforced.
>
> (Easterbrook and Fischel, 1993: 427)

In other words, Easterbrook and Fischel (1993: 438) boldly claim that legislatures, courts, and commissions are struggling to make sense of the term *fiduciary duty* and to formulate a unifying approach while at the same time claiming that there is "nothing to look for"; instead, a fiduciary duty should be understood in strictly contractual terms: "Contract and fiduciary duty lie on a continuum best understood as using a single, although singularly complex, algorithm," Easterbrook and Fischel (1993: 446) say. While being seemingly insignificant, this passage is of central importance for contract theory. Fiduciary duty as central legal term and the basis for, for example, corporate law and what grants directors and managers discretion in making business decisions, is here redefined as form of contract. Easterbrook and Fischel (1993) thus simply try to bypass one of the central legal theory terms by subordinating it to price theory and a free-market theory contract model. This is also indicative of the colonialist tendencies in orthodox neoclassical economic theory (Fourcade, Ollion, and Algan, 2015) to simply suggest, whenever theoretical inconsistencies or competing theoretical frameworks are encountered, that the favoured economic theory overrules all other competing theories including also legislation. Rather than taking competing analytical frameworks seriously and to recognize the practical problems being addressed, or to reconcile alternative theoretical models, the orthodox neoclassical economic theory and the law and economic analysis rely on epistemic conventionalism by referring to shared beliefs communities. Such a view arguably serves to undermine the credibility of the key claims made, and cast doubt upon the wider theoretical framework being advocated. In the end, the attempt to bury fiduciary duties as a legal term by reducing it to a matter of economic contracting is indicative of what Desan (2005: 23) refers to as "[t]he banality employed by economists in describing legal categories."

Taken together, Easterbrook and Fischel (1996, 1993) advocate a contact theory of the firm, rendering the firm a bundle of contracts and enacting shareholders as the firm's investor as the principal and the managers and directors as the shareholders' agents. This contact theory view of the firm thus presents a continuation of the free-market governance model in the antitrust critique and the market for management control theory but now target extant corporate law as what are ineffective in monitoring managers. Before the legal theory response to this attempt to deconstruct the legitimacy of corporate law and court rulings derived therefrom are discussed, a few cases where the contract theory applies without undermining the fiduciary duty concept are examine.

Examples of Contracting Within Corporate Legislation

As corporate law is a constitutional law, a law that prescribes the mandatory rules and relations between the business promoters and the various stakeholders of a new business venture, in the U.S. the individual states can freely enact their own corporate laws that suit regional and local interests and to attract tax-paying companies. *De facto*, it is Delaware corporate law that has been most successful in attracting companies, and close to 90 percent of the companies registered on the New York Stock Exchange (NYSE) are registered in Delaware. As states, technically speaking, compete over firms on basis of its corporate law, the differences between different state legislation is an excellent testing ground for what business promoters and shareholders appreciate in corporate legislation. Lamoreaux (1998: 66) argues that one of the most important consequences of corporate law was to protect contractual parties (say, a group of business promoters) against insiders' claim to divest a firm as soon as they are no longer interested in participating in the business venture. To protect business ventures against such disruptive activities, the firm is *de jure* the owner of its own capital, giving dissatisfied partners who want to liquidize their holdings no opportunity to undermine the business venture. That is, corporate law does not only define the boundaries of the firm and serve to protect it from outsiders, but it factually institutes the firm as an autonomous legal entity for the benefit of all business promoters and other stakeholders.

Still, the degree of protection may differ between states and therefore, Lamoreaux (1998: 66) argues, promoters seeking business charter for their business venture can decide what "degree of firmness" (i.e., how tight or loose legally enforceable protection they want for their venture) they prefer when selecting state for incorporation. As a consequence, Lamoreaux (1998: 70) follows orthodox neoclassical economic theory in emphasizing that the line of demarcation between markets and hierarchies is porous and fluid as the market to some extent is determined by the constitutional rights of corporate law, making market mechanisms an essential feature of the "degree of firmness" being selected. It is noteworthy that even though state-level corporate law differs in content and its degree of legally enforceable rights, state law is still based on the premises that it is the directors who are given the mandate to make independent business decisions within the firm. Managers, who contract theory enacts as the shareholders' agents (just like agency theory does), are on the contrary the directors' agents, but the managers, selected and recruited by the directors, formally speaking, do not operate on basis of contractual terms vis-à-vis the directors but on basis of fiduciary duties that, in turn, justify the reliance on the business judgement rule in court ruling cases. Lamoreaux (1998) demonstrates that the contact theory view is accurate in the early stage activities where the firm is incorporated, providing the business promoters with a "market for corporate law," providing various choice alternatives.

As a practical matter, the actual choices made over time indicate that business promoters prefer conformity and transparency rather than more exotic governance models and thus tend to end up with the Delaware corporate law alternative, a market-based condition that critics of contract theory take as an evidence of the efficacy of existing corporate law and business promoters' unwillingness to experiment with the corporate governance mechanisms, especially in the early stages of new business venturing. If business promoters, who oversee and manage a finance capital raising venture in Manne's (1965, 1967) view, thought they would benefit from a lower degree of firmness in their venture, they would choose to incorporate their business outside of Delaware, but as they do not demonstrate such preferences, American public firms are by and large incorporated in accordance with mainstream corporate legislation.

The Legal Theory and the Economic Views of Contracts

One principal concern in the advocacy of contract theory is that the juridical term contract is strictly defined by legal scholars and therefore denotes something different than it does for an economist, a political scientist, or political philosopher. In classic contract theory in political philosophy, in the seminal works of Thomas Hobbes, John Locke, and Jean-Jacques Rousseau, society is assumed to be based on implicit contracts between the subject and the state (be it a sovereign monarch, as in Hobbes, or the democratically elected parliament, as in Thomas Paine) and the compliance of the subject justified by the benefits, rights, and duties that this contract engenders. For economists, this is essentially the manner in which they invoke the term *contract*, that is, as a metaphorical and loosely defined term. However, as a legal term and a legally enforceable device, a contract is defined as "[a] promise or set of promises for the breach of which the law gives a remedy, or the performance of which the law in some way are cognizes as a duty" (Goldberg, 1976b: 46). For Goldberg (1976b: 49), an economist, the "paradigmatic contract" of neoclassical economic theory is a "[d]iscrete transaction in which no duties between the parties prior to the contract formation and in which the duties of the parties are determined at the formation stage." Unfortunately, for many transactions, there is a large set of contracts for which such simplistic assumptions is a "grotesque caricature," Goldberg (1976b: 49) claims (see, e.g., Riles, 2011). Goldberg (1976b) points at series of complications affecting how well contracts can accommodate all the contingencies they need to recognize:

> Relations to which to take place over a long period of time and in which all parties will have to deal with each other regularly over a wide range of issues (many of them unknown in advance) often are forced in this discrete transaction mold, both in legal and economic analysis.
>
> (Goldberg, 1976b: 49)

The tendency to turn a blind eye to how contracts are practically used to legally prescribe mutual economic responsibilities includes a certain elegance and theoretical parsimony, but it has also misled economists to "suppress the relational aspects of contracts" (Goldberg, 1976b: 49). By the end of the day, economists are left with theory of contracts based on choice that is of limited practical value, while legal scholars and practitioners continue to refine and modify their incomplete contracts to the benefit of practical ends; "[w]hile legal scholars are at least making slow progress towards accommodating long-run complex relations in a broadened theory of contracts, economists have, with rare exceptions, not faced up to (or even perceived) the problems" (Goldberg, 1976b: 49). For Goldberg (1976b: 51), the fallacy that economists succumb to is to treat *all* private-sector exchange as discrete transactions, wherein "firms equate marginal costs to marginal revenue" (based on the zero-transaction-cost hypothesis, per se highly disputed as it is neither easily measured nor proved on basis on empirical data, nor intuitively credible; "it is not likely that a detailed knowledge of that mythical world will be of much practical use," Goldberg, 1976b: 45, suggests). This concept of contract again only applies in highly idealized settings and are therefore of limited use in real-world economies:

> The identity of the parties and the social milieu within which the contract is consummated are irrelevant. The exchange is cloaked in anonymity with one party selling to the market and the other buying from the market . . . [I]n its purest form it has no real world counterpart.
>
> (Goldberg, 1976a: 428)

This suggests that the analyst does not need to be so greatly concerned about *how* marginal costs and marginal revenues are perfectly matched; being consecrated to a theorem, the zero-transaction-cost assumption enjoys protection from the risk of falsification on basis of empirical evidence, as regular conjectures would be:

> Working within the discrete transaction paradigm, economists have developed an elaborate and elegant optimization framework which provides a rigorous definition of economic efficiency. In an administered contracts world we are not so fortunate.
>
> (Goldberg, 1976a: 431)

More important, precisely because economists use the term *contract* as an idealized and metaphorical sense, Goldberg (1976b: 51) continues, the extant contracting practices of, for example, public-sector organizations and government agencies appear to generate distortions including, for example, opportunistic behavior such as gold plating, which, by implication, disqualify such contracting on basis of the predominant efficiency criteria that economists endorse. Unfortunately, the idea that an idealized model of contracts can, at low cost, eliminate the regulatory problems facing agencies is illusory and rooted in theoretical simplifications of real world problems, Goldberg (1976a: 441) argues:

> [I]f the regulatory relationship were replaced by a private contract, the problems faced by the private agent would differ mainly in degree rather than in kind from those that plague regulators and provide a field day for their critics. Indeed, even in a rather simple private sector contract like a university food service contract one can observe on a lesser scale the whole panoply of regulatory horrors.
>
> (Goldberg, 1976a: 441)

That is, contactors would face the same problems regarding unknown futures as regulators do and would thus act like regulators to secure their interests:

> Long-term, flexible pricing contracts with cost-based, profit-limitation features will discourage internal efficiency, discourage hard bargaining with labor and other suppliers, encourage gold plating, and encourage excessive capital formation. That is, the provider will have incentives to act very much like a regulated firm. Likewise, the agent will have incentives to act very much like a regulator, analyzing the cost figures of the provider, determining whether the measured profits meet the criteria laid out in the initial contract, monitoring quality and capital decisions, and so forth.
>
> (Goldberg, 1976a: 444)

Uncertainty about the future (a factual condition most economists accept) in combination with self-interest (a proposition widely endorsed by economists and actively encouraged under the label "instrumental rationality") leads to a convergence in the behavior of the regulator and the contract-holder, Goldberg (1976a) says.

Therefore, in summary, the assumption regarding idealized contracting condition, lifted out from economics textbooks, then leads to the proposition that, for example, public franchising contract are ineffective and poorly designed, arguably because public-sector agents are either incompetent or act opportunistically (and potentially both), a claim that fails to be substantiated but remains a highly tenuous proposition derived from the simplistic assumptions made regarding how contracts are written and how they are modified to accommodate contingencies that were not anticipated when the contract was originally written:

> [S]ome of the regulatory problems perceived by economists are largely illusory; they are the result of stacking regulatory outcomes against irrelevant standards generated by models which suppress the contractual complexities inherent in the so-called natural monopoly sector.
>
> (Goldberg, 1976a: 444–445)

In other words, the "discrete transactional framework" that economists assume is a baseline standard, with no transactions costs involved, leads to a failure to appreciate the complexity of noncontractual arrangements and make economists "unduly sanguine as to the efficacy of private market solutions to many problems" (Goldberg, 1976b: 52). "Economic theory generally ignores the complexity of contractual arrangements by implicitly assuming that most exchange takes place in the discrete transaction form," Goldberg (1976a: 445) summarizes. In brief, based on highly speculative assumptions, economists believe they can, *ex cathedra*, dismiss extant public-sector contracting practices on the basis that they allegedly fail to demonstrate the features prescribed by the normative model derived from the zero transaction zero-transaction-cost theorem. That is, the map is deemed to overrule the actual territory. When Goldberg (2013) summarizes this view, writing close to four decades later, the same argument holds:

> In the economic modeling of the old days the world was characterized by zero transaction costs or, what amounts to the same thing, complete contingent contracts. Under either formulation, the structure of the contracts was irrelevant. The structure does matter, however, if transaction costs (whatever that might mean) are positive or contracts are incomplete.
>
> (Goldberg, 2013: 85)

In a world characterized by an uncertainty about the future and the influence of self-interest, contracts can never be written on basis of a zero transaction costs assumption.

THE QUESTION OF FIDUCIARY DUTIES IN CORPORATE LAW

The Concept of Fiduciary Duties

Easterbrook and Fischel's (1993: 438) treatment of fiduciary duties as a specific contractual relations merit some more detailed discussion. As will be demonstrated, this argument runs counter to corporate law as it is written and enforced in court cases.

In legal theory, the term *fiduciary duty* is a key concept that carries very specific connotations and being associated with defined legal norms and court ruling cases. The term *fiduciary* derives from Latin *fiducia*, meaning *trust*, and the fiduciary is "expected to act in good faith and honesty for the beneficiary's interest" (Lan and Heracleous, 2010: 302). Smith (2002: 1407. Emphasis in the original) defines the term as follows: "'[F]iduciary duty' connotes an obligation to *refrain from self-interested behavior that constitutes a wrong to the beneficiary as a result of the fiduciary exercising discretion with respect to the beneficiary's critical resources.*" Lan and Heracleous (2010: 303) suggest that fiduciary duty law consequently "act by shaping and reinforcing social norms of careful and loyal behavior." DeMott (1988: 880), a legal scholar, argues that the term *fiduciary* should be even more strictly interpreted, being what apply to "situations falling short of 'trust,' but in which one person was nonetheless obliged to act like a trustee." In this stricter sense of the term, the duties of the fiduciary "go beyond mere fairness and honesty"; these duties oblige the fiduciary to "act to further the beneficiary's best interests" (DeMott, 1988: 882). In short, the fiduciary "[m]ust avoid acts that put his interests in conflict with the beneficiary's" (DeMott, 1988: 882).

Moreover, DeMott (1988: 908) argues, fiduciary duties apply to a variety of cases and situations, and as a consequence, the term "eludes theoretical capture"; that is, it is term that cannot easily be formalized into written guidelines and instructions. Smith (2002: 1400) interprets this vague formalization of the term more negatively and argues that "fiduciary law is messy"; as a practical legal matter, "courts routinely impose fiduciary duties in myriad relationships," including trustee–beneficiary, employee–employer, director–shareholder, attorney–client, and physician–patient. Regardless of this "messiness," relationships based on fiduciary duties commonly "[i]nclude the fiduciary's commitment to exercise discretion in a fashion that affects the interests of the beneficiary and the fiduciary's obligation to exercise that discretion on the beneficiary's behalf" (DeMott, 1988: 908). Seen in this legal theory view, fiduciary duties are introduced, prescribed, and legally enforced as a relatively strict term that relies on the fiduciary's willingness to act in accordance with these prescriptions.

The differences between fiduciary duties and "contract relations" (Smith, 2002: 1403) are quite clearly specified. Whereas the fiduciary act in the interest of the beneficiary, that is, follows the "duty of loyalty" prescribed by fiduciary law, and thus should "avoid self-interested behavior that wrongs the beneficiary" (Smith, 2002: 1409), the contacting parties "exercise discretion only with respect to their own performance under the contract" (Smith, 2002: 1403). Expressed differently, the fiduciary must refrain from self-interested behavior that in any way disadvantages the beneficiary, whereas contracting parties "may act in a self-interested manner even where the other party is injured, as long as such actions are reasonably contemplated by the contact" (Smith, 2002: 1410). Frankel (1983: 880) says that in a contractual relation, "no party to a contract has a general obligation to take care of the other, and neither has the right to be taken care of."

At the same time, it is important to recognize that fiduciary law that otherwise stresses the duty of loyalty do recognize the interests of the fiduciary in the relation to the beneficiary: "[F]iduciary duty should not be equated with a duty of selflessness," Smith (2002: 1410) remarks. Regardless of Smith's (2002: 1410) specification, there is a substantial difference between fiduciary and contractual relations, Frankel (1983: 802) says: "A contract society values freedom and independence highly, but it provides little security for its members." In contrast, the "fiduciary society," which Frankel (1983: 802) regards as the more differentiated social order, wherein "affluence is largely produced by interdependence," "[a]ttempts to maximize both the satisfaction of needs and the protection of freedom." This valuation of freedom and independence versus security and satisfaction is of great relevance for corporate law and the corporate governance practices the legislation prescribe and enabled.

Fiduciary Duties in Corporate Law

As a matter of being a component of corporate law, what Eisenberg (1989: 1462) refers to as *fiduciary rules*, "govern the duties of managers and controlling shareholders." More important, it is the directors of the firm, to whom, for example, the CEO is held accountable, who are bestowed with fiduciary duties to protect the interests of the various contributors who participate in what Blair and Stout (1999) call the team production efforts of the corporation:

> A corporation's directors occupy a trustee-like position: unlike trustees, directors do not themselves have legal ownership interests in transferable property beneficially owned by others, but, like trustees, directors are entrusted with powers to use in the interest of others. Invested by corporation statutes with discretionary authority to manage or supervise the management of the corporation's business, directors are bound by fiduciary principles.
>
> (DeMott, 1988: 880)

Frankel (1983: 806) argues that directors "do not fall squarely into the category of either trustee [i.e., fiduciary] or agent." On one hand, like a fiduciary is free from the interference of the beneficiary, corporate directors should be able to manage without the frequent interference of shareholders. This business judgement rule is justified on basis of the efficiency of centralized management, which, in turn, grants discretion to directors; the directors of the corporation should have freedom to make timely decisions without resorting to shareholder approval, Frankel (1983: 810) argues. On the other hand, it is the shareholders who elect the directors, just as principals choose their agents, and shareholders therefore can terminate directors' tenure under "appropriate circumstances" (Frankel, 1983: 806). Such tenure could end through consent (i.e., informally), through a takeover (a market mechanism) or in an election process (by a so-called proxy fight) (Frankel, 1983: 807). Considering these two conditions, directors act as a hybrid construct including fiduciary and agential relations, that is, in a "trustees-like positions" in DeMott's (1988: 880) formulation.

Taken together, the term *fiduciary duty* prescribes that directors hold "trustee-like positions" that prohibit them from acting on behalf of any of the various contributors to the team production activities (including, e.g., the shareholders who supply finance capital). By implication, a similar role is given to the CEO, the board of directors' agent. The legal strictures of corporate law thus make the directors accountable to a variety of stakeholder, whereof the owners of firm's stock represent one category of stakeholders among others. Moreover, fiduciaries (i.e., directors and managers) operate under *preventive rules* that "deter the fiduciary from abusing his power" (Frankel, 1983: 824). Such abuse includes, first of all, self-dealing, which preventive rules prohibit, supervise, and limit. The fiduciary duties of directors and managers, for instance, make insider trading illicit, the situation where individuals access information that are advantageous to hold when participating in open stock market trading. The duty of loyalty prohibits directors and managers from using their position and their access to information to their own benefit as such action may harm the interest of the firm, their beneficiary. Under these strictures, a corporation's confidential information is treated as a property to which the corporation only has an exclusive right, the U.S. Supreme Court have made clear (*United States v. O'Hagan*, cited in Smith, 2002: 1446). Also in more controversial cases this rule applies, as in the Massachusetts state court that granted a tobacco company the right to refuse to disclose the content of its products (Smith, 2002: 1446). Another U.S. Supreme Court case statement expressed this interpretation of corporate law accordingly: "In lieu of premising liability on a fiduciary relationship between company insider and purchaser or seller of the company's stock, the misappropriation theory premises liability on a fiduciary-turned trader's deception of those who entrusted him with access to confidential information" (U.S. Supreme Court statement, cited in Smith, 2002: 1420–1421). Thus, the strictness of fiduciary law applies within corporate legislation. Contractarian arguments cannot bypass or bury the fact that fiduciary rules are mandatory in corporate legislation.

Further Legal Theory Critique of Contract Theory

Needless to say, the idea that the firm is a nexus of contracts and that shareholders are the sole residual risk bearers and therefore entitled to the residual cash flow is not an uncontroversial statement, especially since the propositions underlying such declaration is based on orthodox neoclassical economic theory and in large parts ignore corporate law as it is written and legally enforced. Contractarians advocate an efficiency criterion that corporate legislators never mandate (outside of the specific case when, e.g., takeover bids and mergers are assessed) or even had in mind when they formulated this constitutional law, aimed at creating a legal vehicle for market creation and venturing. As a consequence, a quite extensive legal theory literature presents a critical case against contract theory.

Brudney (1985) objects to contract theory on basis of a combination of legal arguments, empirical evidence, and ideological implications. First of all, contact theory makes use of the juridical term *contract* in ways that legal scholars cannot accept. Contract theory, a corollary to the market for management control, assumes that when a corporation (i.e., its business promoters and, thereafter, the board of directors) issues stock to public investors, the investor "contracts" with the business promoters or the directors. This contract grants the shareholders certain rights. This idea per se is disputed by Brudney (1985: 1411), who claims that this "stretches the concept of contract beyond recognition, when using it to describe either the process of bargaining or the arrangement between investors of publicly held corporations and either theoretical owners first going public or corporate management." Dispersed shareholders, Brudney (1985: 1411) says, cannot and are not given the right to negotiate the terms of their contract with, for example, directors, and therefore, they are formally only the owners of a financial asset, not the firm's contractor as, for example, a supplier or a paying client would be. For Brudney (1985: 1414), contract theory bends the idea of contracts and contractual relations to suit its implied interests—to justify shareholder welfare within a corporate legislation that never included such privileges—and therefore violates legal theory and the business practice. For instance, Brudney exemplifies, shareholders are rarely if ever informed about the managers' duties, rights, and entitlements, and therefore, they cannot negotiate their performance and/or their decisions, which is the privilege of the board of directors. Even if shareholders would had been provided with such information—by no means an impossible to accomplish—shareholders are still not constitutionally given such privileges, possibly because the legislator believes managers should be able to fulfil their formal role—to manage the firm—rather than responding to remarks from shareholders:

> Stockholders do not direct management's activities. Indeed, stockholders are explicitly denied power to interfere in management's activities.

> That they may not, or rationally should not, wish to do so does not detract from the distortion in characterizing management as their agent. (Brudney, 1985: 1425)

Furthermore, in a more recent article published by Brudney (1997: 597), he questions the doctrine that any party are free to contract with anyone else, a fundamental principle in contract theory. This contract law principle violates the mandatory rules of corporate legislation, wherein the sovereign state monopolize the issuance of business charters. That is, the assumption that "[p]arties are as free to 'contract' with one another as they would be in a pre-state world with no such socially-imposed restrictions" is disputed.

To turn to the empirical conditions that would enable the market for corporate control to work as its proponents prescribe, Brudney (1985: 1425) is sceptical, like many other legal scholars, regarding the Efficient Market Hypothesis, rending market pricing the most efficient and unrivalled mechanism for monitoring managerial decision quality. In addition, even if market pricing would operate close to perfection and markets would incorporate all public information (e.g., information-efficiency is assumed), such efficiency per se would still not on its own, Brudney (1985: 1425) argues, "[d]rive management to compete in limiting its rewards or its power to divert assets, or even to be more efficient managers." That is, the "fundamental premise" pointed out by Manne (1965: 112), that there exists a "a high positive correlation between corporate managerial efficiency and the market price of shares of that company," is simply intermediated by layers of decision-making and other factors that slows down the time it takes for substandard decisions to be incorporated into market prices that indicate poor decision-making quality, Brudney (1985) says. That is, it may be or may be not that managers make substandard decisions that affect the firm's performance negatively, at the expense of the shareholders, but simply looking at the market prices of, for example, stocks or bonds reveals little regarding the shortcomings of the corporate governance system.

Finally, Brudney (1985: 1409) criticizes contract theory on a more ideological level for revealing its libertarian roots when questioning or disqualifying of any attempts of the sovereign state to monitor or otherwise regulate allegedly self-regulating markets. Brudney can here be cited art length:

> Apart from the debatable normative consequences generated by the rhetoric of contract in the corporate context, it may be noted that the rhetoric serves an ideological purpose. The evolution of the legal theory of the corporation in the United States, although uneven and complex, proceed from the vision of a 'concession' granted by the state as a special privilege, often to do public good, to that of a contractual arrangement between private parties. That development was part of the process of legitimating corporate freedom of action in the burgeoning industrial capitalism. The notion of private contract implicated lessened public

> concern with the impact of new entrepreneurial giants on consumers, employees, suppliers, and public generally.
>
> (Brudney, 1985: 1409)

Brudney (1985: 1409) here argues that the concept of the contact, a juridical term now subsumed under the vocabulary of orthodox neoclassical economic theory, is introduced to "disconnect" the enterprise from its "dependence upon state authority." As a consequence, the disconnection the firm and the state, from the outset based on the business charter granted by the sovereign state to serve a variety of economic and social ends, downplays the power and interests of other constituencies, including consumers, employees, suppliers, and the public, including median voters and taxpayers (Brudney, 1985: 1409). More specifically, the legal term *fiduciary duty*, granting managers discretion and justifying the business judgement rule in court decisions, is trivialized by contractarians when being portrayed as a significant obstacle to efficiency maximization. Therefore, "the policy aspiration of contractarians is to reduce, if not to eliminate, state-imposed fiduciary restrictions on the power of corporate managers and controllers to engage in conflict of interest transactions or otherwise to serve themselves collaterally at the possible expense of public stockholders," Brudney (1997: 622–623) says. This policy recommendation ignore the fact that the opportunistic behaviour that contractarians postulate as being a predictable behavior among managers is, in fact, already forbid and curtailed by the fiduciary duties, stipulated as a mandatory rule in corporate law (Brudney, 1997: 622–625). To relax one of the key strictures of corporate law would permit *more*, not *less*, opportunistic behavior, Brudney (1997: 622–635) claims: "[T]raditional fiduciary loyalty strictures more rigorously protect common stockholders against opportunistic behavior by managers and controllers than does classic contract doctrine." This ideological separation from the state to embrace the market as the origin and virginal ground for all business ventures is a rhetoric discrediting state regulation and the control of economic activities, per se an ideological stance, rooted in an ahistorical view of the role of corporate law in the constitution of competitive capitalism, Brudney (1985, 1997) summarizes.

Eisenberg (1989), a legal scholar, recognizes the problem of managerial discretion in corporate law (see Eisenberg, 1976) but is nevertheless sceptical regarding contact law as the solution to problems. As Eisenberg remarks, the legal principle of fiduciary duties is a mandatory rule that cannot be compromised in any way: "The general principle . . . is that in publicly held corporations, mandatory legal rules should govern those core fiduciary and structural areas in which the interest of shareholders and top managers may materially diverge" (Eisenberg, 1989: 1480). The same principle applies to closely held corporations, that is, corporations with less dispersed ownership, Eisenberg (1989: 1480) adds. As most of the rules that deals with managerial decision-making, which contact theorists claim produce inefficiencies when not being monitored, are, in fact, mandatory, and therefore, Eisenberg (1989) claims, just like Brudney (1985) does, that the principal idea that contracts should replace fiduciary duties is, at best, misleading:

> The characterization of the corporation as a nexus of contracts is . . . inaccurate. A corporation is a profit-seeking enterprise of persons and assets organized by rules. Some of these rules are determined by contract or other forms of agreements, but some are determined by law, and most are determined by the unilateral action of corporate organs or officials.
> (Eisenberg, 1989: 1487)

Also the weaker form of contracting, so-called implicit contacts, suggesting that *even if* there are no *formal* contracts being written, defining legally enforceable rights, there may be *assumed* contractual relations between, say, managers and shareholders that would render the shareholders the only residual risk bearers, is rejected out of hand by Eisenberg (1989: 1487): "The term 'implicit contacts' is extremely misleading." That is, the contract theory view of the firm does not the problems that legislators have tried to handle. The nexus of contract view of the firm may offer an intriguing set of propositions, but it cannot justify legal reforms.

Gordon (1989) follows Eisenberg's argument closely in stressing that corporate law, as a constitutional law, in fact contains a set of mandatory rules that cannot be bypassed, re-interpreted, or otherwise applied on basis of governance preferences. Gordon here emphasizes that what he calls "normative contractarianism" (i.e., contract theory) includes two principles, the "content" and "opt-out" principles, both being at odds with corporate law as it is written and enforced:

> The first principle is that the content of corporate law, which includes both the statutory law and the common law of fiduciary duty, should ideally be the results that typical parties to the contract comprising the corporation would have reached if bargaining were costless. That will reduce the parties' needs for customized terms and thereby reduce transaction costs. This is the 'content principle.'
> (Gordon, 1989: 1550–1551)

The second, "opt-out" principle suggests that corporate law "[s]hould function as a sort of standard form contract, an 'off the rack' set of terms that parties may use for their convenience but may also freely alter" (Gordon, 1989: 1551). In Gordon's view, the content principle is controversial inasmuch assumes that "the sole purpose of corporate law ought to be private wealth maximization," and therefore ignores the history of corporate law as a legal innovation that grant privileges to business ventures to "aid the provision of public services" (Gordon, 1989: 1551). The second principle violates the mandatory rules of corporate law. However, as proponents of contract theory advocate legal reform to overcome these "inconsistencies," Gordon (1989: 1554) claims that *even if* corporate law would be modified in accordance with contract theory principles, it is a mistake to assume that "full contractual freedom in corporate law would necessarily lead to private wealth maximization." For instance, Gordon (1989: 1597) argues it would be irrational for shareholders "to waive or modify substantially the directors' duty of loyalty," because that would increase the risk of opportunism. In the present legal system, the combination of mandatory rules and the possibility of legal innovation, and the competition between states for incorporation of the business venture (in the case of the U.S.) remains the superior governance model, unrivalled by comparable market-based control.

Clark (1989) follows Eisenberg (1989) and Gordon (1989) in their defence of corporate law and examines the advantages of the "elite rule" of highly specialized, trained, and experienced legal professionals vis-à-vis comparable market-based control. Like the other legal scholars, Clark (1989) stresses the mandatory rules that cannot be bypassed. While contact theory in advocated in the law and economics literature and in some scholarly circles as a legitimate contestant for the governance of the corporate system, in corporate law enforcement and court rulings, there is little evidence of such recognition, Clark (1989: 1706–1707) remarks:

> Practically minded judges and legislators have been known to dismiss these general arguments out of hand. To many who have had experience in the corporate world, it seems obvious that if a corporation adopts a charter amendment opting out of the fiduciary duty of loyalty, the net effects will be clearly bad for investors.
>
> (Clark, 1989: 1706–1707)

The claim that contractual relations between, for example, the shareholders and the managers and the directors would enable Pareto-efficiency, that is, such contracts maximize both the productive and allocative efficiency, is unsubstantiated in the eyes of judges and legislators. In sharp contrast to the contract theory model, Clark (1989) advocates an elite-ruling system, justified on basis of the legal elite's superior knowledge and access to information—a claim that explicitly challenges the neoclassicists' disregard of centrally located agencies, operating as market-makers. Clark (1989: 1723) here defines *elitism* as "[t]he condition in which rules of conduct are actually created and imposed on rule subjects by contemporary elites." Elites also denotes, importantly, individuals with highly specialized professional skills and who have acquired credentials and merits in highly competitive fields, governed by a combination of collegial control and political interests.

The elite model violates most of the free-market model's central principles, including Friedrich von Hayek's idea that no central agency can ever be more efficient than the market pricing mechanism in accommodating and processing large volumes of information. In contrast Clark (1989: 1718) proposes that "[t]he best argument for heteronomy is that elite rule makers may in fact have much better information about what would really promote the welfare of the subjects of a rule than the subjects themselves do." For instance, the Food and Drug Administration (FDA) and the Securities and Exchange Commission (SEC), two primary targets for free-market protagonists as being institutions that "reduce the efficiency" of, for example, new drug development (Clark, 1989: 1718, Footnote 39. See also Nik-Khah, 2014) and the finance market, do in fact play a very central role in collecting and systematizing information in order to make it practically useful in the governance of specific markets and industries. "Arguably," Clark (1989: 1718) exemplifies, "the staff of the Securities and Exchange Commission may have a better based belief than do most individual shareholders about whether charter amendments to create dual class common stock are often in the best interests of shareholders." Clark continues:

> [S]ome antipaternalists follow the odd strategy of arguing against paternalistic regulation on the ground that it is unlikely that regulators know better than the regulated what is in their interests. This is an odd strategy because the reason given for resisting paternalism—no information asymmetry exists—is desperately implausible in many real-world contexts, and because much better reasons for resisting paternalism can be offered.
>
> (Clark, 1989: 1718–1719)

Clark (1989: 1718–1719) rejects the assumptions regarding the efficacy of market pricing on the basis that a centrally located agency can in fact know better (as stated earlier) but also because people more generally have a preference for elite rule over its contestant, the rule of faceless and anonymous finance market actors: "Indeed, many thoughtful people might judge it better to be ruled by a competent bureaucrat who promulgates welfare-enhancing rules simply because it is his job to do so than by a charismatic leader who thinks he is endowed with a consuming altruistic vocation" (Clark, 1989: 1720).

Assuming such median voter preference, Clark (1989: 1720) does recognize that the elite system generates its own agency costs but suggests that for the individual, the elite rule-making have net benefits in comparison to the market-based system. Therefore, Clark concludes that the contact theory of the firm, and its reliance on the finance market for the monitoring of managers, is not a credible contestant for the governance of the corporate system. The efficacy of a contract-based system and prudence of market-based actors are substantially lower than assumed by contract theorists:

> [M]y view is that paternalistic elitism may have decisive relative advantages over contractual rule making in a wide variety of contexts. A good society depends on both autonomy and heteronomy, each present in

> large measure. Theorists ought to face up to this point and then see what headway, if any, can be made in devising principles for setting the optimal mix.
>
> (Clark, 1989: 1726)

The elite rule is thus beneficial as it strikes a balance between efficiency and equity (Elzinga, 1977).

Howard (1991: 5) admits that the contract theory argument is seductive because it is "both simple and elegant," but this parsimonious elegance is accomplished on the basis that it "assumes away" the difficult legal issues at hand and because it sets up a strawman that can be knocked down with what is a "seemingly irrefutable logic." For instance, the primary strawman, the alleged "heavy-handed interference in the affairs of the corporation by government administrators," being claimed to reduce overall efficiency, is little more than a figment in the contractarian's mind, Howard (1991: 5) proposes. In fact, he continues, "nothing could be further from reality." First of all, Howard (1991: 9) emphasizes, like many other legal scholars, that the board of directors is, in fact and in law, the principal decision-making organ of the corporate body. Therefore, neither the directors nor their assigned managers are the agents of the firm's investors, creditors, or any other stakeholder, regardless of how, for example, orthodox neoclassical economic models stipulate their roles. Instead, the directors and managers are, legally speaking, an organ of an "economic and political body" (Howard, 1991: 9). Moreover, even if the law would be modified, as contractarians fiercely campaign for, making their theoretically propositions more aligned with corporate legislation, the accuracy of their models would still be disputed as the political nature of the firm is excluded from contractual relations, Howard (1991: 10) claims:

> [T]he contemporary business corporation, although it is subject to the absolutely unforgiving performance measure of profitability, is not a one-dimensional institution. It is a complex economic and social institution which, if of substantial size, is necessarily 'in politics' in the non-partisan sense that it is compelled to become involved in overall political processes concerning, for example, natural resource use and environmental regulation.
>
> (Howard, 1991: 10)

While the argument in favour of increased efficiency per se is hard to object to, it is complicated to convince sceptical commentators of the credibility of the contractarian argument that there are "money left on the table" (derived from clumsy or heavy-handed governmental market interventions) to be claimed at low or no cost and with no stakeholder losing positions vis-à-vis other stakeholders. The "convoluted argument based on impliedly excessive government regulation, agency relationships, organizational theory and the capital market efficiency hypothesis" (Howard, 1991: 11) that make up contract theory, each accommodating its own disputed assumptions and demanding its own carefully crafted empirical evidence, complemented by "some obvious common sense about the fiction of shareholders maintaining effective control over management," is an insufficient argument when justifying legal reform. Ultimately and contra-intuitively, the theory of the firm that contractarians present underrates the dynamics of the firm—for them, it is only the market that is dynamic, changeable, and capable of generating wealth, a proposition that Howard rejects:

> If one can reify a public business corporation and thus trade it as one more market commodity, the contractarian efficiency model is attractive. If, however, you conceive a corporation as a living, complicated, dynamic social and economic institution—as I do—the contractarian argument is meaningless, a convoluted, oblique attack on political decision-making in the name of 'efficiency,' a result no one could ever prove.
>
> (Howard, 1991: 13)

Therefore, Howard contends, the proposed shift from one legal theory to another is not helpful as it solves few problems but imposes an additional set of problems:

> Neither the logic of economic efficiency nor case law nor business experience justifies such dilution of a legal standard that is well understood and that appears to work effectively to constrain potentially abusive exercise by directors and officers of their sweeping discretion.
>
> (Howard, 1991: 18)

For Howard (1991), just as for Brudney (1985, 1997), Eisenberg (1989), Gordon (1989), and Clark (1989), contract theory do not yet present a logically consistent case accompanied by empirical evidence, jointly justifying legal reform.

More Recent Empirical Evidence Regarding the Robustness of the Contract Theory

As the literature reviewed earlier indicates, in the 1970s, 1980s, and 1990s, the legal theory scholarship committed to contract theory was considerable. The debate has continued ever since, but as the finance market regulation (discussed in more detail in Chapter 5) was rolled back, both in the U.S. and internationally in the 1990s, the contact theory model and its agency theory insistence on shareholder primacy governance became "true by default" as directors started to follow the shareholder value model regardless of its support in scholarly circles. Expressed differently, despite the brittle nature of contract theory and its prescribed practices, its sheer performative force turned the model into the new conventional wisdom, by and large independent of legal reforms and court decisions. With the benefit of hindsight, Klausner (2013) discusses how well contract theory stands up against empirical evidence close to four decades after it was formalized and advocated by legal scholars and economists in the 1970s and 1980s. Unfortunately, in Klausner's (2013: 1329) account, contract theory does not fare well: "On the whole, the empirical literature over the past three decades has provided little support for the contractarian theory. Key pillars of the theory do not match the empirical facts." Klausner explains this failure on basis of a systematic overemphasis on market efficiency:

> Why does the contractarian theory fail to fit the facts? The answer necessarily lies in transaction costs or other market imperfections. The contractarians assumed that the relevant transaction costs were drafting costs, which could not be high enough to undermine the theory in any significant way, and that there were no other market imperfections. But instead, market imperfections are more complex and more important than the contractarians realized. In defining the rights and obligations of the shareholder-manager relationship, general standards are often more suitable than specific rules. Fiduciary duties in various contexts are an example.
>
> (Klausner, 2013: 1330)

Klausner (2013) provides a devastating critique of a "generalized" contract theory" that follow orthodox neoclassical economic theory in its ignorance regarding the intricate corporate governance system that Williamson (1981) emphasized. As neither contractarians, not economists treated the firm as a sufficiently interesting unit of analysis, the firm is rendered a black box that can never accomplish anything that the free market cannot, and therefore, contract theory suffers from a sort of "empirical deficit," "[t]he contractarians paid little attention to actual corporate contracts," Klausner (2013: 1330–1331) says: "A review of a few corporate charters would have revealed that the real-world facts differed in important ways from what the contractarian theory implied." For instance, the IPO (Initial Public Offerings) stage of a business venture, where a previously closely held firm is "going public," that is, it offers public investors the opportunity to buy shares in the firm, is an excellent testing ground for the contract theory. The IPO stage is where the directors and business promoters can demonstrate their appetite for innovative and customized contracting as they believe it benefits the firm and its prosperity and long-term competitive advantage. If directors and business promoters would endorse contract theory and the idea that managers do, in fact, induce considerable agency costs (as stipulated by contract theory and its correlate agency theory), there would be a considerable degree of inventiveness at this stage. Empirical research, however, Klausner (2013: 1338–1339) reports, provides no such evidence, being clearly a disappointment for contract theorists and their allies: "Corporate charters are 'plain vanilla' with statutory takeover defenses commonly added, and nothing more" (Klausner, 2013: 1338–1339).

Furthermore, the market for "business incorporation," which Lamoreaux (1998) predicted, is another testing ground for the practical relevance of contract theory. But once again, there is little evidence of the states competing vis-à-vis one another in terms of providing business charters that protect shareholder rights against allegedly self-serving and incompetent managers:

> There is no race among the states—to the top or the bottom. Whereas commentators on both sides of the race debate had assumed that all fifty states compete with one another in a national market . . . studies found that no such market exists.
>
> (Klausner, 2013: 1343)

For instance, it is widely known that Delaware law as a matter of fact is preferred over other state legislation, but that fact per se does not suggest that the Delaware business charter is more "efficient" than that of other states, Klausner (2013: 1345) says. If there are efficiency gains within the preferred Delaware law, it derives from the sheer conformism of the director's choice to incorporate in Delaware, generating transparency and thus, by implication, reducing the legal costs as lawyers are familiar with Delaware law, which help then provide reliable legal advice more easily (Klausner, 2013: 1345). Thus, the "efficiency" of the present corporate system does not primarily derive from "market efficiencies" but from the conformism of directors, the transparency in the legal system enacted at state level, and the economies of scale in legal services, benefitting from coherent rather than divergent preferences among directors (Romano, 1985). Such empirical evidence is, of course, disappointing for contract theorist and other theoretical orientations that render the free market the source and origin of all efficiency-optimal decisions. Klausner summarizes his argument:

> Widespread Delaware incorporation, therefore, is weak support for the contractarian theory regarding value maximization at the IPO stage. Moreover, the fact that a substantial minority of firms incorporate in their home states, apparently without regard to the content of state law, suggests that market pressure to maximize firm value, if it exists, is not strong.
>
> (Klausner, 2013: 1345)

As proposed by several legal scholars, the mandatory rules of, for example, Delaware law seem to be treated as a minor concern for directors and business promoters.

In addition to the test of contract theory at the IPO stage, the 1970s' contact theory literature was very much concerned about how managers were anxious to protect their interest by establishing "takeover defences" (Klausner, 2013: 1348), including various governance innovations such as "shark repellants," "poison pills," and (in the event of an actual takeover), "golden parachutes" to insulate managers from the economic consequences of job loss that was likely to follow when the new owners bring in their new management team (see, e.g., Rhee, and Fiss, 2014; Fiss, Kennedy, and Davis, 2012; Davis, 1991; Hirsch, 1986). However, the risk of takeover did not effectively serve to entice managers and directors to "initiate agency cost-reducing measures," studies from the mid-1980s to the mid-2000 suggest (Klausner, 2013: 1349). In fact, takeovers were tolerated as a legitimate mechanism with certain systemic benefits, but empirical evidence does not support the normative contract theory view that takeovers benefitted all stakeholders. Instead, Klausner (2013: 1349) says, "empirical research has long documented the fact that target shareholders reap substantial gains from hostile acquisitions" (see, e.g., Bertrand and Mullainathan, 2003; Andrade, Mitchell, and Stafford, 2001; Rosett, 1990).

In summary, the contract theory being put under the heat by Klausner (2013) does not come out very favourably from the test, serving only a limited role in the governance of firms, and the mechanisms it advocates, including takeovers, accomplishes little in terms of initiating efficiency-enhancing activities. If managers were acting opportunistically before, for example, shareholder primacy governance was instituted (per se more of an assumption that an empirical fact and being an assumption that is questionable given the remarkable economic growth in the era of managerial capitalism in comparison to the more recent investor capitalism), there is still no strong evidence that indicates that managers would act with more prudence in the new regime. In his concluding remark, Klausner (2013: 1370) proposes that "[b]oth theorists and empiricists" fail to pay sufficient attention to institutional facts," that is, precisely the wider set of non-market conditions and political interests that corporate law are based on. In the end, therefore, the ambition to reduce the complexity of the contract theory argument to make it manageable and to provide normative recommendations led to a theory that was neither theoretically credible nor practically useful nor converging towards empirical evidence. What contract theory did accomplish, though, based on the previous scholarship criticizing antitrust enforcement and the idea of the market for management control, was to advocate the idea that corporate governance is a matter of determining the relations between managers and shareholders. This proposition is the basis for the agency theory argument that reinforced shareholder primacy governance. As, for example, Bratton (1989: 411) notices, contact theory and agency theory were not successful because they were the outcome from eminent and widely respected scholarship—in fact, quite the opposite was the case—but because these theories "mischaracterize[d] corporate contracts" and made normative and political assertions "in the guise of ontological statements." The proponents of contract theory and agency theory preyed on scholarly standards for theoretical contributions by making the "nexus of contracts view of the firm," a model that essentially "resists empirical verification." All too entangled with theoretical propositions, assumptions, and other ideological beliefs, the very model that contract theory and agency theory advocated was never made amenable for empirical testing. Hence, contract theory could survive longer than a proper theory would under the regular regime of scholarly standards for empirical verification. Consequently, it successfully served as a vehicle for free-market advocacy to the benefit of certain stakeholders well into the new millennium.

Summary and Conclusion

The contractual theory of the firm was advocated despite its deviations from corporate law as it is written, intended, applied, and enforced. More specifically, the contract theory was based on the idea that there is in fact a liquid and well-functioning stock market where the "contracts" of the shares-with-voting-rights could be sold. As Moore and Rebérioux (2011: 88) remark, what the New Dealers, including not least Berle and Means (1934), treated as a concern for the entire economy, that the finance market included speculative elements, was now treated as a "solution" to perceived management-control problems. Operating under the assumptions that stock markets mirror managerial performance without distortions and that shareholders are more efficient investors than any inside manager would be, the last remaining impediment for a full-scale shareholder-welfare model was corporate legislation, whose protagonists subscribed to neither of these foundational assumptions. Roe (1994: 23) argues that the adherents of the contract theory tried to "[s]weep away the remaining mandated terms inconsistent with a contractarian framework, arguing that corporate law *should* be no more than a set of contracts" (Roe, 1994: 23). That is, a conceptual model was advocated as a legitimate source for reform within corporate law. By the early 1990s, Kaufman and Zacharias (1992: 559) say, "a consensus has emerged that state fiduciary incorporation charters should be understood in contractual terms," an accomplishment that needs to be understood on basis of the wider institutional, political, and cultural changes of the 1970s and 1980s, making the idea that the firm is a "self-regulating contractual arrangement among independent bargaining groups" (Kaufman and Zacharias, 1992: 559), both meaningful and socially and politically legitimate in the eyes of its proponents.

In the end, however, legal scholars did neither accept, nor surrender to the neoclassical economic theory view of contracts, making the judicial device of the contract a strict matter of defining property and entitlement. Instead, recent work such as Kar's (2016), "contract as empowerment" model recognizes the legitimately of the coercive power of the state (allegedly posing a challenge to "contractual liberty"; see Kar, 2016: 780) and further assumes that ordinary people not only are "instrumentally motivated" (as stipulated by economic theory) but also "have a sense of justice and interpersonal obligation" (Kar, 2016: 767). That is, the conceptual strictness of the economic contract theory and its "rational contractor" is rejected as the contracting individual is not only assumed to be "merely rational" but also "reasonable"; that is, he or she is "[i]nclined to seek out and abide by a mutually acceptable set of rules for the general regulation of conduct and treat those rules as generating genuine obligations, given an appropriate assurance that all others will, too" (Kar, 2016: 769–770). In this view, a contract not only define rights, liabilities, and obligations but represents a version of contractualism that regards contracts as legal devices that empower people to "[i]nfluence one another's actions and thereby to meet a broad range of human needs and interests (Kar, 2016: 761).

4 1980s

Agency Theory and the Shareholder Welfare Norm

Introduction

The 1950s and 1960s were high-growth decades, and free-market advocacy had to fashion quite intricate and a not-so-easy-to-believe-in argument regarding the perils of state interventions and regulations. It would be fair to say that the 1950s' and 1960s' law and economics scholarship fed on the fear of communism and state-regulated commando economies of the old-school free-market economists and social theorists, including Ludwig von Mises and Friedrich von Hayek, which they projected onto, for example, the New Deal legislation, rather than being rooted in actual economic problems. If there were concerns regarding the post-World War II decades of the 1950s and 1960s, they evolved around issues that neither Mises nor Hayek would ever consider being worthy of attention, that is, the paternalism of conglomerates and the conformism of the American middle-class life, excluding women and minorities from many job opportunities and imposing ready-made consumerist lifestyle choices, the monotonous and repetitive work that the cadre of office workers conducted, and so on. In the latter half of the 1950s and in the 1960s, in particular, the new generation that grew up in the new, affluent classes became impatient with this grinding boredom and uncompromising conformity, and minority groups claimed citizen rights, making the end of the 1960s one of the most turbulent period after World War II.

In the 1970s, the gradual decline of profit levels in American industry was complemented by a series of worrying tendencies, including soaring energy costs, inflation being at a persistently high level, economic stagnation, and high unemployment. The political system in the U.S. was burdened by both the costs for the Vietnam War and the global critique of American foreign policy, and things did not lighten up when the Watergate scandal was publicized by *Washington Post* in 1973, ultimately forcing President Richard M. Nixon to resign on August 9, 1974. The entire 1970s was a hotbed for institutional and legal reform, and members of the free-market community who had advocated a market-based corporate governance model, with shareholder welfare being a central component, were suddenly located at the very centre of the activities and were now able to sell their proposals. The unprecedented economic growth and well-being of the post–World War II period was not a fertile soil for discrediting professional managers—in the eyes of the public, the work they conducted and the corporations they oversaw by and large ensured that yet another television set or refrigerator could be afforded; that is, private ownership and economic well-being seemed intimately connected in managerial capitalism—but as the economic tide changed in the 1970s, the free-market protagonists advanced their positions.

In the 1980s, being an entirely different scene than in the 1960s, the dominant political culture favoured neoconservatism, pro-business arguments, and free-market thinking, that is, precisely the kind of ideologies and policies that, for example, the Chicago school economists and law and economics scholars had advocated since the mid-1930s (with the inception of Friedrich von Hayek's scholarly fraternity the Mont Pelèrin Society in 1937 being one notable event). With winds in their sails and with the long-term critics of Soviet-style planned economies, and with Ronald Reagan now president, ready to serve business interest and to smash organized labour (trade unionism is little more than evidence of a deplorable collectivism in the eyes of the free-market protagonists, and many of them were not especially enthusiastic about representative democracy either), the law and economics argument in favour of shareholder enrichment became increasingly bankable. While much of the antitrust critique was regarded a marginal phenomenon and ideas such as the market for management control was advocated by scholars in the fringes of legal theory, agency theory was advanced on broad front in the 1970s (first under the contractual theory of the firm label), and in the 1980s the theory gained a foothold in primarily business schools, a quite recent institution within the university system and with a somewhat disputed status (not least on the basis of the questionable scientific standard of the research conducted and on which the teaching rested; see, e.g., Fourcade and Khurana, 2013; Khurana, 2007; De Rond and Miller, 2005; Ellickson, 1989; Whitley, 1986). In addition, the growing status of finance theory, developed from the 1950s onwards, had gradually become more widely recognized, and the idea that the finance market metaphorically served as the "brain of competitive capitalism," a calculative centre wherein market impulses were collected and assessed and thereafter processed in decision-making that affected the entire economic system, became popular. However, this biological metaphor, with the "real economy" being some kind of material substratum responsive to the assessment made in the centrally located finance market, was a highly deceiving image of the economy as the cognitive centre of the biological system is relying on the survival of the *entire* biological organism, and therefore imposes risk aversion to secure long-term survival. Expressed differently, if the biological organism fails on basis of inadequate instructions from the brain, nature does not generously "bail out the brain" to make it continue its work.

By the 1980s, the scene looked different than the three previous decades of free market, and with the decline in prestige of Keynesian economic theory, a variety of Chicago-branded economic models, including monetarism, de-regulation policy, and not least shareholder welfare, were now widely endorsed in policy-making quarters. Overseas saving poured into the American economy on basis of the high-interest policy initiated by the Federal Reserve chairman Paul Volcker, which further added to the free-market euphoria of the decade, leading to substantial reforms to better "maximize efficiency." By the end of the decade, the free-market model and shareholder primacy governance were firmly established, not least within the business school setting, as the new conventional wisdom. Enriching shareholders was now just as American as apple pie and Little League baseball. Such entrenched beliefs were indebted to decades of free-market advocacy, including law and economics scholarship, yet, in turn, were being equally persistently criticized by, for example, legal scholars.

"The Deal Decade": Corporate Restructuring in the 1980s

In 1950, the trade union United Auto Workers and General Motors signed a contract that would be referred to as "The Treaty of Detroit," prescribing mutual rights and obligations of the employer and the employees (Davis, 2010: 335). "The Treaty of Detroit," Davis (2010: 335) declares in a somewhat grandiose tone, "was the Magna Charta of the society of organizations." In the vocabulary employed in this book, the treaty was an exemplary agreement indicative of the political climate and economic doctrines dominating in the period. Until at least the mid-1960s, the mass-production/mass-consumption regime ran smoothly, even if commentators such as John Kenneth Galbraith (1971) was concerned about the oligopolistic tendencies in American capitalism. However, "no trees grows to the sky," as the Wall Street adage proposes, and from 1965 the profit rate started to decline in the manufacturing industry: "From 1965 to 1973, the profit rate in manufacturing fell by nearly 41 percent while that of the private business sector fell by 30 percent" (Van Arnum and Naples, 2013: 1160). In the 1970s, the collapse of the Bretton Woods system was followed by the first and the second oil crisis, the Watergate political scandal in the U.S., surfacing on basis of diligent journalism work, and the world economy was cast into a decade-long recession. The pro-business elite did not sit idly during this turbulence but consolidated and mobilized to bring back industry and pro-business policy on the agenda in Washington. By the end of the 1970s, sufficient resources were successfully mobilized to install a neoconservative president in the White House. The Reagan administration recruited heavily from conservative think tanks and institutes (i.e., the American Enterprise Institute and The Heritage Foundation) and listened carefully to what Chicago economists said about the virtues of free markets and de-regulation. "Something seems to have changed in the early 1980s," Greenwood and Scharfstein (2013: 4) say, discussing the advancement of the finance industry. Gordon (2007: 1521) refers to the 1980s as "the Deal Decade." This sea change and the shift to free-market policy translated into a much more dynamic—some would say "turbulent" or even "predatory"—corporate system in the 1980s. Above all, the catchphrase of the Reagan era was corporate or business "restructuring" (Useem, 1990), leading to the de-institutionalization of the conglomerate organization form that had been highly popular in the era of managerial capitalism (Davis, Diekmann, and Tinsley, 1994).

In the 1980s, the corporate system underwent considerable changes, motivated and incentivized by a series of policy reforms to reinforce free-market pricing, and one-third of the 500 largest manufacturing firms disappeared during the decade (Mizruchi, 2010: 132). In addition, "nearly a quarter of the major U.S. corporations received an unwanted [takeover] bid" during the decade (Gordon, 2007: 1521). The de-regulation of the finance market and, for example, the Tax Reform Act of 1981 (Hall, 1994: 132) led to a burgeoning junk bond market, which greatly benefitted a new generation of finance market actors who specialized in intricate financial engineering to extract economic value from underpriced—a curious term in price theory as the market by definition always prices assets correctly—conglomerates: "Debt-financed buyouts increased enormously in the 1980s. In 1979, there were 75 buyouts valued at $1.3 billion; by 1988 there were 214 transactions, exceeding 477 billion" (Kaufman et al., 1995: 76). Despite the term *shareholder value* was not mentioned in *Harvard Business Review* until 1986 (Heilbron, Verheul, and Quak, 2013: 16), the 1980s was a period during which capital owners gained the upper hand over all other corporate constituencies:

> The relations between those who own and control large U.S. corporations—shareholders, mangers, and board of directors—underwent what was arguably an epochal transition in the 1980s and early 1990s, from an era of 'managerial capitalism' to one of 'investor capitalism.'
>
> (Davis and Greve, 1997: 8)

"[S]ince the early 1980s," Rock (2013: 1910) adds, "the U.S. system has shifted form a management-centric system to a shareholder-centric system." The foremost consequence was, over time and through a delicate network of scholarly reasoning, lobbyism and think tank advocacy, and policy reform—almost impossible to disentangle and analyse as free-standing activities—that "managers and directors today largely 'think like shareholders.'" (Rock, 2013: 1910) argues. For instance, Grullon and Ikenberry (2000: 31) say, "It was not until the early 1980s that U.S. corporations began adopting share repurchase programs in large numbers," a practice that serves to transfer wealth to shareholders not as dividends (the conventional transfer mechanism) but through the focal firm intervening into the stock market pricing activities by either announcing that the firm intend to repurchase its own stock or actually purchasing stocks on basis of the claim that the stock is underpriced.

When the "economic and political power shifted in favour of capital, beginning in the early 1980s" (Wolff, 2003: 497), the most significant group to suffer from this new pro-business, free-market regime was labour. First, the blue-collar worker community was losing jobs as "the reigning wisdom on Wall Street" was now that the easiest and quickest way to increase the value of the corporation in the eyes of finance market traders was to either reduce wages or to lay off employees to cut the labour costs momentarily (Goldstein, 2012: 272). For the pro-business and free-market community, now advising the White House, the ulterior motive behind cutting down on labour costs (and thus representing the end of an industrial policy that had dominated since Henry Ford's "five-dollar day" reform, that of raising real wages to boost demand and to generate an upward economic spiral) and laying off employees was to strike a blow on organized labour and unionism, especially in the manufacturing industry:

> Regan restricted the growth of government spending on the poor and the middle class, and simultaneously instituted large tax cuts focused on corporations and the very wealthy . . . The massive unemployment of the first half of the 1980s further undercut union strength. By 1989 only 16% of workers were in unions.
>
> (Crotty, 2012: 84)

In the free-market community, dominated by Chicago school economic theory, trade unions represented little more than the introduction of noise and opportunism in free-market pricing, and trade unions early on became the *bête noire* of free marketeers, fiercely combating what they dismissed as "collectivism."

Second, the employees who were able to keep their jobs were gradually losing their benefits that had been established in the managerial capitalism era and enshrined by, for example, the Treaty of Detroit, leading to both increased economic inequality and direct poverty in working-class families:

> Between the early 1980s and the mid-1990s, the value of pension benefits to current workers dropped in every income group, but by far most rapidly among the lowest paid workers, who already had the lowest coverage levels . . . In addition, tax breaks for private pensions and other retirement savings options heavily favor better-paid employees: Two-thirds of the nearly $100 billion in federal tax breaks for subsidized retirement savings options accrue to the top 20% of the population.
>
> (Hacker, 2004: 255)

The hardship brought by the new pro-business policies and the anti-union campaign in combination with generous reforms benefitting the finance industry led to declining real wage growth (which was solid and continuous in the era of managerial capitalism), and real wage growth was substituted by increased levels of household debt: "From the early 1980s to the present, Americans' debt burden compared with their disposable income has risen considerably" (Sullivan, Warren, and Westbrook, 2006: 248). Prasad (2012: xiv) refers to this finance industry-led, debt-based welfare as "mortgage Keynesianism," a new policy regime enacted in the early 1980s; Americans remained the global economy's great spenders well into the new millennium, an issue that was commonly addressed during meetings between American leaders and leaders of "export-oriented economies" such as Germany and Japan.

Another theme in 1970s' bear markets and thereafter leveraged in the 1980s was to discredit managers. When the American industry seemed to have lost ground in the mid-1970s vis-à-vis foreign competitors (most noteworthy the Japanese automotive industry, which emerged as an overwhelmingly efficient and disciplined competitor by the late 1970s. See, e.g., Vogel, 1979, Pascale and Athos, 1981; Cusumano, 1985), the idea that America needed a new breed of leaders gained a foothold in media and elsewhere. In the late 1970s and early 1980s, a "new-genre leadership" (Avolio, Walumbwa, and Weber, 2009) was formed:

> The image of the postwar corporate executive was that of an almost 'faceless' bureaucrat, yet one who exhibited a calm, statemanlike demeanor, presiding over an organization that understood its responsibility to the larger community. The new corporate leader who emerged in the 1980s was a brash, swashbuckling celebrity, far more colorful than his predecessors, yet often viewed as lacking responsibility to anyone but himself, and perhaps his shareholders.
>
> (Mizruchi, 2013: 216–217)

In a much-cited paper published in 1977, Abraham Zaleznik argued that "leaders" should be separated from "managers" because the former, as opposed to the latter, embodies a venturesome, risk-seeking, and ultimately productive entrepreneurial culture. In Zaleznik's (1977: 70) view, leaders and managers "differ in motivation, personal history, and in how they think and see." Not the least, the leader is not an "organization man," an ideal-type figure that William H. Whyte (1956) introduced in the 1950s; instead, Zaleznik (1977: 72) says, leaders "[w]ork in organizations, but they never belong to them. Their sense of who they are does not depend upon memberships, work roles, or any other social indicators of identity." These professional leaders, who have few personal or emotional bonds attached to the firm they oversee and manage, are the perfect species in the ideal agency theory model, demanding a ruthless commitment to finance market interests and a willingness to avert all the fiduciary duties that corporate law and traditional managerial work have imposed on managers. In Zaleznik's (1977: 72) account, the leader is an autonomous, sovereign figure, transcending the manager's preference "to work with people"—managers "avoid solitary activity because it makes them anxious," Zaleznik (1977: 72) claims. In short, while *leaders* are the movers and shakers of this world, the anti-management narrative of the 1970s and 1980s portrayed *managers* in the Alfred P. Sloan tradition as anxious collectivists, unable to produce economic wealth and well-being but hiding in executive suites and boardrooms and being primarily concerned with serving their own personal interests. No wonder the pro-business community and the free marketeers needed to invent a new breed of leaders who were more comfortable accepting the new rules of the game laid out by free marketeers as the pathway to prosperity. Proponents of what Burns (1978) refers to as *transformational leadership* (by and large consistent with Zaleznik's, 1977, leader) such as Tichy and Ulrich (1983) who spoke with great urgency, not unlike Judge Powell's declaration, about the need to bring forward a new generation of business leaders:

> To revitalize organizations . . . a new brand of leadership is necessary. Instead of managers who continue to move organizations along historical tracks, the new leaders must transform the organizations and head them down new tracks . . . Unless the creation of this new breed of leaders becomes a national agenda, we are not very optimistic about the revitalization of the U.S. economy.
>
> (Tichy and Ulrich, 1983: 59)

No wonder the Reagan campaign's promise of a new "Morning in America"—even though one of the campaigns TV commercials was reputed to include photos from the harbor of Vancouver in British Columbia—was embraced by neoconservatives, libertarians, and many others after the long, painful years of the 1970s. In this environment of anxiety-ridden worries about the future of American capitalism and America more broadly, agency theory was advocated as the latest contribution to the free-market advocacy program that originated in the 1950s at the law school of the University of Chicago.

Agency theory was consolidated in the 1980s (e.g., Fama, 1980; Fama and Jensen, 1983b; Jensen, 1986), but its intellectual roots were developed and published in journal papers in the early 1970s, beginning arguably with the seminal papers of Armen Alchian and Harold Demsetz (1972) and Michael C. Jensen and William H. Meckling (1976). These papers were more explicitly theory of the firm papers, rooted in the idea of the market for management control, but this line of reasoning was indebted to the seminal work of the liberal legal scholar Adolf A. Berle and the statistician Gardiner C. Means, published at the height of the Great Depression and the New Deal rescue program. In the agency theory model, widely circulated and popularized in the 1980s, most of the fine-tuning details that were attended to in the literature on antitrust enforcement, the market for management control, and contract theory were abandoned to streamline a rudimentary but persuasive model that could both inform policy-making and inspire decision-makers in boardrooms and executive suites to abandon the intentions of the legislators of corporate law and to endorse more straightforward efficiency criteria in their day-to-day work. *Arguendo*, the extensive critique of agency theory articulated by legal scholars, management researchers, and economic sociologists, was never really bothering proponents of agency theory as they knew that political, social, and cultural factors would favour their ticket regardless of its theoretical inconsistencies and counterintuitive propositions and assumptions. As all legal scholars know, laws in books are one thing, and laws in practice or real life are quite another (Halliday and Carruthers, 2007). The same can be said of economic theory; dry mathematized modeling of the kind one can find in high-prestige economics journal has little to do with messy and non-linear policy-making, so the ability to sell an argument is not of necessity ultimately a matter of "being right" but of "sounding convincing":

> The popularity of agency theory in governance research is likely due to two factors. First, it is an extremely simple theory, in which large corporations are reduced to two participants—managers and shareholders—and the interests of each are assumed to be both clear and consistent. Second, the notion of humans as self-interested and generally unwilling to sacrifice personal interests for the interest of the other is both age old and widespread.
>
> (Daily, Dalton, and Cannella, 2003: 372)

In this view, agency theory is a textbook illustration of how economic ideas (Blyth, 2002)—no matter of how vague and how disputed they are—can serve as a vehicle for policy reform as they serve the interest of certain actors and their financiers and sponsors. In other words, agency theory is an eminent case of the *performativity* of economic theory (e.g., Mackenzie, 2006).

Jensen and Fama Advocate Shareholder Welfare

The market for management control and the contact theory literature had established the idea of the firm as a nexus of contracts, which, in turn, was monitored by the pricing activities of the finance market actors, buying and selling financial assets issued by the focal firm. That model and theory of the firm per se did not mandate the idea that shareholder welfare was the sole objective of the managers and directors, but this final contribution to the new corporate governance model came essentially from agency theory, Eugene F. Fama and Micheal C. Jensen's refinement and purification (with a generous characterization) of contract theory. However, while contract theory apparently relied on legal theory and the legal concept of *contract*, agency theory finally managed to cut the ropes from legal theory to complete the project to define the firm and its elementary mechanisms exclusively on basis of orthodox neoclassical economic theory. The result was a set of normative propositions that were neither theoretically convincing nor empirically substantiated, yet the message was easy to sell to financiers, think tankers, and policy makers, especially in an era where finance market expansion, propelled by de-regulations and an inflow of overseas savings into the U.S., was taken as evidence of the virtues of free-market pricing—an ideology, despite the alarming increase in financial instability (Charles, 2016; Calomiris and Haber, 2014; Chick, 1997), that would dominate well into the new millennium, until the *annus horribilis* of 2008.

The very core of the agency theory was Berle and Means's (1934) idea that the firm's stakeholders (whereof its investors is a key group) and the salaried managers operate within a principal–agent relationship, where the agent is responsive to the principal's interest only, regardless of the complexity of the business charter. Berle and Means (1934), a law school professor and his statistics-savvy collaborator, serving within the Roosevelt administration, were concerned about the power and influence of the new professional management class and developed a model of the firm where managers were held responsible vis-à-vis outsiders to avoid externalities in the corporate system. This principal-agency model was therefore introduced as a general theory of managerial responsibility that fitted with the overall ambition of the New Deal era policy, putting a faith in the viability and efficiency of competitive capitalism and its corporate system, while being more sceptical regarding a free-market version of this system with no regulatory control or other forms of external monitoring. Therefore, Jensen and Meckling (1976: 311. Emphasis in the original) deviate from Berle and Means's (1934) seminal text and its intentions when they claimed that the firm is "[s]imply one form of *legal fiction which serves as a nexus for contracting relationships and which is also characterized by the existence of divisible residual claims on the assets and cash flows of the organization which can generally be sold without permission of the other contracting individuals.*" For Jensen and Meckling (1976), the principal–agent relationship is not a general model for how managers are held accountable to a *variety* of stakeholders, but they reserve this term for the owners of the assets that can "be sold without permission" and who are granted the right to the residual cash flow. As opposed to Berle and Means's (1934) more sophisticated model, where managers could be held accountable to a wider set of constituencies, Jensen and Meckling (1976) develop their own specific and more narrow version of the theory relying on a more bilateral principal–agent relationship. As will be demonstrated, it is again the neoclassical ideal of "efficiency," defined in quite specific terms as finance market efficiency maximization, that determines this relationship.

Fama and Jensen (1983b) further flesh out the ideas presented in Jensen and Meckling's (1976) article, taking the "nexus of contract view" as its starting point, now regarded as a strictly defined theory of the firm rather than some intriguing but venturesome conjecture in need of further elaboration and/or empirical substantiation. "Our hypothesis is that the contract structure of . . . organizations separate the ratification and monitoring of decisions from initiation and implementation of the decisions," Fama and Jensen (1983b: 302) write in a condensed sentence that indicate that it is decisions and their "quality" that is monitored and assessed within the prescribed model. Once that statement is being made, Fama and Jensen (1983b: 302) proceed to declare that the so-called residual claimant, the owners of stock, are "those who contract for the rights to net cash flow." This statement is, as we will see below, not supported by corporate law or court decisions, but Fama and Jensen are not so much concerned with legal facts and practices as long as the argument follows consistently from their initial neoclassical propositions. In order to bridge the market for management control model, contract theory, and the Berle and Means principal-agency model, shareholders are simply portrayed as the *only legitimate claimants* of the residual cash. This *entitlement* (which is a legal term that differs from a *right*, it should be noticed), which the shareholders do not have *de jure* within the extant corporate legislation), is justified on basis of a quite long series of arguments and motivations, all rooted in orthodox neoclassical economic theory and its constitutional assumptions. First of all, Fama and Jensen (1983b: 304) argues that "agency problems" arise because "contracts are not costlessly written and enforced"—a statement that would speak against the contract theory in the first place, sceptics may object—and therefore include "the costs of structuring, monitoring, and bonding a set of contracts among agents with conflicting interests." In this view, potential and actual deviations between principals (regardless of who they are, shareholders or other social groups) and agents, anticipated in corporate law which defines a business charter as a team production effort naturally generating disputes, is understood not so much as an original problem to be handled but as a condition that induces "costs."

Next, Fama and Jensen (1983b: 304) argue that agency problems are particularly cumbersome when the decision-makers are "not the major residual claimants and therefore do not bear a major share of the wealth effects of their decisions." It should be noticed that "agency problems" are equalized with "agency costs," but to the surprise of commentators, agency costs are rarely, if ever, measured and estimated in actual monetary terms but remain essentially a conceptual term introduced as an ad hoc hypothesis to support the tenuous idea that shareholders are the only residual claimants. This is another noteworthy formulation because it is a key to the normative agency theory argument, based on a truism because the agent is by definition the actor given decision-making authority on behalf of the principal (no matter who the principal is); Fama and Jensen (1983b) do not speak about a *specific* case (i.e., that of the firm as a nexus of contracts) but of principal–agent relations as they are predicated by agency theory in the first place. Despite this lapse of reasoning, Fama and Jensen (1983b: 304) say that the deviation between the decision of the agent and the principal's interests, allegedly caused by the fact that the agent does not carry any risk (a claim being heavily contested by, e.g., legal scholars) justify "effective control procedures." More precisely, this suggests that managerial decision-making quality is best measured in terms of (free-)market pricing, which makes finance-market pricing of firm assets the ultimate check on management malfeasance, as finance markets discipline managers to make decisions that benefit shareholder interest at minimal cost. This is the familiar management for market control and contract theory arguments, lending credence to the efficiency of market pricing vis-à-vis other monitoring mechanisms. Fama and Jensen's (1983b: 304–305) argument may be deeply rooted in orthodox neoclassical economic theory and favour its vocabulary of prices, costs, decisions, and residual cash flow, but they add an emotional, even sentimental stream of thought that is otherwise excluded from economic theory when they portray shareholders and finance market actors more largely as being the victims of self-serving managers, "squandering" and "wasting" the residual cash flow that the shareholders are entitled to, and leaving them without "no protection against opportunistic actions of decision agents." While corporate elites have traditionally, both in theory and in the wider culture, been portrayed as the foremost and, in the best of cases, trusted agents of competitive capitalism, at times benevolent but also ruthless and predatory in cases, but ultimately closely allied with, for example, the finance industry, Fama and Jensen aim to dissolve and separate this industry–finance complex to the advantage of the latter; managers are no longer stateman-like trustees and the fiduciaries of competitive capitalism, into whose hands entire societies have laid their hopes for a more prosperous future—in the eyes of Fama and Jensen, this corporate elite is little more than small-minded and self-serving shirkers whose competence and moral fibre should be doubted. Agency theory and its shareholder welfare governance model are simply founded on the idea that professional managers and corporate elites, responsible for the coordination of the team production activities inside the firm, are, when left unchecked, the gravediggers and destroyers of competitive capitalism. In contrast, the shiny, white knight of Fama and Jensen is the shareholder and the finance market actor, armed with price-setting mechanisms and self-interest and thus capable of curbing the escalating malfeasance of professional managers and corporate elites, disciplining them to minimize the agency costs and to increase the efficiency of the operations.

In the coming decade, Michael C. Jensen, in particular, would be able to market this model of the firm, burdened by incompetent and self-serving managers that withhold (at best) and waste (at worst) the residual cash flow that the shareholders, according to his own model, are exclusively entitled to. For reasons unknown and overtly curious now in hindsight, the "management malfeasance" argument being at the very heart of this line of reasoning was more or less accepted by many policy-makers and even some management scholars, otherwise having a more detailed understanding of the complexities encountering managers. But in the *Deals Decade*, when finance theory and finance market expansion and de-regulation was widely embraced in neoconservative and libertarian quarters and translated into policy, the think tankers and functionaries recruited from institutes that had the same financiers and sponsors as Rochester University and Jensen himself, Jensen's ranting about agency cost-inducing managers and their detrimental influence on competitive capitalism was bankable. Jensen (1986) continued to drum this massage with great persistency:

> Free cash flow is cash in excess of that required to fund all projects that have positive net present values when discounted at the relevant cost of capital. Conflicts of interest between shareholders and managers over payout policies are especially severe when the organization generates substantial free cash flow. The problem is how to motivate managers to disgorge the cash rather than investing it at below the cost of capital or wasting it on organizational inefficiencies.
>
> (Jensen, 1986: 323)

Given that Jensen and other orthodox neoclassical economists have a rather scant interest in what happens inside the firms—the firm is after all only a continuation of the market, in this view[1]—he has surprisingly clear opinions about the quality of, for example, internal management control system:

> Firms often do not have good information on their own costs, much less the costs of their competitors; it is therefore sometimes unclear to managers that they are the high-cost firm which should exit the industry. Even when managers do acknowledge the requirement for exit, it is often difficult for them to accept and initiate the shutdown decision. For the managers who must implement these decisions, shutting plants or liquidating the firms causes personal pain, creates uncertainty, and interrupts or sidetracks careers. Rather than confronting the pain, managers generally resist such actions as long as they have the cash flow to subsidize the losing operations.
>
> (Jensen, 1993: 848)

Needless to say, accounting scholars and strategic management scholars would reject this proposition out of hand and certainly as a *general proposition* introduced to justify reforms in corporate governance. As large conglomerates and divisonalized organizations, was widely regarded as a problem for all sorts of commentators and policy-makers in the 1970s, Jensen (1993) continues to declare his unreserved support for takeover activities and accompanying corporate restructuring. This is a theme that is familiar from the market for management control and the contact theory literature, rendering, for example, takeover bids serve as a mechanism that revitalize inefficient corporations and incentivize and discipline managers to better respond to marker changes and the demands of the finance market actors. Jensen is greatly enthusiastic when it comes to the effects of corporate restructuring in the 1980s:

> Total factor productivity growth in the manufacturing sector more than doubled after 1981 from 1.4 percent per year in the period 1950 to 1981 to 3.3 percent in the period 1981 to 1990. Nominal unit labor cost stopped their 17-year rise, and real unit labor cost declined by 25 percent. These lower labor cost came not from reduced wages or employment but from increased productivity: Nominal and real hourly compensation increased by a total of 4.2 and 0.3 percent per year respectively over the 1981 to 1989 period.
>
> (Jensen, 1993: 836)

Therefore, Jensen (1993: 837) summarizes, "during the 1980s, the real value of public firms' equity more than doubled from $1.4 to $3 trillion." Not all commentators were equally sanguine about the takeover wave (see, e.g., Schneper and Guillén, 2004: 263), coinciding with the de-industrialization of America in the Reagan era and the fortification of finance engineering activities, aimed at short-term economic value extraction (which, it should be noticed, perfectly well follows the neoclassical efficiency criteria. See, e.g., Zhang and Gimeno, 2016). In contrast, for Jensen, advocating shareholder welfare the measure of all things, the takeover wave was not only beneficial but also welcome. "The capital markets [is] an effective mechanism for motivating change, renewal, and exit," Jensen (1993: 852) claims:

> The evidence from LBOs, leveraged restructurings, takeovers, and venture capital firms has demonstrated dramatically that leverage, payout policy, and ownership structure (that is, who owns the firm's securities) do in fact affect organizational efficiency, cash flow, and therefore, value.
>
> (Jensen, 1993: 868)

Takeover and mergers are, despite its alleged efficiency-inducing virtues, relatively complex legal, financial, and managerial processes, and the very threat of takeover is an equally efficient mechanism for increasing "management decision quality." Therefore, Jensen suggests that the shareholder welfare objective should not only be enforced indirectly but needs to be established as *the sole legitimate objective* of the managers and the directors. Consistent with his limited regard for professional managers, Jensen makes the claim that, for example, stakeholder theory, proposing that firms serve a variety of stakeholders whose internal interests are not of necessity aligned or brought into harmony at low cost, is an inadequate corporate governance model as managers are incapable of handling more than one objective, and that would be to maximize the efficiency of the team production activities: stakeholder theory, Jensen (2002: 237) writes, is "[f]undamentally flawed because it violates the proposition that any organization must have a single-values objective as a precursor to purposeful or rational behavior." Jensen (2002: 237) continues: "[F]irms that adopt stakeholder theory will be handicapped in the competition for survival because, as a basis for action, stakeholders politicize the corporation,[2] and leaves its managers empowered to exercise their own preferences in spending the firm's resources." Once Jensen (2002: 238) has declared that "multiple objectives is no objective"—a declarative statement unaccompanied by factual evidence—he adds that "maximizing the total market value of the firm" is one "objective function" that resolve "the trade-off problem among multiple constituencies" (Jensen, 2002: 239):

> With no criteria for performance, managers cannot be evaluated in any principled way. Therefore, stakeholder theory plays into the hands of self-interested managers allowing them to pursue their own interests at the expense of society and the firm's financial claimants. It allows managers and directors to invest their favorite projects that destroy firm-value whatever they are (the environment, art, cities, medical research) without having to justify the value destruction.
>
> (Jensen, 2002: 242)

In other words, if, and only if, managers embark on the project to enrich one constituency (the shareholders), all other tradeoffs and responsibilities will be solved as a consequence therefrom. This one-size-fits-all argument in combination with the one-best way argument is the very basis for Jensen's shareholder welfare advocacy. Again, the familiar arguments run as follows: shareholder value creation, apparently benefitting *a few*, is allegedly *good for all*, and if nothing else, it serves to discipline the salaried managers who are claimed to induce agency costs that are not only *considerable* but also being higher than *all other relevant costs*; that is, agency costs overshadow all other benefits of the corporate system.

All these propositions can be disputed, but the concept of *agency costs* is particularly complicated to accept as the intuitive understanding would accept that there may be, under certain conditions, *some* agency costs but that they are at worst moderate and that they are well compensated for by other efficiency-inducing activities in of the extant governance model. For the commentator not committed to agency theory and the theoretical baggage its carries with it, the idea of agency costs may or may not be present (some—but not the majority and certainly not all—managers may after all, history learns, be both incompetent and inclined to serve their own interests), but the magnitude and distribution of agency costs (whereof most parts are already implied and thus accepted by the principal–agent model as such) cannot justify the claim that shareholders should suddenly receive all the free cash flow. The Jensen argument thus seems tenuous, counter-intuitive, and overtly draconian in addition to its conspicuous ignorance of corporate law and legal practice. More specifically, why Jensen assumes that corporate law ignores agency costs would merit some explanation. Over the decades, there are little new evidence that been brought forward that have benefitted Jensen's argument. On the contrary, agency theory as it is presented by Michael C. Jensen and Eugene F. Fama remains an enigma in the corporate governance literature: How could this poorly designed, simplistic, and speculative theoretical model rise to prominence and be treated as legitimate contestant for the analysis and design of governance practices? The answer must be sought in neither scholarly circles nor the corporate system per se but in the institutional milieu that was emerging in the mid-1970s to the mid-1980s, promoting the interests of the owners of finance capital at the expense of other constituencies.

The Legal Theory Critique of the Agency Theory Shareholder Welfare Model

The agency theory view of shareholders as the principals of the firm (i.e., its investors singlehandedly carrying the residual risk) and managers being their agents have been fiercely criticized by legal scholars. As there are as many theoretical and practical objections to agency theory as there are propositions and assumptions made by its protagonists, the literature is quite extensive and addresses a variety of themes. First of all, Coffee (1986: 26) is sceptical towards the proposition in orthodox neoclassical economic theory that "market forces alone will result in the installation of the optimal level of monitoring devices and incentive systems that bring agency costs down to an irreducible minimum" (Coffee, 1986: 26). As this is an axiomatic principle in agency theory, yet based more on a line of reasoning on basis of further propositions and assumptions than factual evidence, this is a key argument against agency theory. In fact, the very reliance on jurisprudence rather than market contracting in the first place is indicative of many externalities of market-based pricing that now, suddenly, when everything else is in place in the corporate system, is claimed to triumph over any other competing governance system. As Bratton and Wachter (2010: 675) comment, the idea that "shareholder empowerment" will cause agency costs to decline and capital to flow to its best use (i.e., the two key objectives, consistent with the efficiency criterion, that proponents of shareholder welfare invoke to justify their position vis-à-vis sceptics) implies that the corporate governance systems "leave big money on the table," an assumption, Bratton and Wachter (2010: 675) say, that is "counterintuitive." If managers were such terrible decision-makers, concerned to primarily enrich themselves and to otherwise squander cash, how come the economic growth during the era of managerial capitalism were maintained at unprecedented levels for decades, being in fact the longest period of stable economic growth in competitive capitalism? For legal scholars, such factual evidence sides poorly with the propositions of agency theory.

Second, Coffee argues persuasively (as discussed in Chapter 2) that shareholders have a different risk-utility function than managers do. Shareholders for most parts keep well-diversified holdings, while managers do only "have one job" and are compensated on basis of firm or industry-specific expertise that contains some irreducible hard-to-transfer know-how and skills. Therefore, the divesture of the firm would entail a loss or a profit for the shareholder but would have much more pervasive consequences and implications for the manager, especially for top managers and executives who can easily suffer reputational losses from failing their responsibilities. On basis of this micro-economics argument, Coffee (1986: 26) suggests that it is more costly to align the shareholders' and the managers' risk appetite than agency theorists admit:

> Do these [market] forces work to align the manager's risk-aversion level with those of the shareholders? It seems extremely doubtful that the contractual devices described by Jensen and Meckling do anything like this. Take, for example, the use of outside directors. If anything, they have reason to be even more risk averse than managers. This is because their economic stake in the corporation is relatively small while their potential personal liability may be significant once the corporation becomes financially distressed.
>
> (Coffee, 1986: 26)

Therefore, Coffee (1986: 28) concludes, the Jensen and Meckling model "generally overestimates the willingness of managers to bond themselves in order to increase the firm's stock value." As a consequence, even if, say, a conglomerate firm is successfully taken over through takeover bids—an agency theory textbook case of managers being disciplined, leading to a new "management team" taking over the executive function—there is nothing in the agency theory model to neutralize the basic fact that the new management team would have an entirely different utility function. Instead, the new management team would demonstrate a similar risk aversion as their predecessors, and no solution to this systemic corporate governance problem, engendered by the market for management control, the use of contact theory, and the shareholder welfare model, is in sight:

> [A]lthough Jensen's emphasis on the managerial incentive to hoard 'free cash flow' is correct, the bonding process that he believes will cure this problem has yet to show durability. Once the momentary threat has passed, the same agency-cost problems will return when new shares are issued, making the process more circular than permanent.
>
> (Coffee, 1986: 37)

One solution to this problem is of course, as have been frequently implemented, to design economic compensation package to managers so that they are incentivized to tolerate and take more risk and thus to fundamentally alter their risk-utility function, but the use of generous compensation, lavish bonuses, and extraordinary pension packages has little to do with the alleged superior market efficiency that justifies the shareholder welfare model in the first place but is little more than a less than subtle method for making managers serve the short-term goals of the shareholders. The empirical evidence of the soaring economic compensation accruing to managers—one of the most conspicuous and heatly debated empirical phenomenon in the era of investor capitalism (Frydman and Jenter, 2010; Lord and Siato, 2010; Bebchuk and Grinstein, 2005; Bebchuk and Fried, 2004)—is, in fact, indicative of the failure of the agency model and its inability to "bond" (in Coffee's, 1986, phrase) shareholders and managers. Elementary risk-utility functions remain unchanged until managers are insulated from all the downside risks they have historically been motivated to avoid.

Third, Stout's (2002, 2003, 2013) work addresses some of the legal theory implications of agency theory, pointing both at the ignorance towards the historical roots of corporate legislation and some of the inconsistencies that follow from the agency theory model. First of all, Stout (2002) argues that the proposition that the shareholders are the only residual risk bearers, first advanced by Frank Knight, a leading figure in the first generation of Chicago economists, is incompatible with, for example, finance theory and, more specifically, option-pricing theory (see, e.g., Black and Scholes, 1973) that render the debtholders as a legitimate risk bearers:

> Options theory teaches us that once a firm has issued debt (as almost all firms do), it makes just as much sense to say that the debtholders 'own' the right to the corporation's cash flow but have sold a call option to the shareholder, as it does say that shareholder 'owns' the right to the corporation's cash flow but has bought a put option from the debtholders. Put differently, option theory demonstrates that bondholders and equity holders each share contingent control and bear residual risk in firms.
>
> (Stout, 2002: 1192)

Generally speaking, the role of the firm's creditors is downplayed in the shareholder welfare argument. Creditors are, similar to the shareholders, operating on a finance market and rely on market pricing mechanisms in their day-to-day work, but unlike the shareholders, the creditors contract for a predefined, fixed yield. Therefore, creditors have no interests in speculation and are consequently more risk averse as upside risk is not compensated and downside risk jeopardize the termination of the contract. Therefore, increased risks that follow from higher leverage, promoted within the shareholder primacy governance model, is a way for shareholders to transfer risk to creditors, who do not benefit from this leverage. That is, the shareholders' potential gain is always of necessity the loss of the creditor, measured in terms of increased risk of default but with the yield being constant. The widely pronounced "shareholder value is good for all" argument is therefore not even beneficial for other principals and finance markets actors, operating within the *de facto* market for management control and on a contractual basis. Agency theory therefore fails to pass even the most elementary resilience test.

Moreover, as a legal matter, "shareholders of a public corporation are entitled to receive nothing from the firm *unless and until the board of directors decides that they should receive it*" (Stout, 2002: 1194. Emphasis in the original). While agency theorists and contractarians have at least accepted this elementary statute of corporate law, they claim that the shareholders are the firm's investors, and therefore, the argument proceeds, the shareholders are the residual risk bearers, which, in turn, entitle them to the residual cash flow. But this argument leads back to the finance theory and the option-pricing model objection that admits no such privileges for the shareholders. Ultimately, agency theory (and its predecessors, the market for management control and the contact theory literatures) recourse to sheer policy advocacy as a way out of these overwhelming theoretical and legal complexities, unfolding as a self-referential, circulatory argument: "[C]orporate law *ought* to incorporate shareholder primacy (or so the argument goes) because shareholders *ought* to be the firm's sole residual claimants" (Stout, 2002: 1195). Agency theory thus falls prey to the so-called is-ought fallacy (commonly credited to the Scottish philosopher David Hume), making a daring epistemological leap from what is presented as factual conditions to normative statements but without recognizing this addendum.

Despite this fragile theoretical model, agency theorists are keen on providing advice on how to make firms shareholder value-generating ventures. As agency theorist mistrust managers—even more than so: underperforming and incompetent managers are postulated to be a structural feature of corporations—agency theorists have ben animated by the idea that outsiders (i.e., finance market participants) and academics (i.e., followers of orthodox neoclassical economic theory but, importantly, not legal scholars failing to subscribe to the favoured models or management scholars) have "better insight into how to run businesses than businesspeople themselves" (Stout, 2013: 2007). To capitalize on this alleged insight, agency theorists have strongly advocated outside directors as the remedy to poor managerial decision-making and discipline. Unfortunately, this claim has been poorly supported by empirical evidence (Bhagat and Black, 2002: 263; Davis, 1991: 607; Useem, 1990: 700; Brudney, 1982: 638): In fact, some studies indicate that firm with higher degree of so-called independent directors perform worse than firms with a higher degree of internally recruited directors (Almandoz, 2014: 458). In addition, firm with independent directors recruited from the finance industry on the board perform worse than do firms that does not include such directors. This evidence suggests that independent directors do not solve the agency cost problems that agency theorists regard a major concern for the corporate system.

Stout (2013) points at some of the wider and more far-reaching consequences of the agency theory model. First of all, like many other legal scholars, Stout (2013) questions the assumption that business promoters that raise capital to finance their venture—recall that Manne (1965, 1967) justifies the entire idea of the market of management control on basis of the argument that the firm is a finance capital raising vehicle—are attracted by the idea that shareholders, who believe they have exclusive right to the residual cash flow and who campaign for a maximal payout, are given the authority to influence their day-to-day work. If that would have been an attractive feature of the firm being incorporated, new business charters would have been written in ways that would have ensured shareholder rights or, alternatively, states with higher degrees of "shareholder protection" would have been chosen for incorporation. Again, there is little evidence of such beliefs in the efficacy of market pricing as an internal mechanism for monitoring managers. More widely speaking, the entrenchment of shareholder value ideologies and practices seems to make the entire idea of the public corporation, the foundation for the corporate system based on dispersed ownership and tradable voting rights following the stock, unattractive. If the entire entrepreneurial function, as conceptualized by Richard Cantillon and Joseph Schumpeter, an activity based on calculated risk taking, is burdened by the persistent claim from shareholders that the firm should be divested as soon as any setback occurs, there are few possibilities for renewal within the corporate system and, by implication, competitive capitalism per se. The shareholder welfare model may affect, Stout (2012: 54) says, corporations' willingness to "have public investors at all." Especially for start-ups, this is not a trivial matter, Stout says:

> [S]takeholders rationally distrust dispensed shareholders who can personally profit from threatening to expropriate or destroy the value of stakeholders' specific interests. This makes it harder for shareholder-focused public corporations to attract dedicated employees, loyal customers, cooperative suppliers, and support from local employees. Shifting public corporations from the managerial model to the shareholder-centric model thus can produce a one-time increase in 'shareholder wealth,' while simultaneously eroding public corporations' long-term ability to generate profits, just as fishing with dynamite produces a one-time increase in catch size while eroding long-term fishing returns.
>
> (Stout, 2013: 2016)

Reporting data from the Business Dynamics Statistics and the Longitudinal Business Database, maintained by the U.S. Census Bureau, for the 1976–2011 period, Decker, Haltiwanger, Jarmin, and Miranda (2014: 4) show that the share of US employment accounted for by young firms has "declined by almost 30 percent over the last 30 years." The statistics Decker et al. (2014: 16) present indicates a declining importance of new firms (and not only "new establishments," oftentimes confused in entrepreneurship research) and a waning entrepreneurial spirit in the U.S.:

> Firms aged five years or less made up about 47 percent of all firms in the late 1980s, but this number declined to 39 percent of all firms before

> the start of the Great Recession, and has declined further since then. Similarly, the share of employment at firms less than five years of age declined from an average of 18.9 percent in the late 1980s to an average of 13.4 percent at the cyclical peak before the Great Recession. Finally, firms that were five years old or less contributed 39 percent of all new jobs in the late 1980s, but about 33 percent of all new jobs before the Great Recession.
>
> (Decker et al., 2014: 16)

Decker et al. (2014: 18) remark that the "incentives to start new businesses appear to be declining in all sectors," and especially in the retail sector. This, in turn, substantially reduces the business dynamics in the American economy and leads to the share of employment provided by "young firms" now being in decline in "all 50 states": [S]tates with business climates as different as California and Texas exhibit large and similar declines in entrepreneurial activity, Decker et al. (2014: 18) summarize. Unfortunately, there is no credible theoretical explanation for this faltering American entrepreneurialism, but Decker et al. (2014: 19) claim that an understanding of the causes and consequences of this decline "should be a high priority."

In addition, the decline of IPOs (Davis, 2013: 292. Figure 3) and the slowdown in newly listed companies in the 1997–2009 period, the high noon of shareholder primacy governance, provide further evidence that support the hypothesis that shareholder governance is comparatively unattractive (or, alternatively, that finance capital is possible to acquire elsewhere at low cost): In the period, "[t]he number of public companies listed on stock exchange has declined by 39 percent in absolute terms, and by a whopping 53 percent when adjusted for GDP" (Stout, 2012: 54). Also the time a stock is being held is substantially lower today, making "long-term and committed owners" a rare species in corporate ecology: "It is estimated that the typical Fortune 5000 company had a "life expectancy" of seventy-five years early in the twentieth century but now has one of only fifteen years (and the number is declining)" (Stout, 2013: 2021).

Stout's concluding remarks suggests agency theory provide no legitimate basis for prescribing either "positive" or normative corporate governance practices:

> Shareholders' rights turn out to be illusory. Executives and directors own a fiduciary duty of loyalty to the corporation that bars them from using their corporate position to enrich themselves as the firm's expense. But thanks to the business judgement rule, unconflicted directors remain legally free to pursue almost any other goal. Directors can safely donate corporate funds to charity; reject profitable business strategies that might harm the community; refuse risky projects that benefit shareholders and creditors' expense; fend off hostile takeover bids in order to protect the interests of employees or the community, and refuse to declare dividends

> even when shareholders demand them . . . Shareholders in public companies cannot successfully sue directors simply because those directors place other stakeholders' or society's interest above shareholders' own.
> (Stout, 2012: 44)

Stout's (2012) advocacy of a board-centric corporate governance model is substantiated by empirical data for the 1978–2011 period, reported by Cremers and Sepe (2016). These data demonstrate that boards with stronger decision-making authority (so-called staggered boards, boards that include directors being grouped into different classes, with each class of directors standing for reelection in successive years, a procedure which in turn makes shareholder activism more complicated; Cremers and Sepe, 2016: 76–77) is positively associated with firm value and thus with economic well-being. The increased risk of managerial moral hazard, commonly justified as the *raison d'être* of shareholder activism, is substantially lower than the costs of the short-termism amplified by shareholder activism; that is, the board-centric model offers the benefit of "committing shareholders more strongly to long-term investment projects" (Cremers and Sepe, 2016: 124). Cremers and Sepe (2016: 135) summarize their argument: "Unsurprisingly, shareholder advocates are not satisfied with the gains they have already made. Notwithstanding the remarkable success they have had in advancing their reform agenda, they see shareholder empowerment as not yet accomplished." Cremers and Sepe (2016: 142) reject this expansion of shareholder activism on empirical and legal grounds and thus advocate legal reforms that would transform the use of staggered board into "into a quasimandatory rule" (Cremers and Sepe, 2016: 75): "[I]t is time to reverse the *j'accuse* of shareholder advocates," Cremers and Sepe (2016: 142) announce.

Management Studies and an Empirical Testing of Agency Theory

The agency theory model of the firm is based on the assumption that incompetent managers make substandard decisions that reduces the shareholders welfare as the residual cash is reinvested in low-yield projects. In other words, the *raison d'être* of agency theory is that it justifies the disciplining of firms that suboptimize the use of its resources. The question is then, What kind of firms that are being targeted in tender offer bids? Davis and Stout (1992) report empirical data that undermine agency theory assumptions as the data reveal that it is not poorly managed, poorly performing, and otherwise inefficient firms that are targeted by bidders. In fact, it was firms with low levels of debt—generally seen as an indication of sound householding as the firm can generate its own cash to finance its operations—that were regarded attractive takeover bids: "[T]hese results conform to the notion of takeover discipline poorly performing management only to the extent that one has faith in the efficacy of capital markets in evaluating management and one believes that lower debt is a sign of poor management," Davis and Stout (1992: 626) summarize. In addition, given the credence given to finance-market pricing, Davis and Stout's (1992) finding that firms with a CEO recruited from the finance industry "significantly increased the risk of becoming a takeover target" was unexpected and did not support the agency theory argument. Rather than demonstrating prudence and a close attentiveness to market interests, finance CEOs apparently failed to counteract takeover threats: "This suggests that finance CEOs, rather than being particularly skilled at running the firm to serve shareholder interests, were carriers of a conception of control that no longer met their own standards of keeping their share price up" (Davis and Stout, 1992: 627). On the other hand, as Davis and Stout (1992) noticed, if it assumed that low levels of debt is a measure of "good managerial decision quality," it may be that finance CEOs are in fact "good managers," but that conclusion would undermine the agency theory argument that predicts that only "poor managers" are disciplined by finance-market actors, who are claimed to know better than insiders.

Interpreted either way, the agency theory model does not fare well. In addition, the presence of "slack" (Davis and Stout, 1992: 627) in the firm, a buffer against the volatility of the market, understood by agency theory as evidence of "empire building" or "sandbagging," the managers' tendency to protect themselves rather than to distribute the residual cash to the shareholders, attracts takeover bids. But if such firms are approached by tender offer bidders, it is not so much with the intention to discipline self-serving managers as it is to extract economic value from well-functioning firms, the ambition to discipline managers are at best secondary (and possibly a negligible incentive) to the goal to extract economic value form the targeted firm; if that is the case, the market for management control is given an entirely different meaning and function, which undermine the agency theory argument and instead justify a reliance on corporate law that grants managers discretion on basis of fiduciary duties. Davis and Stout (1992: 627) summarize their argument:

> [A]gency theory fares rather poorly as an empirical theory, despite its imposing status as normative theory . . . Agency theorist seriously misconstrue the extent to which boards can be seen as vigilant monitors looking out for their shareholder principals—if anything, boards' interest are much more closely tied to those of managers . . . Without takeovers and vigilant boards, the foundations of agency theory as an empirical theory is weak, as the null to modest effects reported here attest. Thus agency theory, as it stands, does not provide a credible alternative theory of organizations.
>
> (Davis and Stout, 1992: 627)

More recent studies sides with Davis and Stout's (1992) seminal work. "[T]he predictions of agency theory are not precise and detailed enough to guide empirical research," Farre-Mensa, Michaely, and Schmalz (2014:

17–51) suggest. Empirical studies of, for example, the banking sector indicate that agency theory–based management control and incentives systems justify excessive risk taking that generate no additional value but leverage the risk to levels that most shareholders, or would creditors and other stakeholders, would not approve. Fahlenbrach and Stulz (2011: 12) examine how well banks performed during the 2008 finance market crisis and find no support for agency theory: "[O]ur result shows that no evidence exists that banks with better alignment of the CEO's interests with those of the shareholders had higher stock returns during the crisis" (Fahlenbrach and Stulz, 2011: 12). Since agency theory rests on rational choice theory and the calculative practices developed on basis of market pricing, rational agents consistently expect to receive compensation in parity with increased risk exposure, *ceteris paribus*. In Fahlenbrach and Stulz's (2011) study of banks, increased levels of risks were not accompanied by higher compensation, thus undermining the agency theory model (see also Sanders and Hambrick, 2007: 1073–1074).

In addition to the poor empirical support of agency theory, management scholars frequently remark that agency theory present a non-contextualized model of managers and the firm, and therefore fails to incorporate institutional factors. Aguilera and Jackson (2003: 448–449) identify at least three institutional factors: First, the theoretical assumptions within agency theory "[o]verlook the diverse identities of stakeholders within the principal-agent relationship" (Aguilera and Jackson, 2003: 448–449). Second, agency theory overlooks "[i]mportant interdependencies among other stakeholders in the firm" (Aguilera and Jackson, 2003: 449). This, in turn, implies what Aguilera and Jackson (2003: 449) refer to as "a type of dyadic reductionism," wherein only the relationship between principals and agents matters in the team production activities inside the firm. Third, and finally, agency theory "[r]etains a thin view of the institutional environment influencing corporate governance" (Aguilera and Jackson, 2003: 449); that is, Aguilera and Jackson (2003: 449) argue, "shareholder rights do not capture the entire complexity of institutional domains by limiting actors' financial behavior to the effects of law." In the end, Aguilera and Jackson (2003: 448) summarize, agency theory "[f]ails to sufficiently explore how corporate governance is shaped by its institutional embeddedness." This failure includes a robust model explaining how diverse governance models produce high output in different countries and regions, failing to explain, for example, the success of German and Japanese manufacturing industry, based on a governance model that deviate considerably from the model prescribed by agency theory.

Fligstein and Choo (2005: 66) add to this criticism and claim that "systems of corporate governance" result from political and historical processes rather than from "efficient solutions to the functional needs of the owners of capital who seek to maximize profits for themselves." The focus on efficiency and the interest for shareholders exclusively do not provide a sufficiently detailed model that can explain varieties in the corporate system and its institutional setting. Furthermore, Fligstein and Choo (2005: 66–67) suggest that the "one best way" argument of agency theory is simplistic and fails to explain regional differences in performance:

> [T]he fact that many societies appear to have experienced comparable economic growth without converging on a single form of corporate governance (i.e., that of the united States) suggests that there is no set of best practices of corporate governance but rather many set of best practices, and that the relationship linking these institutions to good societal outcomes like economic growth is more complex than agency theory would allow.
>
> (Fligstein and Choo, 2005: 66–67)

In this view, agency theory neglects "the broader intercorporate environment in which management acts," and thus imposes "an atomistic or undersocialized view of managerial action as largely divorced from social context" (Davis, 1991: 591). As opposed to the view of managers and directors in corporate law, making fiduciary duties the best legal device to underline and encourage the role of the manager as a social actor who serves many interests and who needs to balance many trade-offs in his or her decision, agency theory strictly follows a rational choice model wherein behavior is "motivated solely by pecuniary self-interest" and where "cooperation indicates a contract among self-interested parties" (Davis, 1991: 591). This map only partially and highly selectively represents the territory, management scholars and economic sociologists have repeatedly pointed out.

The question is ultimately, again, Why has agency theory managed to rise to prominence? Weinstein (2013: 46) suggests that agency theory "must be regarded as a 'performative' theory," a theory that *prescribes* rather than *describes* the objects, outcomes, and relations that it embodies, a common theme in the analysis of economic and finance theory in the social science literature (see, e.g., Mackenzie, 2006). Agency theory advanced a "quasi-financial conception of the corporation" (Weinstein, 2013: 53) at the perfect moment in time, at the intersection between the era of hegemonic Keynesianism and the new era of free-market policy, in a period of time where policy-makers, pundits, and even scholars were clutching at straws to get hold of a new economic model that would stabilize the economy and possibly also produce economic growth and prosperity. As Peck (2011) stresses, the entire Chicago School free-market theory upon which agency theory rests was able to surf the wave of discontent with the *ancien régime* in the late 1970s, and the success of the Chicagoans was not so much a matter of "being rights" as it was a selling of a free-market argument that has now been the guiding light for more than three decades:

> Notwithstanding all the talk of the 'power of ideas,' the influence of the Chicago School essentially rose in lockstep with the misery index—a

> simple measure of the late-Keynesian ordeal of unemployment plus inflation—the historic peak of which coincided, exactly, with the presidential election of 1980.
>
> (Peck, 2011: xlix)

Now in hindsight, it is apparent that agency theory has accomplished little more than to fuel the financialization of the economy and the corporate system, which has led to plummeting economic growth, increased financial instability, and economic inequality levels being back on the 1920s' level. Writing in hindsight, Kaufman and Englander (2005: 9) are concerned that agency theory, despite its fragile and incredible theoretical constitution and its weak empirical substantiation, continues to inform corporate governance practices: "[F]inancial agency theory's shareholder-maximizing motto actually encouraged the managerial misbehaviour of the 1990s. And, to our bewilderment, this mantra still guides reforms for correcting the very problems it helped cause" (Kaufman and Englander, 2005: 9). What can be learned from the case of agency theory prominence is that, as Elzinga (1977: 1210) remarked, "bold statements always have appeal, even when they are incorrect."

Summary and Conclusion

Ideas about market efficiency, an effective market for managerial control, and a contractual theory of the firm rendering, for example, fiduciary duties and the business rule principle obsolete, were all brought into the agency theory model being advocated in the late 1970s and 1980s. While these ideas have been undermined and discredited by legal scholars at every single point they have been introduced, the very idea that the corporation is a primary vehicle for shareholder enrichment, the essence of the agency theory argument and justified basis of a set of assumptions, propositions, anecdotes, and ideological beliefs cobbled together into a "theory," perfectly suited the "pro-business agenda" of the neoconservative upsurge in the U.S. in the early 1980s. Agency theory was, despite its fragile construction, suddenly preached at business schools all over the world (as Fourcade and Khurana, 2013, remark, free-market theorists were commonly excluded from the prestigious economics departments at, for example, MIT, Princeton, and Harvard, but found a new home in the business school setting and economics departments funded by wealthy pro-business sponsors). What was a widely taken for granted business practice, for example, to invest in R&D and production capital, was now dismissed as a form of managerial indulgence and a way to withhold residual cash from the owners of stock. Agency theory was thus a key tool in the hands of the anti-union campaign that the Reagan Administration endorsed. The quick de-industrialization of the U.S. in the 1980s (Bluestone and Harrison, 1982), very much an effect of the high-interest rate policy that overrated the dollar and undermined the competitive position of

American industry, was met with limited interest and concern in Washington as the new class of economic advisors regarded the finance industry as the new motor of the American capitalist economy. In this milieu of neoconservatism, pro-business agendas, and free-market theorizing, agency theory's weak logical consistency and lack of satisfying empirical evidence, were not a problem; instead, agency theory provided an easy-to-tell, easy-to-sell narrative and model for how to rehabilitate the American economy on basis of the new allegedly brainy and hyper-competitive (some would say ruthless) finance industry professionals. If the past was manufacturing, managerial capitalism, and a below-optimal efficiency, from which many rather than a few stakeholders benefitted, the future was to be shaped by finance industry monitoring, competition, and maximal efficiency, proponents of agency theory and related models and accompanying reforms claimed. Three decades later, it is possible to examine the consequences of this campaign.

Notes

1. "[I]t makes little or no sense to try to distinguish those things that are 'inside' of the firm (or any other organization) from those things 'outside' of it. There is in a very real sense only a multitude of complex relationships (i.e., contracts) between the legal fiction (the firm) and the owners of labor, material and capital inputs and consumers of output," Jensen and Meckling (1976: 311) declare in a statement that captures the orthodox neoclassical economic theory view of the firm, understood as a production function that adds little value to what the omnipresent market has already done, besides the minimization of transaction costs as stipulated (not never empirically proven) by the Coase theorem.
2. This statement is particularly complicated to accept by critics of agency theory as the entire governance model proposed is part of the campaign to turn the corporation into a vehicle for shareholder enrichment, thinly veiled as a concern for "efficiency" but an efficiency measured solely on basis of finance-market pricing and thus being, as the numerous bank and finance market crises after 1980 indicate, an autopoetic and self-recursive procedure to price financial assets on basis of expectations.

Part II

Into the Wild

The 1990s and Into the New Millennium

5 Finance Market De-Regulation and the Decline of New Deal Policy

Clinton-Era Free-Market Reforms

Introduction

Free-market ideology was gradually entrenched over the four decades of the 1950s to 1980s, aimed at making the corporate legislation and its idea of the firm as a socially sanctioned team production efforts, involving many stakeholders and relying on fiduciary duties, suspicious of being inefficient and to portray regulatory oversight as being little more than political interests meddling with jurisprudence in ways that harm market efficiency. The critique of antitrust enforcement, the introduction of the market for management control, the advocacy of contract theory, and, finally, the agency theory claim that managers induce excessive agency costs on basis of their sheer incompetence and proclivity to enrich themselves, was a four-stage procedure that landed in the straightforward claim made by agency theorists that shareholders should be given the residual cash because that would be the best way to optimize the use of resources and assets generated by the corporation. Capital owners do not only know better than insiders in the firm, agency theorists stipulate; they are also inclined to transfer the money to high-growth sectors of the economy where they are the most likely to receive a yield. Needless to say, this four-stage entrenchment of the free-market model, ultimately rooted in the idea that "economic freedom" trumps all other societal and political objectives. Furthermore, the orthodox neoclassical economic theory doctrine that mandated that economic equality is not only irrelevant but also corrupting as a measure of economic performance as it misleads, for example, policy-makers to engage in activities that either reduce overall efficiency or pose a threat to the economic freedom of the individual—and most likely do both.

As economic freedom, as opposed to other definition of liberal freedoms, is defined negatively, as the very absence of a sovereign intervening into economic matters, the orthodox neoclassical economic theory doctrine bundling efficiency and economic freedom is tautological: only when the state stays away from markets (i.e., the economic freedom criteria is fulfilled) can efficiency be maximized, which, in turn, is defined on basis of market-pricing activities devoid of state intervention. As have been demonstrated in the four previous chapters, in every domain of free-market advocacy there has been detailed objections to this model articulated by legal scholars, economists, management scholars, and economic sociologists, emphasizing both theoretical inconsistencies in the arguments and models proposed, the ignorance of historical conditions shaping corporate law, a less that satisfying attention to corporate law statutes and actual court ruling cases, and the omission of empirical data and intuitive understandings that speak against the orthodox neoclassical model of governance. Despite this failure to present a theory of how to govern the corporation that a wider set of scholars, policy-makers, and commentators, not of necessity subscribing to free-market orthodoxies and price theory, the shareholder primacy governance model that was the end station of this stepwise elaboration have been remarkably influential; in fact, it would be adequate to speak of it as the single most successful managerial innovation over the last four decades. This is a puzzling phenomenon that business historians and many others may be capable of explaining, but one factor that certainly benefitted the enactment of new corporate governance principles is that the free marketeers were heavily backed by wealthy financiers that had an interest in funding academic, semi-academic, and pseudo-academic work that acted in concert with or was tangential to their interests. In the American political system, money increasingly translates into political clout, and therefore, free-market theory could see their speculative theories regarding the mysterious money-making machine of the free-market translate into policies and law in the 1990s and beyond.

While the 1980s has been portrayed as the "the Deals Decade," the 1990s that followed and brought with it a new Democratic president, symbolically breaking the dominance of neoconservatism that reigned in Washington for 12 years, and an information technology revolution including the Internet, has been referred to as the "decade of deregulation" (Andrade et al., 2001: 104). By 1990, shareholder welfare governance seemed well entrenched and was embraced by industry, not primarily because managers and directors believed in the efficiency-enhancing virtues of shareholder enrichment but because they were increasingly incentivized and economically compensated on basis of their ability to boost stock prices. In addition, to lay off people, slash divisions, and sell of subsidiaries were fashionable, not least supported by the new transformational leadership ideal being in vogue. In addition, "industrial restructuring" (i.e., a euphemism denoting the decline of the manufacturing industry) was widely preached to be a perfectly normal order of things as North American and European economics should now produce more advanced "professional services" and similar, whereas former Eastern bloc countries and burgeoning South-East Asian economies were now entrusted with this "low value-added production." The early 1990s was a period of great expectations, where the future looked bright and the 1970s' economic hardship and bear markets on the global stock markets seemed long since left behind.

The free-market advocacy had enacted the market as the purest and most well-functioning, almost-perfect (or at least as perfect at this world would permit) pricing mechanism. Of the various markets at hand, the finance market, dealing directly with market prices on basis of calculative practices, was given a specific status as "the market to rule them all." For instance, this was Friedrich von Hayek's view of the capital market, Sotiropoulos, Milios and Lapatsioras, 2013: 102. Original emphasis omitted) suggest: "Hayek's perspective renders capital markets central to the organization of capitalism as a system of exploitation. Finance has a crucial role in disciplining economic behaviour according to the inner norms of the system"

In the 1980s and 1990s, the institutional ownership grew steadily; that is, ownership became less dispersed or, perhaps better, dispersed only indirectly through the ownership of shares in, for example, pension funds and mutual funds, and therefore, the shareholder welfare governance model greatly benefitted the finance industry. Profits generated throughout the economic system were piped into the finance sector, which grew remarkably. In addition, as the finance industry was understood and defended as an embodiment of pure and sound economic rationality, embedded in rational choice theory and calculative practices, politicians and policy-makers were instructed by the new generation of economic advisors trained in the orthodox neoclassical free-market doctrine to de-regulate finance markets, again for the benefit of every Tom, Dick or Harry who would be able to harvest the efficiency-gains brought by the elimination of costly and unnecessary regulatory oversight. There was a certain beauty in this fairytale-like story about treasures available at the end of the rainbow, ready to be collected if only policy-makers and others would understand and embrace the wonders of free-market capitalism.

However, despite the de-regulatory frenzy of the Clinton era, the Reagan-era de-industrialization (Bluestone, Harry, and Harrison, 1982) had left the members of the blue-collar worker community jobless and disenfranchised as, for example, trade unions were destroyed, leaving certain parts of the population less enthusiastic about the prospect of continuing on the pathway of de-regulation and free-market policy. The Reagan-era policy provided, for example, popular music artists such as Bruce Springsteen with ample material to exploit when writing songs about towns such as Youngstown, Ohio, or Mahwah, New Jersey, suffering from policy-induced blue-collar job loss. Still, it was not until the first decade of the new millennium that a more comprehensive understanding of where the free-market model had taken the corporate system and competitive capitalism. In the 1990s, at least on American soil, orthodox neoclassical economic theory could safety influence polity and jurisprudence through the extensive network of academic institutions, institutes, financiers, think tanks, lobbyists, and activist groups that worked to further fortify the free-market model.

In this chapter, the de-regulatory reforms that followed from the shareholder welfare governance model are examined; "Why stop here?" free marketeers seemed to have asked themselves, echoing Mae West's famous *bon mot* that "too much of a good thing can be wonderful!" In order to understand how the two major reforms passed at the very end of the decade and century and in the latest hours of the Clinton presidency, The Financial Services Modernization Act of 1999 (FSMA) and Commodity Futures Modernization Act of 2000 (CFMA), the wider scenery of the 1990s economic and political landscape needs to be examined. This chapter thus leaves the more intramural academic discussion in economics, legal theory, and management studies to address institutional conditions.

The Institutional Environment in the Decade of De-Regulation

The 1970s' economic conditions were characterized by high inflation in combination with growing unemployment and economic stagnation, a brew that the dominant Keynesian doctrine could neither explain on basis of its theoretical framework, not practically curb. In fact, it may be adequate to say that the free-market model was successful in taking over the role as the leading economic policy framework because its proponents claimed it could prescribe a remedy for the inflation problem. Milton Friedman's so-called monetarist theory argued that all economic crises were caused by monetary instabilities, an explanation that challenged Keynes's argument that crises were self-perpetuating as economic downturns create a further loss in demand, which, in turn, justifies state intervention such as investment in infrastructure projects to turn the tide. The monetarist theory was never really convincing outside its narrower clergy, but the inflation problem remained. In 1979, President Jimmy Carter named Paul Volcker as the chairman of the Federal Reserve and assigned him the explicit role of bringing down inflation. Volcker was reputedly not convinced about Friedman's monetarist theory, and neither were his closest staff, but they initiated a high-interest policy to push down inflation by making the cost of credit higher and saving more attractive. Unfortunately, Volcker's cure did little to restore the economic vitality and what became known as the "Volcker shock" of 1979 (Levitt, 2013a: 167), which raised interest rates above the 10 percent level, led to an overrated dollar, which undermined the U.S. export industry's competitiveness and made unemployment rates soar to Depression-era levels (Van Arnum and Naples, 2013: 1161). "Today, the recession is forgotten, and Volcker is praised for his inflation fighting," Stein, 2011: 265) writes, "but during 1982, GDP fell 2.2 percent. The Volcker policy generated an the inflow of overseas savings in combination with the decline of American manufacturing industry—an industry that actually increased its productivity by over three percent in 1984 and 1985 but saw those accomplishments being consumed by a politically initiated 63 percent rise in dollar value (Stein, 2011: 269) further accentuated the novel idea that the finance industry was the future of American competitive capitalism.

Once inflation was stabilized at tolerable levels by 1983, low inflation has remained the primary economic policy objective, enforced by a series of institutional reform such as the establishment of autonomous central banks in many advanced economies (Major, 2014: 5; Kogut and Macpherson, 2011; Zelner, Henisz, and Holburn, 2009; Polillo and Guillén, 2005). While many commentators regard the low-inflation economy the crowning achievement of the new economic policy, several commentators, including Madrick (2011), emphasize the draconian effects of always prioritizing low inflation (which, it should be noticed, is in the interests of the finance industry as low inflation makes their operations more transparent and lower risks) at the expense of any other macroeconomic or monetary objective:

> Many economists hailed the resulting low inflation that began in the 1990s as the beginning of a new stable age of ideal growth . . . Much the opposite is more likely. The anti-inflationary policies were adhered to too firmly, and contributed significantly to slower rates of growth, higher levels of unemployment, the disappointing growth rate of productivity until the late 1990s, and stagnant wages. Extreme speculative excesses arose in other areas while Friedman's anti-inflation heirs were in charge—in high-technology stocks in the late 1990s and mortgage finance in the 2000s, to take the starkest examples. Freidman's assurance that financial deregulation would work turned out to be an empty promise, with disastrous consequences. Since the early 1980s, the financial markets have been far more unstable than in the 1950s and 1960s.
> (Madrick, 2011: 49)

For instance, to substantiate and illustrate Madrick's (2011) claim regarding "slower rates of growth," Stein (2011: 282) reports that at the beginning of 1994, when inflation had fallen from 3 to 2.6 percent in the previous year, the Fed "[r]aised interest rates because it believed that an unemployment rate below 6.2 percent would set off inflation." Needless to say, the 6.2 level of unemployment would have been treated as major failure and arguably an indication of "limited dynamics" in the regime of managerial capitalism and Keynesian economic policy, but after the sea change of the 1980s, this level unemployment was simply business as usual, also under a Democratic administration. The primary benefactor of this policy was, of course, the finance industry, a fact that became even more salient over time and with the benefit of hindsight. As Milberg (2008) notices, making the fundamental economic measure of "money supply"—a statistical measure of the size of stock of capital in an economy—to weight the growth of the finance industry between mid-1990s and mid-2006. In this period, the U.S. inflation rate was stabilized at around 2 percent, consistent with the underlying theory and the policy it generated, but the money supply rose by a factor of more than 7 percent per annum (Milberg, 2008: 428). If inflation was initially curbed by high interest rates but also undermined the competitiveness of American export industry, the low inflation policy that followed benefitted the "weightless economy" of finance unproportionately at the expense of all other sectors.

The Clinton Presidency

When William Jefferson "Bill" Clinton was elected president in 1992 and installed in January 1993, it represented a return of a Democratic head of state in the White House and, importantly, a Democratic president who did not inherit as dour economic conditions as Jimmy Carter did in 1977. The charming and relatively young President Clinton to some extent reminded many elderly Democratic voters of John F. Kennedy, a president that Clinton shared more with than both Kennedy's running mate Lyndon B. Johnson and the competent peanut farmer (a business inherited from his father after his untimely death) and "Dixiecrat" Jimmy Carter. In addition, Clinton was also understood to end the Reagan-era conservatism, which was smeared by some scandals and crises such as the allegations of weapon smuggling to Iran and finance industry crises and instabilities (i.e., the "Black Monday" on October 19, 1987, and the savings-and-loans industry crisis in 1984) but otherwise essentially delivered what neoconservative and libertarian voters have hoped for above all—lower taxes for not least higher higher-income groups. But if there were any hope that Clinton would take an entirely different route, such expectations never materialized. Richard Nixon had declared in the early 1970s, at the height of hegemonic Keynesianism, that "We're all Keynesians now!" and Clinton perhaps never declared that "We're all free marketeers now!" but it would have been a fine historical parable if that would have been the case. Maney (2016) emphasizes that the 1990s were the salad days of free-market capitalism:

> The economy was growing at an annual rate of 4 percent; unemployment, including unemployment among minority groups, was the lowest in a generation; and wages were increasingly (though not at the same rate) for all income groups. Yet—and this was the puzzle—inflation and interest rates were lower and more stable than one would have expected in a well-stoked economy.
>
> (Maney, 2016: 211)

This upsurge in economic activity in combination with the "economic fundamentals" being under control led to an almost unprecedented optimism among Clinton's economic advisors. In the final report issued by the Council of Economic Advisors, published in December 29, 2000, the idea of a "new economy," characterized by endless growth and stability was introduced as a serious contestant for a new economic conditions: "Over the last 8 years . . . the American economy has transformed itself so radically that many believe we have witnessed the creation of a New Economy" (Council of Economic Advisors Report, cited in Maney, 2016: 210).

The 1990s was above all the decade of deregulation, but the economic growth was essentially propelled by the global implementation of information technology. Total Factor Productivity (TPF) growth stayed at the level of

0.58 in the 1972–1995 period and thereafter jumped to 1.43 in the in 1996–2004 to again slow down to 0.54 in 2005–2008 (Gordon, 2015: 55). Gordon (2015) proposes that this upsurge in TFP, beginning in the mid-1990s, can be explained by what economic historians refer to as a "delayed effect" from computer science and computer industry investment made in the 1970s and 1980s: "Productivity analysts have credited the dot.com revolution, which married the computer with communications and developed e-commerce and search engines, for the productivity growth revival of 1996–2004" (Gordon, 2015: 55). Such statements can be substantiated by labour market statistics, testifying to the growth of employment in the telecommunications industry: Between 1992 and 2001, this industry generated "two-thirds of all new jobs and one-third of new investments" (Maney, 2016: 211). "The Internet had been under development for decades, but it was during the nineties that it came into its own—in much the same way radio in the thirties and television in the fifties came into their own," Maney (2016: 211) argues; as numerous commentators have pointed out, the 1990s were great years for Anglo-American competitive capitalism, and the Clinton administration anticipated economic growth and stability for a foreseeable future.

Despite the optimism, the neoconservative and libertarian mobilization initiated in the early 1970s had put its mark on policy-making, restricting political initiatives: "Government interventions that would have been taken for granted in the Nixon Administration became far too radical for the Clinton and Obama Administrations to even consider," Mizruchi (2010: 127) notes. Once the free-market genie was out of the bottle—a metaphor for the institutional build-up of free-market thinking and activism in the 1970s, the 1980s, and beyond—it is not so easy to push it back in. "Many figures on the Clinton administration were as receptive as their Republican predecessors to request for limited intervention," Hacker and Pierson (2010a: 195) remark. This bipartisan embrace of free-market ideology is not the least mirrored in the frantic reform work of the 1990s' Congress. "[T]he neoliberal political decisions that promoted financialization in the Reagan era, coupled with added financial deregulation during Clinton's tenure," Jacobs and Myers (2014: 767) say, paved the way for an unprecedented expansion of the finance industry in the 1990s and in the new millennium. Congress records speak for themselves: In the period between 1979 and 1992, "just over 600 laws were passed per session," in the seven sessions of Congress, whereof "34 pertained specifically to finance." During the Clinton years (1993–2000), the number of new laws fell to 293, whereof "on average 94 finance laws were passed," increasing from around 5% to 25% of all legislation (Martin, 2002: 28). This shift in legislative practice either coincided with or was a direct consequence of Wall Street funding the Clinton campaigns and supplying co-workers to the administration: "The Clinton administration had been rife with Wall Street tycoons," Mayer (2016: 323) notices.

Unlike in the 1950–1990 period, free-market advocacy was no longer a matter of academic theorizing and legal reasoning but had moved to the heart of American politics, the Congress of the Republic. Of all the reforms and legislations of the Clinton era, two acts being passed at the very end of the decade deserve special attention as they represent the ultimate triumph of the free-market ideology as a major New Deal legislation was repealed. In the following, the Financial Services Modernization Act of 1999 and the Commodity Futures Modernization Act of 2000 are examined.

Market Deregulation Policy

As various and heterogeneous actors are involved in policy-making, policy is rarely if ever based on the blueprint of clear-cut theories and accompanying empirical evidence but is, to the contrary, a quite covert process of "muddling through" (as political scientists Charles Lindblom, 1959, puts it), including bargaining and numerous considerations within different time horizons, including unanticipated consequences and the risk of enabling loopholes. While academic theorizing may appear sleek and parsimonious—at least when the work is finally put into print—policy-making is messy and include power games and wider socio-cultural elements, not of necessity related to the political matter at hand. In this fog of war of policy-making, think tanks and lobbyists play an increasingly central role in turning know-how and information into easy-to-communicate-and-sell packages that reduce time and effort on part of the policy-makers (e.g., senators and congressmen and -women). In many cases, the mangling of policy leads to diluted version of original ideas, being finally enshrined by law and regulations, at times to the of consternation of certain groups and activists, and indicating the validity of the expression "This what was politically possible to accomplish for the time being."

Policy-making in finance market matters is no different besides the sheer amount of money being involved in the lobbying in support of certain ideas as the economic consequences of, for example, de-regulation are considerable. Flaherty (2015: 434), for instance, makes a connection between finance industry reform and the growth of the share of total aggregated income that top income groups have managed to secure for themselves: "Banking sector liberalization, banking sector supervision and financial reform are all associated with growth in top income shares." By implication, Flaherty (2015: 435) proposes, finance industry reform and the wealth concentration it has engendered historically "must be interpreted in terms of relative class-based and institutional power resources." That is, to put it to the point, as finance industry reform tends to benefit certain groups at the apex of the finance industry, the reform work that precedes a more liberal legislation cannot be assumed to operate in isolation from the resources that the social class benefitting from the reform can mobilize. However, no democratic and transparent political system tolerate a straightforward and linear connection between, for example, financial donations and laws being enacted, but "in real life" resources are informing the policy-making work in indirect and at times oblique ways:

> [B]argaining asymmetry is driven by a variety of factors beyond fiscal policy alone, such as regulatory control, class-based power resources, financial globalization and institutional weakening. Whilst the weight of financial sector profit and productivity has continued its upward climb relative to other economic sectors, in many countries—including social democracies such as Denmark for example—it continues to outstrip the real economy in terms of its contribution to productivity and growth.
> (Flaherty, 2015: 435–436)

In the case of the U.S., generous donations from wealthy capital owners and industrialists to support, for example, de-regulatory advocacy and practical policy-making work, led to strong conservative advantages in terms of political influence: "By the mid-1990s, there were two conservative think tanks for every liberal one." Wisman (2013: 938) says. In the case of the FSMA and the CFMA, it is no secret that the finance industry, but also other industries (such as energy companies, including the by-then heroic business phenomenon Enron), poured significant amounts of money into the Washington political apparatus to have their favoured policies enacted. For some commentators, this role of money in polity and, by implication, jurisprudence is a legitimate way to let citizens freely support the policy work that benefit their interest, while for other commentators, mostly on the centre-left flank, this permissive view of donations is little more than what has been called "vending-machine politics" (Froud, Johal, Papazian, and Williams, 2004: 905)—a form of clientelism (Hicken, 2011; Lemarchand, Rene, and Legg, 1972) or "crony capitalism" (Rosas, 2006), wherein wealthy donors can have policy tailored to suit their own interest with little regard to wider social concerns. If one are includes to be sceptical about how "class-based and institutional power resources" inform policy-making, and leads to "bargaining asymmetry" (Flaherty, 2015: 435), the de-regulation of the finance industry in the late 1990s and in 2000 is exemplary of how "big money" cannot be neglected in policy-making.

THE FINANCE INDUSTRY REFORMS

The Financial Services Modernization Act of 1999

During the Great Depression, more than 1,000 banks failed (Funk and Hirschman, 2014: 677), and the fragility of the financial system was widely regarded as one of the contributing factors to the system-wide decline of the American economy. The New Deal program thus aimed to restore a functional capitalist economic system and to rehabilitate the confidence in such a system. The Glass–Steagall Act of 1933 and the Securities Act of 1934 that created the Securities and Exchange Commission, the finance industry's regulating body, were political responses to the failure of the finance industry to regulate itself (Hilt, 2014: 8–16). The Glass–Steagall Act established firewalls between commercial banks, insurance companies, and investment banks and served to promote what would be known as "managerial capitalism" (Rock, 2013: 1912). The statutes of Glass–Steagall Act would last into the end of the decade, but there were changes in the finance industry regulation enacted by Congress in 1956, 1967, 1977, 1989, 1994, and 1999 (Grant, 2010: 380. Table 1), indicating that political bodies were eager to amend legislation as economic and institutional conditions changed. Not least were the Clinton administration's economic advisors more than willing to further deregulate what seemed to be sound and supposedly self-regulating financial markets, Maney (2016: 220) proposes: "Believing a new economy was in the offering, [Clinton's economic advisors] were looking for even more ways to release, in a controlled way, the creative energies of the private sector. Deregulation of telecommunication was done. Banking was next."

In the 1990s, finance industry representatives targeted the Glass–Steagall Act as a particular piece of legislation to repeal: "The American Bankers Association played a significant role-and had a significant interest-in the passage of the Gramm-Leach-Bliley Act" (Grant, 2010: 384).[1] The finance industry investing heavily in lobbying and think-tank activities to overturn the Glass–Steagall Act, the official objective of the reform was to work in the interest of the American people. "Gramm-Leach-Bliley was intended to create one-stop-shopping for financial consumers. It was to be what Costco and Wal-Mart are to retail shoppers," Grant (2010: 384–385) remarks. Here, it should be noticed that this concern for consumer welfare was also invoked in the antitrust enforcement critique of the 1950s' law and economics scholarship, testifying to the continuity of the free-market argument, where clumsy or self-serving governments were claimed to undermine the welfare Americans. The fact that business tycoons and others were more than willing to finance such scholarships and campaigns unfortunately indicates that more than heartwarming philanthropy was at stake. As Thomas Frank (2012) notices, this populist credo rhymed poorly with the gains that major campaign sponsors such as the then-on-the-rise Texas energy company Enron foresaw and quickly capitalized on as soon as the FSMA was passed. "Remember," (Frank, 2012: 108) says, referring to Phil Gramm (R-TX), the senator benefitting the most from generous campaign donations from the finance industry, "Phil Gramm did it all for the little guy." As accounted for by Grant (2010), some Democratic senators questioned the idea that FSMA would be in the interest of the American voters. For instance, Senator Barbara Mikulski (D-MD) was sceptical regarding the substance of this argument:

> We have already seen the trend toward mega-mergers, accompanied by higher fees, a decline in service, and the loss of neighbourrhood financial institutions. This bill accelerates that trend. With a globalization of

> financial resources, the local bank could be bought by a holding company based in Thailand. Instead of the friendly teller, consumers will be contacting a computer operator in a country half-way around the globe through an 800 number. Their account will be subject to financial risks that have nothing to do with their job, their community, or even the economy of the United States. I know impersonalized globalization is not what banking customers want when we talk about modernization of the financial services.
>
> (Senator Barbara Mikulski, D-MD, during a Senate debate preceding the enactment, cited in Grant, 2010: 393)

The liberal Senator Paul Wellstone (D-MI) addressed another concern, the concentration of economic power, and warned that deregulation of the finance industry would "aggregate a trend toward economic concentration that endangers not only our economy, but also our democracy" (cited in Maney, 2016: 223). The congressman Ed Markey (D-MA) perceived deregulation a threat to privacy that overshadowed the alleged consumer benefit the new legislation would engender: "If commercial banks, investment banks, and insurance companies could combine their activities, they could also combine all the personal information they each had on customers, including medical records, financial status, and purchasing preferences" (cited in Maney, 2016: 223–224). This was an argument that struck a chord in conservative quarters, wary of personal integrity and privacy as constitutional rights. Another objection was raised by Senator Russell Feingold (D-WI), who remarked that the sheer volume of the political contributions from actors with vested interests indicates something more than a concern for the well-being of the consumers:

> And this lobbying campaign has left a trail of political contributions that is nothing short of stunning. A recent study by Common Cause put the political contributions of these special interests at $187.2 million in the last ten years.
>
> (Senator Russell Feingold, D-WI, during a Senate debate preceding the enactment, cited in Grant, 2010: 393)

Grant (2010: 411) argues that financial crises are frequently caused by credit oversupply in the economy, leading to speculation and ultimately to "bursts" that are more harmful for wider economy than for the finance industry that quickly recovers. Despite the concern regarding the fragility of a high-leveraged finance industry and the increased moral hazard risk, the proponents of the FSMA advocated a repeal of the Glass–Steagall Act:

> Supporters of Gramm-Leach-Bliley recognized that too-big-to-fail firms posed a risk of taxpayer bailouts. Their concerns were soothed by a

> belief that market discipline, combined with innovative ways to reduce risk-namely derivatives like credit default swaps would mitigate the danger. We now know that discipline failed and the innovations actually amplified risk greatly.
>
> (Editorial, *Questions for Reform*, New York Times, March 29, 2009, cited in Grant, 2010: 411)[2]

The idea that derivatives would serve a stabilizing role was not substantiated by reliable evidence as historical time series of derivatives prices over the economic cycle are needed to better understand how derivative are affected by the ups and downs in the economy. Derivatives did not serve a stabilizing function but, to the contrary, further amplified the leverage in the finance industry and contaminated the global finance system. Anyway, when the FSMA was finally passed in the House and the Senate—the FSMA was passed 362 to 57 in the House and 90 to 8 in the Senate, revealing an overwhelming support for the bill (Maney, 2016: 225)—the Glass–Steagall firewalls that served to "separate banking, securities, and insurance activities in the financial services industry" (Grant, 2010: 413) were torn down. The finance industry was for the first time since the depression era given a *carte blanche* to expand its activities into new domains, with a significant concentration of power and a conglomeration of large finance institutes—a tendency that other industries did not demonstrate, as they were now monitored by the finance market:

> Large banks have strayed from their core business mission of banking by extending their tentacles into increasingly complex lines of business, in an effort to become true 'one-stop shops' for customers. The repeal of Glass-Steagall and passage of Gramm-Leach-Bliley in 1999 made possible the conglomeration and expansion of a handful of banks.
>
> (Grant, 2010: 419)

As being an eminent case of "over the counter policy," where wealthy donors can have their interests translated into legislation through financial donations and lobbying, the repeal of the Glass–Steagall Act not only marked an ending of the New Deal regime but also opened the full-scale financialization of the U.S. economy (and by implication, the global economy) that would lead up to the finance market collapse of 2008. The so-called Troubled Asset Relief Program (Blinder, 2013; Barofsky, 2012), initiated and managed by a former Goldman-Sachs executive, the Bush administration's secretary of Treasure Hank Paulson (Blinder, 2013), was ironic and sided poorly with the free-market protagonist's adage "Rational markets can take care of themselves" (as Alan Greenspan put it, cited in Palma, 2009: 831). As Grant (2010: 393) notices, "lessons from America's past show that it is unwise to let banks get too big in the first place; instead, American law should reform to limit the scope and reach of banks." Unfortunately, the FSMA/Gramm–Leach–Bliley Act of 1999 was passed on basis of the belief in the virtues of unregulated financial markets, demonstrating superior efficiency on basis of market pricing and alleged extraordinary intelligence and acumen of finance actors. Rather being conducive to increased efficiency, the FSMA/Gramm–Leach–Bliley Act opened up for various types of opportunistic behavior: "[T]he Gramm-Leach-Bliley Act created incentives and opportunities for managers to inflate parent companies' balance sheets," Prechel and Morris (2010: 338) summarize. The efficacy of the new legislation was thus compromised by the loopholes it failed to anticipate.

One of the most remarkable things with this late Clinton-era de-regulation project was how this fundamental shift in policy and regulatory control of the finance industry, representing a historical break with New Deal policy, basically took place in the fringes of the otherwise detailed and animated American political and economic journalism and debates, Maney (2016) argues:

> Perhaps the most striking thing about the bank reform was the disproportionality between its importance and the public attention it received. It had been under almost constant consideration for nearly two decades. Along with health-care and telecommunications reform, it was the most heavily lobbied issue on Capitol Hill and showering members of the commission with millions of dollars in campaign contributions. In contrast to the deliberations that led to Glass-Steagall, the debate that led to its repeal was largely confined to the back pages or business sections of most newspapers. Neither a passage of Gramm-Bliley-Leach nor the president's signing statement got more than twenty seconds on the evening newscasts. Not surprisingly, a poll conducted shortly after the bill became law disclosed that most Americans had never heard about it. President Clinton was himself partly responsible for the news blackout. At no time did he try to explain in everyday language the workings of the modern banking system and what reform would mean to the average person.
>
> (Maney, 2016: 225)

Maney's (2016) remarks are supported by new evidence made public in 2014, According to formerly previously restricted papers, including 7,000 document pages, released by the Clinton library on Friday, April 18, 2014, and examined in *The Guardian* on April 19, 2014, it was Clinton's economic advisers who pushed for a quick political decision and repeal of the centrepiece of the New Deal legislation. Already in 1995 and 1997, there were two attempts to "hurry Clinton into supporting a repeal of the Depression-era Glass Steagall Act," The *Guardian* journalist Dan Robert reports. Senior adviser John Podesta, who later worked for the Obama administration, gave Clinton only three days in 1995 to decide whether to back a repeal of Glass-Steagall. As this attempt failed, a similar event occurred in 1997 when Treasury secretary Robert Rubin's close ally Gene Sperling, director of Clinton's National Economic Council and serving the same role for the Obama administration, again gave no more than three days to make a decision. In a letter to the president, received on May 19, 1997, Sperling stated that "Secretary Rubin intends to introduce the proposal in a 21 May speech," if the draft would have been approved by the president. In an accompanying letter, the Treasury secretary assured that the reform would not demand much attention from the president: "Should you approve our recommendation to move forward, the proposal would be a Treasury initiative, and would not require a significant time commitment from the White House"; "I and my staff will manage the process of advancing the proposal," Rubin added. Taken together, the 7,000 pages of documents reveal "little discussion of internal opposition to repealing Glass-Steagall." Clinton's advisors instead "repeatedly reassured him that the decision to let Wall Street dismantle regulatory barriers designed to protect the public after the Great Depression simply represented inevitable modernization," Dan Robert (2014) summarizes.

Given this relatively lukewarm interest in enlightening the American voters regarding the new rules of the game, it is perhaps little wonder that Alan Blinder, one of Clinton's economic advisors, argued in 2013 that the finance industry meltdown of 2008 was like a bolt out of the blue for many Americans: "*The American people still don't quite know what hit them*, and why it happened, or what the authorities did about it—especially why government officials took so many and unusual and controversial actions," Blinder (2013: xvi. Emphasis in the original) says. Policies enacted behind closed doors and accompanied by limited ambition to communicate the implications to the voters are unsurprisingly leading to what a cynic may call ignorance on part of the voters, and what others may choose to refer to in more euphemistic terms, such as policies suffering from "democratic deficits." No matter what labels being used *ex post facto*, much of the FSMA and its implication were possibly never fully understood by the median American voter.

Commodity Futures Modernization Act of 2000

The underlying rationale or the two major reforms at the end of the millennium was that finance theory, developed by economists on basis of neoclassical economic theory since the late 1950s, presented models that portrayed finance traders as being both rational actors responding to risks and uncertainty (carefully separated by Frank Knight in the 1920s) and being disciplined by the market pricing mechanism that imposed a penalty excessive risk taking. For instance, the Capital Asset Pricing Model (CAPM), a backbone finance theory model, "assumes that every investor rationally balances risk against reward" (Topham, 2010: 133). After the FSMA repealed the Glass–Steagall Act of 1933, Topham (2010: 133) suggests, "[e]conomic theory, legislation, and financial industry lobbying efforts consistently pushed towards financial deregulation," and eventually complementing FSMA with the CFMA in 2000. Topham (2010) says that "the mood" of the 1990s were very favourable to free-market reforms. The economy grew, not the least on basis of the information technology and digital media industry emerging from California's Silicon Valley, inflation had been under control for a considerable time, and de-regulation and free-market thinking had by now become widely established as the new pathway to prosperity:

> From an economic standpoint, the millennial mood was one in which all the market mysteries had been solved and monetary policy would prevail indefinitely. Efficient markets thrived, economic actors were consistently rational, and asset prices (such as real estate) reflected all available information in the marketplace.
>
> (Topham, 2010: 141)

CFMA de-regulated the issuance of derivatives, and the Federal Reserve board chairman Alan Greenspan had for a long period endorsed the use of derivatives as a class of financial assets that further enhanced the efficiency of finance markets and that served the auxiliary beneficial function to stabilize and self-regulate the finance industry. In short, derivatives were nothing short of a magic potion that could vivify the strong and heal the sick. In addition, in Greenspan's view, greater concentration in the finance industry was not a concern as the market—always first and last the market—would discipline actors that deviated from the market pricing and risk/reward trade-offs (Topham, 2010: 142). "People are smart, especially in finance, the mantra goes; the best way to police financial markets is to let them police themselves," Akerlof and Shiller (2015: 8) summarize the end-of-the-millennium attitude among proponents of finance market de-regulation and policy makers more widely.

As Topham (2010: 136) remarks, "derivatives have existed for thousands of years and do play a useful role in hedging risk, particularly interest rate fluctuations." Swaps, hedges, and securities are some examples of derivative instruments that share risk and thus provide certain benefits for finance market actors and their clients. And yet some derivatives are very complex to trade as they are complicated to price over the economic cycle and therefore become illiquid (as discussed in the next chapter). The finance industry again demonstrated a great deal of interest in the CFMA as they spent "[o] ver $5 billion from 1998–2000 to lobby for an overhaul of Glass-Steagall in the Gramm-Leach-Bliley Act and enact the more obscure CFMA" (Topham, 2010: 142). While the FSMA was arguably the main dish, the CFMA was perhaps better understood as the dessert, targeting the use of certain "hybrid instruments," such as "securit[ies] having one or more payments indexed to the value, level, or rate of, or providing for the delivery of, one or more commodities" (Topham, 2010: 145). The CFMA aimed to extend regulatory exclusions for such instruments, that is, to further reduce the regulating agency's jurisdiction in terms of monitoring the derivatives trade. As with the FSMA, the CFMA caused several commentators to address the moral hazards and "too big to fail" issues that they believed the new legislation would engender: "[T]hat which is true in the 1930's is true in 2010 . . . [W]e have now decided in the name of modernization to forget the lessons of the past, of safety and of soundness," the *New York Times* columnist Stephen Labaton argued (*Congress Passes Wide Ranging Bill Easing Bank Laws, New York Times*, Novmber 5, 1999, cited in Topham, 2010: 140).

Under all conditions, as a case of policy-making and legislative practice, the passing of CFMA is a very interesting and arguably odd case. The bill had been circulating on Capitol Hill for the better part of a year when it was pass in the House (Maney, 2016: 235), but when it went to the Senate, Senator Phil Gramm (R-TX) (more details about Gramm and his career shortly) wanted assurances that the trade of Collateralized Debt Obligations (CDOs), a class of derivatives currently being subject to regulatory control, should be beyond the reach any regulatory agency, including the SEC, the primary New Deal institution overseeing the finance industry; "After two months of negotiations between Gramm and [Larry] Sumners [Clinton's secretary of Treasury], Gramm got most of what he wanted," Maney (2016: 235) writes. In addition, just like in the case of the FSMA, news media was by and large not interested in covering the policy-making process or even debating the implications from the new legislation in the making: "At the time, the CFMA attended little public attention. Aside from a few trade publications and industry newsletters, no mainstream newspaper assigned a reporter to the measure. Not the *New York Times* or the *Washington Post* or even *Wall Street Journal*" (Maney, 2016: 235). In hindsight, this modest concern regarding derivatives trade and its regulatory control emerge as one of the genuine enigmas of the Clinton era, regardless of the turmoil and "newsworthiness" of the impeachment of the president that followed the sordid Monica Lewinsky affair, an event that cast a long shadow over Clinton's final days in office.

The FSMA undermined the regulatory framework that was institutionalized in the Great Depression era, and the CFMA further paved the way for the use of increasingly exotic financial assets on broad front. The primary benefactor of this liberal legislation was a relatively small group of Wall Street conglomerates, data from close to ten years after the passing of the CFMA indicate:

> [A]ccording to third quarter 2009 figures compiled by the Office of the Comptroller of the Currency, just five U.S. banks hold 97% of all U.S. bank derivatives positions in terms of notional values, and 88% of the total net credit risk exposure in event of default. The total notional values of the derivatives held by these commercial banks topped $204 trillion, dispersed among JPMorgan Chase ($78 trillion); Goldman

> Sachs ($42 trillion); Bank of America ($40 trillion); Citibank ($32 trillion) and Wells Fargo ($4.5 trillion).
>
> (Topham, 2010: 148)

Needless to say, such reforms played a key role in the events of 2008's finance industry systematic meltdown, but regardless of this system-wide collapse, CFMA paved the way for opportunistic behavior: "The 2000 Commodity Futures Modernization Act created opportunities for management to transfer much of the risk to unsuspecting investors by using complex financial instruments in unregulated equity markets," Prechel and Morris (2010: 350) argue. Also the massive and growing literature that sorts out the events of 2008 address the CFMA as a centrepiece of the new brave world of unregulated finance markets. Alan Blinder, for instance, a leading American economist at Princeton, emphasizes Clinton's Secretary sf Treasury, the Harvard economist Larry Summers, culpability in the passing of the CFMA. Blinder does not shy away from using quite harsh terms:

> As the Secretary of Treasury in 2000, Larry Summers championed the passage in the Commodity Futures Modernization Act, an outrageous piece of legislation that actually *banned* the regulation of derivatives. The CFMA effectively declared that this particular zoo should have no zookeepers at all. Market discipline—that old oxymoron—was supposed to take care of everything.
>
> (Blinder, 2013: 279)

However, the Clinton presidency ended as what could be described as the "free marketeer's delight," the finance market traders' license to act precisely as they wished. And that was precisely what these finance industry conglomerates did, both given an orthodox neoclassical theoretical sanction to do so as long as they operated on de-regulated markets, fortified by the full and unconditional political support from political institutions. In some cases, the truth was stranger than fiction as in the case of Goldman Sachs benefitting greatly from the Greek economic crisis by undermining its own client's interests:

> Goldman Sachs and other Wall Street banks quietly assisted Greece in masking billions in debt with interest rate derivatives in 2001, and in 2009 immediately prior to Greece's default. Simultaneously, a Goldman Sachs subsidiary exchange in London facilitated heavy trading in CDS's on Greek debt, signaling a rise in the cost of these insurance contracts, which made it harder for Greece to sell bonds and in turn affected their ability to borrow. In essence, Goldman Sachs profited from the original derivative package, and then profited from CDS contracts on a debt catastrophe they engineered.
>
> (Topham, 2010: 149; see also Augustin, Subrahmanyam, Tang, and Wang, 2016)

On the other hand, concepts such as "greed" is excluded from the rational choice theory and dismissed (as Ronald Coase called it) as a case of "aesthetics and morals." In the cold-hearted (or, perhaps better, "no-hearted") world of the utility-optimal seeking *homo oeconomicus*, there is no room for such unnecessary complications; in the world of Ronald Coase, Aaron Director, Milton Friedman, Alan Greenspan, *et consortes*, morality is a curiosity or at best a residual explanation in heterodox economic theory or in suspicious social science frameworks. Only the market, the original arbiter, determines the nature of human relations, and it does so strictly in terms of efficiency and pecuniary values and rewards.

Regardless of this worldview, appealing only to an inner circle of free-market Savonarolas and neither credible nor desirable for few others, the consequences of the CFMA did not exactly helped to sell the free-market argument more easily: "Barings Bank, Enron and countless other financial and nonfinancial firms have failed under the weight of derivatives on their books," Topham (2010: 136) can remark with the benefit of hindsight. Regardless of these failures, extending into the global collapse in 2008, Topham (2010: 158) sees little political ambition to amend the present situation: "Political posturing and vast amounts of lobbying dollars continue to abate any real transformation of derivative markets, while banker bonuses reach record levels and the U.S. economy remains on questionable footing." Clinton enters the pantheon of history as a Democratic president who greatly benefitted Wall Street and served its interests.

A Question Concerning Bargaining Asymmetry: The Passing of FSMA and CFMA

That the wind of pro-business policy of the Reagan era continued to inform policy-making into the end of the 1990s indicates that the free-market argument had strong bipartisan appeal in Washington and elsewhere. The story of how free markets offered many benefits and would do the job for free for politicians and that would release resources committed to regulatory control is in many ways a beautiful story of the benefits of human collaboration and mutual trust. The crux is, as, for example, Mirowski (2013) has emphasized, that if markets are a "naturally occurring" phenomenon being greatly beneficial for mankind at large—the claim to promote consumer interest is frequently at the heart of the free-market argument—why is it that there is such a massive involvement of financial donations and campaign contributions when reinforcing free-market policies? The paranoid and broad-sweeping claim that "socialist" or "collectivist" ideologies are lurking (see, e.g., Bork, 1978) in political and regulatory entities does not really hold water as the benefits of competitive capitalism and the well-being it generates should be evident by now to even left-wing communities. The sceptics' concern is that the free-market advocacy may be suspicious of not only advocating efficiency-enhancing reforms but may use such arguments to advocate specific industry interests. Not the least the presence of a dense network of lobbyists, think tankers, and academic researchers funded by neoconservative and libertarian pro-business sponsors, among others, underlines that markets are emerging and forming on basis of the work of market-makers and that these market-makers seem, in turn, to be incentivized by pecuniary interests and not more noble sentiments.

The role of Texas Senator Phil Gramm, playing a central role in the passing of the FSMA and the CFMA, is an illustrative case of the problem of "bargaining asymmetry." Senator Gramm was dedicated to the free-market cause and early on developed close ties with Wall Street benefactors. "From 1989 to 2002, [Gramm] was the top recipient of campaign contributions from commercial banks and in the top five for donations from Wall Street," Perrow (2010: 318) reports. When Gramm left the Senate, he was even able to donate $1 million from his funds to encourage other senators to "pursue his agenda," Perrow (2010: 318) adds. In the work that preceded the passing of the two acts of 1999 and 2000, Gramm received generous grants from Wall Street and from the by then highly successful energy company Enron, a firm, which business guru writer Gary Hamel (2000: 211) described as a company that "revolutionized international power plant development," by using innovative finance market operations and thus having a "spectacular success."[3] Enron money was omnipresent in both Washington and in Texas, more specifically, so Gramm was not alone in accepting campaign contributions. Furthermore, Gramm's connections to Enron did not end with the transfer of money. His wife, Wendy Gramm, referred to as the "Margaret Thatcher of financial regulation" by *Wall Street Journal* (12 November 1999, cited in Froud et al., 2004: 907), was a long-term associate of Enron: before the inauguration of Bill Clinton in 1993, Wendy Gramm "was appointed to the Enron Board and audit committee from which she received between US$ 915,000 and 1.85 million in salary, attendance fees, stock option sales and dividends from 1993 to 2001" (Froud et al., 2004: 907). It would thus be fair to say that the Gramms had close bonds with Enron and that they benefitted greatly from the money that Enron earned on basis of questionable business practices, whereof some were piped into Phil Gramm's campaign funds.

In the aftermath of the events of 2008, *Time* magazine compiled a list of the "25 People to Blame for the Financial Crisis" and unsurprisingly Phil Gramm, "the chief architect of the Financial Services Modernization Act," was included on the list (Grant, 2010: 410). In Professor James Cox's account, a renowned securities and derivatives scholar at Duke University School of Law, "Phil Gramm was the great spokesman and leader of the view that market forces should drive the economy without regulation . . . The movement he helped to lead contributed mightily to our problems" (cited in Grant, 2010: 410). Gramm himself admits no faults on his parts, maintaining the idea that he cherished while in office and that bestowed great financial resources upon him, that "regulatory oversight of the financial services industry is not the answer" (Grant, 2010: 411), is still correct. For Gramm, as for many other free-market campaigners, the efficacy of free markets is not a testable hypothesis but is leveraged to the status of theorem—it is an axiomatic principle not amenable for empirical testing. Consequently, it is not possible to admit, for example, "degrees of market efficiency" in market pricing without seriously putting the entire analytical framework at risk, and that is, the philosophy of science literature suggests, neither possible on basis of epistemological principles, nor behavioural theories.

Regardless of the role of Gramm and his soft money in the passing of the act of 1999 and 2000, the concern regarding bargaining asymmetry remains a major issue in American policy-making. In what political scientists Jacob S. Hacker and Paul Pierson (2010a, b) call "winner-takes-all-politics," the massive inflow of finance capital to fund free-market advocacy in Washington and at university departments endorsing the free-market model leads to a "democratic deficit" as wealthy financiers and business tycoons (e.g., the Koch brothers of Koch Industries, with headquarters in Wichita, Kansas; see Mayer, 2016) can orchestrate a vending-machine politics apparatus where pay-for-policy arrangements are normalized. Against this background, it is beyond irony that the former vice president of Lehman Brothers, Lawrence G. McDonald, writes in his autobiographical account that he now, in hindsight, wished that "President Clinton had never signed the bill repealing Glass-Steagall," adding that he personally "never thought he much wanted to sign it." "In less than a decade," McDonald continues, "this act would be directly responsible for bringing the entire world to the brink of financial ruin" (McDonald and Robinson, 2009: 7).[4]

The long-term consequences of this influence of orthodox neoclassical economic theory in polity and in jurisprudence are arguably considerable and potentially undermine the long-term viability of the regime of competitive capitalism and its corporate system. The case of Phil Gramm and his sponsors is thus an illustrative case of how "winner-takes-all-politics" is no longer a dystopian scenario in the mind of the paranoid defender of liberal democracy but an actual reality with substantial and tangible consequences.

Leaving the Century: The "Decade of Deregulation" in Hindsight

The passing of the FSMA and the CFMA triggered a line of research among economists to assess the efficacy of the new legislation in terms of stock market responses, a sort of self-referential operationalization of the term "efficiency" to assess "legislative quality" wherein the market is always already defined as the superior arbitrator, a form of Archimedean point, which operationalize raising stock prices as the *prima facie* evidence of a qualified piece of legislation being passed. Akhigbe and Whyte (2004) examine how the FSMA affected the level of total and unsystematic risk in banks and insurance companies (traditionally relatively stable business in terms of risk exposure) and in securities companies (traditionally less stable on basis of their high leverage and risk exposure). Akhigbe and Whyte (2004: 445) found evidence that the FSMA led to "a significant increase in total and unsystematic risks for banks and insurance companies." In contrast, securities firms experience "a significant decline in both total and unsystematic risks" (Akhigbe and Whyte, 2004: 445–446). The FSMA thus served to transfer risks and to distribute them over a larger number of finance market actors. As the securities business is "generally riskier" than the bank and insurance businesses, this effect do not violate intuitive thinking. At the same time, Akhigbe and Whyte (2004: 446) warn, "bank and insurance company expansion into the securities business is likely to increase risk." Akhigbe and Whyte (2004: 446) provide strict policy recommendations and say that "[r]egulators should carefully monitor and supervise bank activities in this new era of financial modernization to mitigate adverse effects from the increase in risk"; "our results suggest that regulators must be vigilant to ensure that the safety of the financial system is not compromised," Akhigbe and Whyte (2004: 446) emphasized in the middle of the 2002–2005 subprime market expansion. The increased level of risk in the entire finance industry was also complemented by another issue, that of increased *illiquidity*—or, rather, the *signaling* of market actors such as public companies that market liquidity was not optimal or in decline—which led to an increase in stock repurchase announcements.

The Question of Liquidity

In the 1990s, the propositions of price theory that had animated the antitrust enforcement critique and that justified the market for management control and contract theory started to play a more marginal role. While price theory rested on the proposition that market prices accommodate and process all public information for the benefit of the market-based agent, capable of reaping the efficiency gains generated by free-market pricing, in the 1990s and especially in the new millennium, the question of illiquidity was surfacing. In hindsight, the theoretical scaffold of price theory was deconstructed as soon as the shareholder primacy governance was established. "Efficiency" started to mean something entirely different than in the 1950–1980 period, defined as the "efficiency through market pricing of assets." Now, by the end of the 1990s, "efficiency" meant the unmonitored right to transfer risks to other stakeholders. In the 1990s, stock repurchases was the primary evidence of the abandoning of price theory, a new practice based on the argument that the market may *de facto* underrate the value of stocks (for some reason, as critics have remarked, the opposite position is never announced—that stocks are *overrated* in the eyes of the insiders), which, in turn, justify that firms repurchase its own stock to boost share prices. In addition, in the new millennium, discussed in more detail in the next chapter, the growing aggregated economic value of securities issued was indicative of how another essentially illiquid financial asset, speaking against the price theory argument that had dominated over four decades of free-market advocacy, became the most prominent vehicle for finance market expansion.

Carruthers and Stinchcombe (1999: 358) remark that liquidity and illiquidity are not the effect of "a kind of economic 'state of nature,'" but is part of the market-making process that "depend on specific institutional features and organizational activities." The market-maker is here "an individual or (more usually) an organization that takes an illiquid asset and turns it into a more liquid one" (Carruthers and Stinchcombe, 1999: 358). The liquidity of an asset is therefore not some innate or essential feature of an asset but, instead, rests on the supply of capital and not least on the collective ability to price the asset, preferably over the economic cycle. A significant body of empirical work has demonstrated that few markets are ever persistently "frictionless" over time, which, in turn, indicates that, for example, standardized financial assets cannot be bought and sold without transaction costs (Pitluck, 2011: 27).

Amihud (2002) argues that "stock excess returns," *de facto* more of a theoretical construct rather than an empirically testable concept as it is complicated to determine a baseline return for a fictional "standard stock," are widely considered compensation for risk in finance theory. For instance, Amihud (2002: 35) exemplifies, "stock expected returns are negatively related to size"; that is, owners of stock issued by large firms receive fewer returns than do owners of stocks in smaller companies, *ceteris paribus*. Amihud (2002: 35) regards this stock excess return as a "proxy for liquidity": larger firms have more outstanding stocks, and therefore the number of buyers are higher; that is, the stock is easier to sell off if the holder of the stock is unsatisfied with its valuation or identify more lucrative investment opportunities. Following from this theoretical model, stock excess returns also accrue to owners of illiquid stocks, and Amihud (2002: 32) argue that his empirical data are consistent with this hypothesis. At the same time as Amihud (2002: 33) seeks to measure liquidity, it remains, he warns, "an elusive concept": "[Liquidity] is not observed directly but rather has a number of aspects that cannot be captured in a single measure." This, in turn, implies that empirical research is dependent on credible and robust proxy measures that capture illiquidity. One such proxy is to measure stock market liquidity in terms of "turnover velocity" on basis of cross-national statistic, a "ratio of the total value of shares traded relative to the total value of the stock market" (Pitluck, 2011: 31). If the turnover velocity is high, the market is liquid, while a lower turnover velocity indicates illiquid markets. A legitimate and frequent critique of this measure, drawing on what the renowned French mathematician Henri Poincaré (2001) refers to as *conventionalism* (Ben-Menahem, 2006; Nye, 1979), such a proxy tend to confuse *measures* and *definitions*, that is, cause and effect: rather than measuring degrees of liquidity, turnover velocity is the very definition of liquidity per se, making this proxy self-referential and thus incapable of measuring what it purports to measure in objective terms.

Chordia, Sarkar, and Subrahmanyam (2005) examine the illiquidity of the U.S. stock and bond markets for the 1991–1998 period. As Chordia et al. (2005: 86) notice, "the vast majority of equilibrium asset pricing models do not consider trading and thus ignore the time and cost of transforming cash into financial assets or vice versa." That is, mainstream neoclassical finance theory simply assumes that markets are liquid without substantiating this proposition. However, if markets were liquid, there would be no or only limited volatility in stock and bond prices over the trading week or the annual seasons. The data reported by Chordia et al. (2005: 126) reveal that there are "weekly regularities in stock and bond market." More important, these regularities "closely mimic each other," that is, stock and bond markets, trading different financial assets, demonstrate intra-trade regularities that suggest that markets are illiquid over substantial period of the week: "Friday is the lowest-liquidity day of the week for both markets. Further, liquidity in both stock and bond markets tends to be higher during the summer/early fall months of July to September" (Chordia et al., 2005: 126). Pitluck (2011: 32) provide further evidence:

> [I]n the United States, if we measure liquidity by the volume of trading, liquidity exhibits a ∩-shaped curve so that it is highest at the beginning and the end of the trading day, and exhibits an ∩-shape across the trading week, with the highest liquidity on Tuesdays and Wednesdays . . . Over the course of the calendar year, US liquidity peaks in July through September.
>
> (Pitluck, 2011: 32)

Unfortunately, Chordia et al. (2005: 126) say, "[t]here is no theory on linking movements in liquidity across equity and fixed income markets," and the very question of illiquidity per se "[h]as largely remained unexplored" (Chordia et al., 2005: 126).

Pitluck's (2011) empirical study of an illiquid market (Malaysia's Stock Exchange in Kuala Lumpur) sheds further light on the illiquidity problem. In such stock markets, Pitluck (2011: 27) argues, "[f]und managers in firms such as pension funds and investment banks are typically forced to trade slowly, plotting a string of contingent trades across days, weeks and even months." Moreover, larger and more international funds are "[a]t an even greater disadvantage, plodding while smaller or local investors can be relatively nimble" (Pitluck, 2011: 27). As a consequence, such a market cannot immediately reflect, for example, the decision-making quality in underlying corporations that issue stocks or bonds being trading, professional finance trading is less a matter of carefully monitoring stock prices that purports to carry immaculate and undistorted informational content as it is a quite political and practical skill to sell off stocks in ways that does not harm the valuations of one's holding. This is, in short, an entirely different view of the market and finance trading than the idealized image of orthodox neoclassical economic theory, portraying the market as a "giant brain" that accommodates and processes public information:

> In response to the economic incentives created by illiquid times, traders must attend as closely to their decisions on *when* to trade as their decisions on *what* to trade. If stock markets were liquid, professional investors would execute their orders in whole as soon as the decision is made.
>
> (Pitluck, 2011: 36)

Taken together, the works of Amihud (2002), Chordia et al. (2005), and Pitluck (2011) indicate that also finance markets, the most refined and "pure" of all markets, operating directly on basis of numerically stated valuations of financial assets being issued, are characterized by significant degrees of illiquidity. As markets have underwent considerable de-regulatory reform, including much more detailed finance reporting, it is not plausible that the finance markets of the 1950s and 1960s were more liquid—or, *arguendo*, if they were, it is precisely because the use of complex derivatives advocated by the finance industry itself did not distort market liquidity—and therefore the initial claim that markets can effectively executive a check on managerial decision-making quality was never a credible proposition outside of orthodox neoclassical modeling. The illiquidity of markets is thus the free-market protagonist's demon, frequently explained on basis of the last remaining regulatory control, but such arguments leads into an infinite regress that never resolve the initial conundrum regarding the sources of market illiquidity. In other words, illiquidity of markets is the primary *aporia* of free-market theory.

Regardless of such objections, by the end of the day, for orthodox free-market protagonists, liquidity is not a major concern because it is assumed that the market will take care of this pricing of the asset on basis of the sheer volume of the transactions, but for more moderate commentators the finance industry will always be attracted to illiquid assets as they may offer a price premium on basis of the fact that they are by definition costly to price and thus to trade:

> [A]s the 'plain vanilla' transaction becomes more liquid and amenable to being transacted in the market, banks are moving on to more illiquid transactions. Competition forces them to flirt continuously with the limits of illiquidity.
>
> (Rajan, 2006: 500)

This was precisely what happened during the first years of the new millennium, leading to the finance industry collapse when trillions of hard-to-price (i.e., illiquid) securities lost its value when the subprime mortgage market came to a halt in 2008. In hindsight, the new recognition of the illiquidity problem, not so much in theory as in practice, was foreboding the long-term consequences of the repeal of the Glass–Steagall Act of 1933.

Explaining Stock Repurchases

Kahle (2002: 260) addresses the "sudden and drastic increase in repurchases in the 1990s," as an indication of new calculative practices in the boardrooms in American corporations. Stock repurchases are widely understood as a means for the board of director to distribute the residual cash to shareholders (as prescribed by agency theory) by intervening in the stock market to boost the stock price by either announcing that the firm intends to buy its own stock (which frequently raises the stock price as traders assume there is insider information not yet mirrored by the market price),[5] or actually buying it stock. In other words, rather than choosing to distribute the residual cash as dividends (the conventional channel for the transfer of the residual cash) the shareholders benefit "indirectly" as they can take advantage of raising stock evaluations and can thus chose to sell a proportional amount of stocks that corresponds to the stock price appreciation if they wish to liquidize their holdings. In this view, there is a trade-off between dividends and stock repurchases but the consequences are the same: shareholders benefit from the firm distributing its residual cash.

Already in 1982, during the free-market reforms of the Reagan era, the SEC had adopted Rule 10b-18, reducing the "ambiguities" regarding stock repurchases (Grullon and Ikenberry, 2000: 34), but it was not until the early 1990s that stock repurchases programs were implemented on large scale. In the five-year period from 1995 to 1999, U.S. corporations "[a]nnounced intentions to repurchase roughly $750 billion worth of stock" (Grullon and Ikenberry, 2000: 31), and in 1998—for the first time in history—U.S. corporations "distributed more cash to investors through share repurchases than through cash dividends" (Grullon and Ikenberry, 2000: 31). Over time, these changes are significant, Grullon and Ikenberry (2000: 34) demonstrate: "[T]he average dividend payout-ratio [in the U.S.] fell from 22.3% in 1974 to 13.8% in 1998, while the average purchase payout ratio increased from 3.7% to 13.6% during the same period." Why the stock repurchase strategy displaced the dividend strategy remains unclear for some commentators, but Kahle (2002: 260) postulates that the performance—reward systems implemented in U.S. corporations to support shareholder primacy governance is key to the new payout practice: "In the 1990s, stock options have encouraged firms to repurchase shares both to maximize managerial wealth, since repurchases do not affect the value of managerial options but dividends do, and to fund increasingly prevalent employee stock option programs." Also Grullon and Ikenberry (2000: 34) believe that performance—reward systems provide a credible explanation for the sudden preference for stock repurchases over dividends in the boardroom:

> [T]he increased use of executives stock options is a major factor in the general increase in purchase activity in the 1990s . . . managers intent on maximizing the value of their options might be tempted to eliminate dividends entirely—and we rarely see companies take such an

> extreme step. Nevertheless if the corporation is compelled to pay out capital to shareholders for whatever reason, managers who are heavily compensated through options may feel more inclined to choose a share repurchase over a cash dividend.
>
> (Grullon and Ikenberry, 2000: 34)

Regardless of how the residual cash is transferred to shareholders, the 1990s was the decade where corporate payout policy changed dramatically: "[t]otal corporate payouts in share repurchase programs during the period 1972–1983 amounted to less than 4.5% of total earnings. Over the period 1984 to 1998, this same ratio exceeded 25%" (Grullon and Ikenberry, 2000: 34). Taking a leap forward into the coming decade, Lazonick (2013: 497) reports that from 2001 to 2010, S&P 500 companies, which account for about 75 percent of the market capitalization of all U.S. publicly listed corporations, spent in excess of 50 percent of their net income on stock repurchases. In addition, Lazonick (2013: 497) adds, these companies "[d]istributed dividends equal to about 40 percent of net income over the decade, bringing a total payout ratio (buybacks plus dividends) to well over 90 percent." These figures show the magnitude of the shareholder primacy governance entrenchment by 2010. At the same time, it is also indicative of how the underlying price theory model and the idea of market efficiency are no longer a valid basis for board room decisions as the market's capacity to value the firm's stock is systematically distrusted. Suddenly, once shareholder enrichment was fortified as the new conventional wisdom in corporate governance, the very theoretical foundation for this model and its principal arguments were undermined. Even more perplexingly, agency theorists remained silent about the boardroom decision to bypass the market pricing mechanisms once it primary objective was accomplished: to provide a theoretical justification for shareholder enrichment. That is, it is as if price theory and the efficient market hypothesis were little more than theoretical scaffolds that would be disassembled as soon as the shareholder primacy governance model was erected. Once the shareholder primacy governance model was in place and supported by performance-reward systems and recruitment routines that secured shareholder-minded executives and directors, the concern for more speculative and intricate orthodox neoclassical theorems and principles waned. After all, the cynic may say, the pro-business community paid for robust practical effects, not for scholarly theses and theoretical arguments of interest merely to seminarists and other academic insiders. Agency theorists and free-market protagonists may have lost their theories when stock repurchases was implemented on broad basis, but they won the war nonetheless.

The Democratization of Stock Ownership

In the 1990s' political climate, the finance industry in combination with the burgeoning computer science and digital media industry were widely regarded as core industries of the shiny future of competitive capitalism. What has been euphemistically referred to as the "democratization of credit" in the 1980s (referring to, e.g., the junk bond market that provided capital to firms and business that were historically excluded from the venture capital market, dominated by traditional finance institutions such as investment banks) was now complemented by the "democratization of stock ownership." At the beginning of the 1990s, "about 21 percent of the American adults owned stocks" Harrington (2008: 12) writes. Seven years later, the percentage had "more than doubled," rising to 43 percent, and by 1999, "the figure was 53 percent" (Harrington, 2008: 12). Studies show that the finance industry already in the 1910s initiated campaigns to make stock ownership a matter of concern for a wider share of the population (Ott, 2009; Hochfelder, 2006), and by the Wall Street crash of 1929, sharing stock investment recommendations had become a public pastime, to the point where the core of the finance capital owners realized that a bubble was on its way to burst, as too many speculated too much and therefore pushed the finance system to extraordinary high levels of systemic risk. In the 1990s, the situation looked different, with more people being "financially literate" and with computer-based systems that provided presumptive stock-owners with new financial services.

At the same time as stock ownership became more dispersed, and encouraging, for example, George W. Bush, who took office in 2001, to make the slogan "the ownership society" the political vision for his presidency, the 1990s was essentially a decade of increased economic inequality:

> There was in fact a redistribution from the poorest to the wealthy over the course of the 1980s, and this continued in the 1990s under Bill Clinton and Tony Blair . . . [n]eoliberal policies tended to affect the most vulnerable members of society in the harshest ways.
>
> (Jones, 2012: 338)

More specifically, in the early 1990s, the Reagan-era deconstruction of welfare state institutions had led to a situation where $41 billion were spent annually on unemployment benefits. In contrast, $91 billion were spent on courts, police, and prisons, dwarfing the welfare provision costs. In the U.S., the 1990s was a period where this gap between welfare provisions and punitive action costs continued to grow: "By 1996, 1.63 million people were being detained in American prisons and jails—a threefold increase from 1980 . . . These figures suggest that incarceration generated a sizeable, nonmarket realocation of labor, overshadowing state intervention through social policy" (Western and Beckett, 1999: 1031). In other words, the decade of de-regulation was also the decade wherein economic inequality was accentuated and became normalized, no longer being a top priority in policy-making or being part of the responsibility of the board of directors as companies gradually transformed the employees' benefits and pensions into shareholder value, economic value that some part of the population (53 percent more precisely; Harrington, 2008: 12) was able to access only through stock ownership in these corporations.

Still, 47 percent of the Americans did not own stocks, and for them it would have been beneficial if the balance of power between finance capital owners and labour would have been less asymmetric. When the new millennium arrived, finance capital owners had established a new conventional wisdom rooted in free-market theory that suggested that finance-market expansion was indicative of a sound and socially beneficial capitalist economic system that foresaw a bright future. By the end of the century, the "Morning in America" that Ronald Reagan had promised seemed to finally have arrived, albeit with a Democratic president at the helm and a Labour Party leader at No. 10, Downing Street. Lewis E. Powell's memorandum, wherein the forthcoming Supreme Court judge worried that "the enterprise system are in deep trouble, and the hour is late" (Powell, 1971: 7), now seemed like a delusion, left behind in a distant past.

Summary and Conclusion

In August 1979, when President Carter appointed Paul Volcker as the chairman of Federal Reserve, the low-inflation rate policy was established as a primary political tool to stabilize the economy and to promote economic growth. This policy has also been heavily campaigned for by free-market protagonists, claiming, for example, that an independent central bank is a key mechanism that would counteract political opportunism (Polillo and Guillén, 2005). A low-inflation/low-interest policy is also highly attractive for the finance industry as low interest is conducive to an increased supply of cheap capital that can be invested in more high-risk or speculative ventures: "[F]inancial instability is reinforced when the interest rate is low" (Charles, 2016: 433). Unfortunately, when speculation grows in proportion, the financial instability of the economic system follows suit, at times to the point where the market collapse (see, e.g., Kindleberger, 2007). The shareholder welfare society is therefore not the outcome from the successful demonstration of the superior performance of the unregulated market, but is instead a matter of informing and shaping policy-making and legislative action to create a new regime of economic accumulation that reduce governmental regulation to a minimum and yet render the state as a key actor in market creation activities; the shareholder welfare society is not so much an outcome from a stabilization of naturally occurring markets as it is a man-made fabrication based on extensive theorizing, lobbying, and think-tank activism.

One of the foremost implications from the policy changes in the 1990s was the growth of economic inequality, a tendency that has continued ever since and today shows no signs of abating. "[O]ne of the decades in which growth was the 'smartest' (innovation led)—the 1990s—was a decade in which inequality continued to rise," Lazonick and Mazzucato (2013: 1094) write. Wray and Pigeon's (2000: 826) analysis reveals that over "the entire Clinton expansion," less than 2 percent of the new jobs were created "[f]or the half of the population that has not attended college." One factor, in particular, worthy of attention was the soaring compensation of top management, representing "a new cultural norm of mega pay," Erturk et al. (2004: 709) propose. Given that the entire shareholder primacy model has been based on the idea that managers underperform in predictable ways, either on basis of unchecked self-interest or sheer incompetence (the distinction between these two vices are never fully made clear in, e.g., the agency theory literature), the outcome that this group would be one of the primary benefactors in the shareholder welfare society is surprising. On the other hand, as managers now are claimed to serve as the shareholders' agents and can assume no other legitimate objective than to serve shareholder interests, thus burying all claims that corporate executives would consider a wider variety of interests, higher compensation may be justified by their former detractors (i.e., agency theorists) as shareholders now dictate the content of managerial decision-making (at least in theory, albeit perhaps not so much in practice, empirical research indicates; see, e.g., Crilly, Zollo, and Hansen, 2012; Westphal and Graebner, 2010; Westphal and Bednar, 2008; Westphal and Clement, 2008). Under all conditions, the 1990s was the decade that paved the way for the finance-market expansion of the first years of the new millennium, not least being propelled by securities issuance to make illiquid holdings (e.g., home mortgage loans) become liquid and tradable assets.

Notes

1. The FSMA is at times referred to as the Gramm–Leach–Bliley Act to honor the senators and congressmen who drafted the bill and made it pass in Congress.
2. Credit Default Swaps (CDS) is one class of derivative instruments that has been surrounded by much controversy. While proponents of derivative instruments emphasize the risk-sharing benefits of such financial assets, Augustin et al. (2016: 184) emphasize that the CDS market "remain largely under-researched so far," leaving finance market actors, policy-makers, and regulators in the dark regarding the long-term consequences of CDSs. At the same time, Augustin et al. (2016: 178) argue that "[t]here is sufficient anecdotal evidence to suggest that CDSs affect the prices of the underlying securities; change the economic incentives of the key agents in the financial system; and alter the behavior of investors, firms, and regulators." This, in turn, is evidence of "substantial market frictions" that would have been intolerable for, for example, financial economists even two decades ago" (Augustin et al., 2016: 178). For instance, some commentators have discredited CDSs as vehicles for "speculating against other investors' or governments' assets by accelerating default on the underlying debt" (Augustin et al., 2016: 179). For instance, "sophisticated investors" such as hedge funds have been accused of buying "default insurance" without having any economic ownership in the underlying debt, thus participating in default speculation (Augustin et al., 2016: 179). In addition to the introduction of new sources of frictions in finance markets that affects asset prices and economic incentives, CDSs may also have unintended consequences for "the rule of law"; that is, there are "legal details inherent in CDS contracts that introduce distortions and uncertainties into decision-making processes and asset prices" (Augustin et al., 2016: 184). In the end, such concerns render CDS a controversial and disputed class of derivative instruments, very much in need for more scholarly attention.

3. Quite soon after the publication of his book praising Enron, Hamel had good reason to regret such statements as they were unflattering for Hamel's analytical capacities and integrity. After the company's bankruptcy in December, Enron was widely portrayed as a stronghold of mind-boggling greed and fraud, a site "[l]argely comprised of incredibly immoral, arrogant, and mercenary individuals that created a milieu of sleaziness and greed," as one commentators, Carol Devine Molin (cited in Seeger and Ulmer, 2003: 69), put it.
4. In the end, when Lehman Brothers had filed for Chapter 11 bankruptcy protection, announcing bank debt of $613 billion and $155 billion in bond debt, the largest in U.S. history, MacDonald, despite his stated belief in the market, subscribed to what Paul Krugman referred to as "lemon socialism." In this economic regime, Krugman (cited in Palma, 2009: 863) says, "taxpayers bear the cost if things go wrong, but stockholders and executives get the benefit if things go right": "All my life I have been a laissez-faire Ronald Reagan/Margaret Thatcher capitalist, swearing by the market, taking the risks, and devil takes the hindermost. But this one time I was looking for a government rescue, and wasn't going to get it" (McDonald and Robinson, 2009: 7).
5. Studies (e.g., Farre-Mensa, Michaely, and Schmalz, 2014; Kahle, 2002) indicate that this beneficial effect tend to diminish over time, a fact that suggest the stock repurchase arrangements has a "cry-wolf effect" that is discounted over time.

6 The New Millennium
Volatility, Crises, and Austerity

Introduction

In the free-market euphoria of the 1980s and 1990s, propelled by overseas savings overflowing the emerging American investor capitalism, and the information technology and digital media revolution that spurred an upswing in the economic growth in the mid-1990s, the free-market idea was gradually accepted as the new conventional wisdom. Policy-makers, media pundits, and others chose to turn a blind eye to the recurrent small- and larger-scale financial crises in the global finance system and treated them as minor events that in no way overshadowed the aggregated efficiency gains made. In the U.S., the old millennium ended with two pieces of legislation that more or less gave free reign to finance market actors to issue securities as it suited their interests and therefore broke down the New Deal firewalls between banking and what would easily become speculative finance. The dot-com bubble, ending by the spring of 2001, indicated that the money supply in the finance system had now reached unprecedented levels, but such warning signals were interpreted on basis of the novelty of the information technology industry and its venturing activities rather than being seen as what carried any particular significance pertaining to the finance industry. The market model developed imposed a minimal form of regulatory control on, for example, securities markets, based on the work of privately owned credit rating agencies (CRAs). The CRA regulation was deemed to be the right way to balance free-market enterprising and venturing with regulatory control on basis of privately owned corporation, now monitoring the prudence and risk moderation of their very own paying clients. Over time, and especially after the events of 2008, the CRA model became subject to detailed scrutiny, revealing that these hopes for paying clients listening carefully to their suppliers of market ratings were based on an overoptimistic view wherein professional integrity and uncompromising ethical principles would withstand the sheer and unrestrained self-interest of finance market actors and others. Expressed in relatively modest, even anodyne terms, and with the benefit of hindsight, a U.S. Financial Stability Board (FSB) report published in 2014 (cited in Harnay and Scialom, 2016: 418) stated, "[T]he area of greatest concern remains institutions' inability to consistently produce high quality data." That is, the entire CRA-based regulation framework rested on incomplete and unreliable data. For commentators more prone to speak their heart than most authors of governmental reports dare to do, such as Thomas Frank (2012: 11), "[f]ree-market theory has proven itself to be a philosophy of ruination and fraud." Much cash had flown under the bridges of the global finance industry before such declarative statements could be made without being treated as hysterical populist and anti-business outbursts. Yet, once the levees broke in 2008, also some hardcore free-market protagonists and law and economics scholars such as Judge Richard Posner (2009), who have persistently applied economic theory to explain non-economic phenomena, for example, the amount of abortions in the U.S. society and the presence of children in foster care as a "regulated market problem" (Landes and Posner, 1978),[1] admitted that competitive capitalism perhaps, after all, demanded some kind of sovereign state to monitor and regulate economic activities.

In hindsight, it is easy to think that the entire free-market advocacy, putting all its eggs in the basket of free-market pricing, is based on a simple category mistake. As Richard Stallman, a renowned computer programmer remarks (cited in Boyle, 2003: 8), "'Free' as in 'free speech,' is not 'free' as in 'free beer.'" Free-market protagonists believed that regulated market of the managerial capitalism, the economic model based on New Deal policies and reform, would leave much money on the table—curiously enough in an era characterized by unprecedented economic growth and welfare—and that the de-regulated market would without additional cost do the job that previously demanded cadres of professionals and their expertise. The market efficiency did not provide any free lunches, we know now, and "free markets" are comparable to "free speech" inasmuch they provide some benefits and opportunities but they do not *per automata* lead to socially beneficial or desirable outcomes. As in the case of free speech (as Søren Kierkegaard, 1992: 43 knew), the value derived therefrom is a matter of whether people have something worth saying, and in the case of free markets, the virtues of free markets cannot be defined *a priori* but is a matter of how humans make use of such provisions. Hence, confusing the use of free in "free beer" and in "free speech," rooted in the epistemic realism of orthodox neoclassical economic theory, led to serious misjudgement of the instabilities of global financial markets, a fact that was widely discussed *post festum* in 2008 and beyond.

Financial Innovations and Market Efficiencies

The two acts of 1999 and 2000 basically eliminated the regulatory control of the securities market and advanced derivatives and provided the finance industry with an historically unique ability to expand its basis globally. Goldman Sachs, one of the most iconic Wall Street finance institutes, well connected to the Washington, D.C., political system (see, e.g., Mandis, 2013; Cohan, 2011), increased its capital stock more than 500-fold between 1970 and 2005 (Akerlof and Shiller, 2015: 26): "In 1970 the Goldman partnership had $50 million; in 2005, it was more than $28 billion." In contrast, U.S. GDP (in inflation adjusted dollars) increased only 12-fold over the same period. That is, the capital accumulation in Goldman Sachs was close to 42 times faster than in society at large, *ceteris paribus*.

The pre–Great Depression finance industry was primarily local and regional, and there were no digital media that could create (through IOU issuance) or transfer economic value within in fractions of a second, so there was a certain inertia that made the finance industry relatively separated from what at times is called the "real economy." On the other hand, many policy-makers and commentators, including Louis D. Brandeis, worried about the finance industry's ability to claim the benefits of the work accomplished by, for example, entrepreneurs. By the end of the twentieth century, many policy-makers and office holders did not share these concerns as they were convinced that markets contained self-stabilizing mechanisms making them robust over the economic cycle.

Effectively translating this adage into the end of the millennium acts of 1999 and 2000, the future was now open for novel finance industry innovations. Frame and White (2004: 118) address what they refer to as *financial innovations*, which they group into "a new product (e.g., adjustable-rate mortgages, exchange-traded index-funds); new services (e.g., online securities trading, internet banking); new 'production' processes (e.g., electronic record-keeping for securities, credit scoring); or new organizational forms (e.g., a new type of electronic exchange for trading securities, internet-only banks)." Following the free-market credo, Frame and White (2004: 118) suggest that finance is "[a] facilitator of virtually all production activity and much consumption activity" (a proposition that is correct only if policy-makers and legislators assign finance actors this role, i.e., it is more a *de jure* than a *de facto* matter; Pistor, 2013) and add that it therefore follows that "[i]mprovement in the financial sector will have direct positive ramifications throughout the economy," an affirmative proposition *a priori* that demands empirical substantiation. For Frame and White (2004), finance innovations are good for both industry and consumers. Still, as they argue next, regulation tend to influence innovation activities, either positively or negatively, and therefore, Frame and White (2004: 121) add, "[i]t is impossible a priori to assign a positive or negative sign to the connection between the stringency of regulation (however measured) and the pace of financial innovation." For Frame and White (2004), finance innovations are complicated to assess *ex ante*, but by and large, they are assumed to contribute to overall efficiency and are therefore socially beneficial.

Baker and Smith (1998: 2) add to this argument by pointing out that innovators, the "financial entrepreneurs" including, for example, junk bond market pioneer Michael Milken and the law firm Kohlberg Kravis Robert & Co.

that developed the leveraged buyout practice in the 1980s, "are rarely held in esteem by Americans." In Baker and Smith's (1998) affirmative account of financial entrepreneurs, this new breed of finance industry actors cannot do anything wrong as they add to the overall efficiency that orthodox neoclassicists hold in esteem. If the wider public and policy-makers refuse to accept the creativity of financial entrepreneurs, it should be seen as the sour grapes of the loser. Just like in any other innovation activities, there may be long-term benefits, but there are also potentials risks that reveal themselves only over time and with the change of the economic tide. One such example is the expanding securities market that was inflated after 2000, certainly putting its mark on the first two decades of the new millennium. The "securitization" of virtually everything that occurred after 2000 represented a new form of financialization of the economy, now trading all sorts of assets. While the rationale for this new class of finance assets followed consistently from the orthodox neoclassicist free-market model, neoclassic theory did not fully recognize the illiquidity of the asset in the downturn of the economic cycle. Needless to say, the consequences of the finance industry were disastrous[2] and brought with it what is now being referred to as the Great Recession, lasting well into 2017, more than 10 years after the by now-notorious subprime mortgage loan market retracted.

Increasing the Leverage: The Securities Market Expansion

Bluhm and Wagner's (2011: 194) define securities as financial assets that "[t]urns asset cash flows into marketable securities." In order to accomplish this process of turning a future cash-flow (derived from e.g., a mortgage loan interest payment) into an asset, "derivative technology and financial modeling" are used to construct a security. A security is a derivative, connected to an underlying financial assets that is held by the issuer of the security, say, a bank that holds a stock of home mortgage loan contracts that will generate interest payments over a longer time, *circa* 30 years. Shin (2009: 310) suggests that securitization facilitate greater credit supply to "ultimate borrowers at the aggregate level," but the leverage of the return on equity is still dependent on the stability of the finance market. In "benign financial market conditions," when measured risks are low, financial intermediaries "expand balance sheets" as they increase the leverage, primarily by keeping the level of equity intact and adjusting the size of total assets (Shin, 2009: 310). In order to expand balance sheets, new borrowers must be recruited; when all prime borrowers already have a mortgage, banks have to "lower their lending standards in order to lend to subprime borrowers" (Shin, 2009: 310). When subprime borrowers are invited to participate in the expansion of balance sheets and the accompanying securitization, "the seeds of the subsequent downturn in the credit cycle are thus sown" (Shin, 2009: 310).

As Shin (2009: 311–312) remarks, securitization has long been seen as "a positive development for the resilience of the financial system by enabling the dispersion of credit risk." However, after the "credit crisis" of 2007 and 2008, a less sympathetic view of securitization has been established, emphasizing "the multi-layered agency problems that took hold at every stage of the securitisation process, starting with the origination of the loan the sale, warehousing and securitisation as well as the role of the credit rating agencies in the process" (Shin, 2009: 311–312):

> The motto would be that there is always a greater fool in the chain who will buy the bad loan. At the end of the chain, according to this view, is the hapless final investor who ends up holding the hot potato and suffers the eventual loss.
>
> (Shin, 2009: 312)

Securitization therefore serves to expand credit supply and contribute to finance market stability as long as financial intermediaries do not compromise their risk-management standards and invite subprime borrowers to expand their balance sheets. Unfortunately, empirical evidence indicates that the tendency to increase the return on equity by higher leverage is an industry-wide phenomenon, rooted in the incentive structure of the finance industry. Shin (2009: 331) uses the image of an inflating balloon that is filled with new assets; as the balloon expands, banks search for new assets to fill the balloon, but once they have exhausted all the second-rate borrowers, they turn to other borrowers, even subprime ones, to enable further balance sheet expansion. As risks increased with the leverage, especially if the "balloon" is filled with sub-prime mortgage loans, securitization no longer serves the role to stabilize the finance market; quite the contrary, it contributes to instabilities and uncertainty as the pricing of securities become more complicated; that is, securities become more illiquid.

Under favourable market conditions, derivatives such as securities enables the holder of illiquid, long-term contracts to develop a financial asset to be traded over the entire contract period:

> The growth of securitization, or 'structured finance,' has been one of the most important developments in finance in the last twenty-five years. The basic idea of securitization is that bundles, or 'pools,' of income-producing financial assets, usually loan-like obligations such as mortgages, corporate loans, auto loans, or credit-card receivables but potentially also revenue sources such as royalty streams, are sold to an entity (a 'special purpose vehicle') that issues claims on the pool income to investors. Once the claims have been sold, the underlying assets have been 'securitized.'
>
> (Hunt, 2009: 117)

When operating as under stable conditions, the costs for the home mortgage loan lender is reduced as the firm issuing the security can capitalize on this illiquid asset. That, in turn, is theoretically reducing the costs for various stakeholders, including, for example, home owners financing their purchase through home mortgage loans. In the end, though, the use of securities on large-scale basis easily incentivizes finance traders to take increasingly risky positions on the market, and as securities are essentially illiquid—that is, not easily priced or traded at low costs—during the downturn in the economic cycle, widespread ownership of securities lead to high levels of systemic risks at this stage.

An extensive literature reports how the securities market has expanded over time. "[T]he securities industry grew from 0.4 percent of GDP in 1980 to 1.7 percent of GDP in 2007," Greenwood and Scharfstein (2013: 7) say. However, the holdings of finance industry are measured in entirely different figures: "In 2006 banks issued $1.8 trillion in securities backed by mortgages, credit cards, auto loans, and other debt. More than half of the credit card and student loans in the country were securitized" Tabb (2012: 96) writes. Between 1980 and 2000, "securitized debt expanded 50-fold, whereas bank loans expanded 3.7-fold," Wisman (2013: 926) adds. Especially in the 2002–2005 period, where the U.S. subprime home mortgage loan market expanded greatly, the issuance of so-called Mortgage-Backed Securities (MBS) grew proportionally. Empirical evidence (discussed in the following) suggests that a substantial share of such loans and their accompanying securitization were instituted on basis of relaxed, substandard risk-assessment methods, and therefore, there were evidence of what has been referred to as "predatory lending"—lending that serves the sole purpose to benefit the lender, while the borrower carry all of the risks while acquiring no benefits beside the claim to own a real estate that the borrower cannot financially maintain until the termination of the contract (Engel and McCoy, 2001, 2007).[3] Securitization is thus playing a key role in the expansion of the finance industry and in further reinforcing the shareholder primacy ideology as securities is a mechanism that turn illiquid holdings into tradable (i.e., liquid) assets.

Why Securities Matters

The acts of 1999 and 2000 was based on the premise that finance industry ultimately rest on self-regulatory mechanisms, where, for example, increased levels of risks will always be punished by the market, and therefore, finance traders have a strong incentive to carefully monitor their risk leverage. Unfortunately, this self-disciplinary introspection is, in turn, based on the idea that it is possible to separate different finance assets into risk classes, a belief that poorly translates into actual accomplishments. This, in turn, is based on the fact that it is complicated to distinguish what Mehrling (2011: 48), drawing on the work of Hyman Minsky, refers to as "speculative" and "productive" credit: "[U]nder American conditions, the money market and the securities market have *always* been completely intertwined and, as a consequence, it was *never* been possible to distinguish speculative from productive credit." Chick (1997: 358) predicted at an early stage that increased possibilities for securitization would lead to more speculative finance market activity: "With both the banks and firms turning to more securitized lending, the markets have a greater role in financing deficit expenditure as well as funding the capital stock, the influence of speculative behavior is increased." In addition, Chick (1997: 358–359) points at the co-production of securitization and off-balance-sheet activity, which leads to the demands regarding "the degree of prudence" being "greatly reduced." Off-balance-sheet activity serves to "help banks evade restrictions" (Chick, 1997: 359), which were originally enacted and enforced to avert excessive speculation.

It is complicated enough for individual finance traders to assess their own risk-leverage and their own risk-profile (i.e., to monitor their personal risk preference), but as finance trading performance assessment is commonly based on *relative performance*, that is, not the performance estimated given a certain personal risk-utility function, the *individual* risk-profile remains a moot question (Rajan, 2006: 501). In the fog of war of finance market trading, where sound versus speculative positions are complicated to determine, especially on short notice, all financial traders will demonstrate, albeit to various degree, so-called *herd behaviour*—the preference to act in concert with other traders, that is, follow the market index (Froot, Scharfstein, and Stein, 1992). In addition, the more illiquid the assets held are (as in the case of certain classes of securities in bear markets), the larger the risks, and the higher the presence of herd behavior; if finance traders hold a portfolio of stocks, the value of the portfolio may never fall below a certain level as it is easier to estimate what is referred to as the "fundamental value"[4] of the stocks (Bryan and Rafferty, 2013), but when it comes to securities, such "fundamental values" are fictive and poorly correlating the value of the underlying assets.[5] By implications, the securities markets have proved to work best at the upward turn of the economic cycle (when economic growth favours credit expansion), while the downward to a higher degree turn renders securities illiquid. Therefore, securities have served to increase the supply of credit and to expand the global finance market, but this new class of financial assets has also brought new levels of risk. In fact, as Gammon and Wigan (2015: 113) remark, "securitization not only redistributed credit risk, it redefined it."

The risks derived from the issuing of securities derive from a number of sources. First of all, the rating of securities has traditionally been assigned a small group of CRAs, whereof three privately owned corporations (Standard & Poor, Moody's, and Fitch) make up a *de facto* credit rating oligopoly. Unfortunately, the work conducted by the CRAs have proved to be quite inefficient in curbing the risk leverage of finance traders. The CRAs ratings are published only once, when the finance asset is being issued on the market, but finance traders themselves need to constantly monitor the value and risk of the security during the entire period the asset is held or until it terminates.

The work of the CRAs and the finance traders are thus operating within different time horizons and serve different purposes, and this fact leads to an underestimation of the risks of holding securities. Moreover, a more pressing concern, related to what (Downer, 2011: 748) refers to as *epistemic accidents* in the field of aviation, is that the lack of robust empirical data prove certain assumptions and estimations to be erroneous only *after* an accident or serious event has already occurred, as such data or evidence only reveal itself on basis of real-world experience. In the case of securities, the pricing of this class of financial assets are dependent on long-term data series but as also new financial assets issued were rated mostly favourably (and possibly on basis of the widely held assumption that markets have an innate capacity to stabilize themselves) but without the benefit to access such data. When the economy grows, favourable securities evaluations translate into a further expansion of the securities markets and offerings, which, in turn, are understood as an indication of the early-stage evaluation being correct, leading to a tendency to overrate securities vis-à-vis other finance assets (e.g., stocks) over time. In 2007 and 2008, most MBS lost all their value, a market response that points at both institutional factors (CRAs and finance traders have different objectives and work within different time horizons) and epistemic or calculative factors (no robust time-series data was available when the first securities were rated, and thereafter, there was little effort moderate the initial assessments as the market grew):

> [A]gencies did not know what they were doing on a fundamental level, at least with respect to some (but not necessarily all) novel securities . . . *if* rating agencies do not know what they are doing, they are likely to find it to be in their interest to issue ratings on novel products anyway.
> (Hunt, 2009: 117)

Hunt's (2009) bold claim regarding the credit rating agencies' inadequate performance can be substantiated by data provided by Hirsch and Pozner (2005), indicating that CRAs do not consistently act in ways that discipline investors to value prudence and to moderate their risk exposure. In March 2000, "at the height of market mania" (Hirsch and Pozner, 2005: 231), the CRAs issued 92 buy recommendations for every sell recommendation. By the end of July 2001, when the S&P 500 index had fallen 12 percent and the NASDAQ index by 59 percent, CRAs still continued issuing buy recommendations in 65 percent of the cases (Hirsch and Pozner, 2005: 231). Such data indicate that CRAs are better understood as the finance market's cheerleaders than its foremost control mechanism.

Paredes (2003) argues that securities regulation is by and large based on the idea of the virtues of transparency derived from mandatory disclosure, that is, practices that are designed to even out informational asymmetries in the market for the benefit of overall market efficiency. But to assume that the production and dissemination of information per se are conducive to a more efficient and/or resilient finance market is a fallacy, Paredes (2003) argues; without holding robust theoretical models that show the significance of the information and data generated, mandatory disclosure is a relatively ineffective legal device in the monitoring of the securities market. First of all, Paredes (2003: 418) argues, "relatively little attention is paid to how the information is used"; that is, there is no proper analysis of how investors and securities market professionals "[s]earch and process information and make decisions based on the information the federal securities laws make available." Unless such practices are unveiled and related to empirical data, structured into time series and over the economic cycle, mandatory disclosure remains a relatively blunt regulatory tool. Second, substantial evidence suggests that human actors tend to suffer from an overconfidence bias. That is, they overrate their own abilities in predictable ways, especially in comparison to indices and other aggregated performance measures (Paredes, 2003: 457). Given such behavioural biases, the disclosing of securities information does not make a difference as a market regulation mechanism. Third, social-psychological phenomena such as herd behavior materializing as "stock runs" or "bank panics" (see, e.g., Greve, Kim, and Teh, 2016), where "good" and "bad" companies and stocks are increasingly complicated to distinguish in the turmoil of a quickly falling stock index and when stock is sold off at a high pace regardless of underlying substantial value, are poorly counteracted by mandatory disclosure. Paredes (2003) exemplifies:

> The stock market collapse of 2001 and 2002 following the scandals at Enron, WorldCom, Adelphia, Tyco, and elsewhere illustrates the point. After these scandals came to light, investors began to discount stocks as a whole because of corporate governance concerns. Investors were unable to discern the honest, well-run (*i.e.*, 'good') companies from the dishonest, poorly-run (*i.e.*, 'bad') ones, and so punished all companies indiscriminately, even those with good, honest management teams.
>
> (Paredes, 2003: 470)

Furthermore, mandatory disclosure does not really support what Paredes (2003) refers to as *shaming* (and free-market protagonists speak of as "reputational-capital" or "reputation costs"; Hunt, 2009; Partnoy, 1999), that is, market actors' sense of professional standards and pride and serving to reinforce prudent behaviour. In a situation where too-lax regulatory control becomes separated from meaningful professional identities and norms and values, these regulatory efforts cease to execute a disciplinary function. The medium- to long-term consequences are, Paredes (2003: 468) says, a decline of the efficacy of the regulatory system and a loss of faith in the integrity of capital markets and the finance industry. By and large, Paredes (2003: 469) concludes, "[i]nvestors often assume that the federal securities laws provide more investor protection than the laws really do."

These issues are of key relevance as historical records reveal that market self-regulation has been a quite blunt tool in evading bubbles,[6] economic crises, and instabilities in the economy (Gerding, 2005). The six historical cases that

Gerding examines are unflattering evidence for policy-makers and regulators, showing that cycles of de-regulation and re-regulation frenzy do not so much follow the intentions of political bodies as they occur whenever policy-makers and regulators are overwhelmed by economic volatility they no longer fully control. Gerding (2005: 418) proposes a correlation between deregulation during the rise of a bubble and "political reaction and re-regulation in the aftermath of a bubble." Such evidence is unflattering because rather than political and legislative bodies being able to demonstrate integrity and prescience, they in fact actively contribute to and reinforce the volatility of, for example, securities markets: "[D]eregulation and deteriorated securities laws improve conditions for both an outbreak of widespread securities fraud and the further inflation of the speculative bubble. Bubbles and regulations are thus locked in a tight, symbiotic relationship" (Gerding, 2005: 418). Market booms and bubbles, coincide with "periods of laissez-faire economic policy and financial and securities deregulation" (Gerding, 2005: 421). Such failure to anticipate and neutralize market booms and bubbles is, in turn, explained on basis of "behavioral biases" that afflict not only finance traders but also policy-makers and regulators. Finance traders demonstrate "overoptimism and overconfidence" when assessing their own investment ability, and they tend to justify that they discount "the probability of being defrauded and overestimate their ability to detect fraud" (Gerding, 2005: 421). Policy-makers and regulators, in turn, demonstrate similar behavioral biases that downplay the risks of new economic instabilities or even breakdowns on a systemic level: "[A]s time passes since the last financial crisis, regulators and policymakers discount the potential for new crises and the need for regulations to avert those crises. This creates a condition that scholars of international financial crises have labeled 'disaster myopia'" (Gerding, 2005: 422. See also Cole and White, 2012). Once bubbles burst and the financial market comes to a halt, which in many cases is also contaminating other sectors of the economy, in most cases demanding much longer periods to rehabilitate themselves from sharp economic downturns, there is a "strong political reaction against speculation" accompanied by a public demand for new laws and regulations to "punish malfeasance in the market" (Gerding, 2005: 423). In fact, empirical studies demonstrate that most securities laws and regulations are responses to "collapsed bubbles, stock crashes and related financial crises" (Gerding, 2005: 423).

Securities are issued and traded in the borderland of liquidity and illiquidity. As finance traders can only perform better than their competitors if they successfully exploit modestly illiquid assets, this class of assets will always attract speculative activities.

MBS and the Subprime Market: The "Democratization of Credit" to Fuel Securitization

While the old-school free-market theorists considered the market a naturally occurring mechanism for pricing commodities that must not be distorted by regulatory oversight, the new generation of free-market protagonists took a more pragmatic view of the market, admitting, for example, that liquidity, being a key condition for, for example, stock market to be able to assess managerial decision quality as proposed by the market for management control literature, in fact, cannot be taken for granted; markets do not per se imply liquidity unless assets are standardized and the supply is accompanied by a reasonable demand. Illiquidity is thus an empirical condition that by and large discredits much of the claims made regarding market pricing and efficiency. Once finance markets have been de-regulated, there were new opportunities to issue essentially illiquid assets such as MBSs. The MBS serves a specific role in the new millennium as they were the vehicle *par preférénce* to transform "a relatively illiquid commodity (a commercial mortgage) into a liquid and tradable security" (Gotham, 2006: 262). Gotham continues: "Financial institutions unbundle, repackage and pool commercial mortgages into securities that investors can buy in capital markets." Engel and McCoy (2007: 2045) describe securitization as follows: "In securitization, investment banks take pools of home loans, carve up the cash flows from those receivables, and convert the cash flows into bonds that are secured by the mortgages." As MBS made it more lucrative to issue credit as mortgage loans as risks were spread on a global securities market,[7] it is inadequate to say, Coffee (2009: 3) argues, that a real estate bubble was overwhelming the capital markets;[8] in fact, the opposite, a form of reverse credit expansion process, more based on securities market "pull" than credit demand "push," was the case—"an erosion of discipline in the capital markets destabilized the real estate markets" (Coffee, 2009: 3):

> [T]he rise of asset-backed securitizations led major investment banks to acquire large portfolios of mortgage loans in order to securitize them and sell debt securities collateralized by these portfolios to investors on a global basis. In so doing, they abandoned diversification as the usual governing principle of prudent financial management and at the same time recklessly pursued increased leverage.
>
> (Coffee, 2009: 3)

The orthodox, free-market story was that a government-sponsored real estate bubble brought down the economy, but rather than portraying the home owners who saw their homes being foreclosed when they could no longer pay their subprime mortgage loans as being culpable, it is possible to examine the role of securities in this speculation-led debacle. Engel and McCoy (2007: 2039) call for attention to "the harms caused by securitization to debtors whose loans are securitized." As Bryan and Rafferty (2014: 891) point out, in a financialized economy that favours liquidity and short-term yields, anyone who hold illiquid assets (e.g., jobs, houses, health) tend to be "subordinated" to capital accumulation processes, not only in classic Marxist terms of the "extraction of a surplus in the workplace" but also making households the "systemic 'shock absorbers' in global financial markets." In such an economy, the ability to accumulate finance capital is the foremost objective, legitimized by a vaguely defined and essentially fluid term "efficiency," supposedly beneficial for all constituencies.

To turn to the facts, between 1997 and 2006—the period of finance market de-regulation and expansion—the so-called S&P/Case-Shiller Index of home prices rose by approximately 125%, whereas the U.S. Consumer Price Index rose by only 28%; "by the early 2000s, there was a widespread belief that housing prices could only go up," White (2013: 104) says. Leading free-market spokespersons such as the Princeton economist Ben Bernanke, soon to be named Alan Greenspan's successor as the chairman of the Federal Reserve, were not a bit worried about such inflated housing prices but saw them as being indicative of a sound and well-functioning economy: "Housing prices has risen by nearly 25 percent in the past two years. Although speculative activity has increased in some areas, at a national level these price increases largely reflect strong economic fundamentals," Ben Bernanke declared in his role as the chairman of the Council of Economic Advisors in a speech before Congress in October 2005 (cited Mian and Sufi, 2014: 78). Mian and Sufi's detailed analysis of the decline of home mortgage loan assessment standards on the ZIP (i.e., postal) code level reveals that the soaring housing prices had little, *pace* Bernanke, to do with "strong economic fundamentals." Instead, the period 2002–2005 was the only period wherein credit growth was *negatively correlated* with income growth (Mian and Sufi, 2009: 1453). In a sound and well-managed housing markets, credit growth and income growth correlate, so that loan takers are likely to be able to repay their loans, but at the height of the subprime loan expansion, the demands on the mortgage loan borrower were substantially relaxed (Rona-Tas and Hiss, 2010: 137).

The explanation for this more "generous" assessment of presumptive loan-takers, a "democratization of credit" for it sponsors, is its role in the security market: "From 2002 to 2005, private-label securitization soared. As a percentage of all MBS issued, it increased from less than 20 to over 50 percent from 2002 to 2006, before collapsing entirely in 2007" Mian and Sufi, 2014: 92). In Mian and Sufi's ZIP-code level data, it is possible to examine how "subprime ZIP code areas" (in California and in Florida, in particular) relied on securitization to extract value from the high-risk contracts:

> [T]he increase in the rate of securitization is much stronger in subprime ZIP codes compared to prime ZIP codes during this period, and the relative increase is driven primarily by securitization sold to financial institutions not affiliated with the mortgage originator.
>
> (Mian and Sufi, 2009: 1453–1454)

In other words, the subprime market was fuelled by the leaders' ability to repackage these high-risk loans into securities that could be sold on the global finance market, thus spreading local risks (housing market pricing is, in most cases, with a few metropolitan areas as exceptions, reflecting local economic conditions) into globally dispersed risks. If just a few such securities are issued and overrated by CRAs, the harm done is relatively modest and easily absorbed by the finance market, but if the securitization of high-risk loans is conducted on an industrial basis on the macro-scale, the risks amplify and infect substantial shares of the global finance industry. That was precisely what happened in the period, partially leveraged by the official doctrine that finance markets have the capacity to stabilize itself as excessive risk taking is punished in the end and because rational actors are concerned about escaping such punishment. Sadly, as zoologist and paleontologist Georges Cuvier once remarked, what makes "good poetry" rarely make "good science" (Riskin, 2015: 297), and in this case, the master narrative regarding the free market's capacity to regulate itself failed its protagonists:

> [D]efault rates increase significantly more from 2005 to 2007 in ZIP codes that experience an increase in the fraction of mortgages sold in private securitizations or to noncommercial bank finance companies from 2002 to 2005. This results hints at moral hazard on behalf of originators as a factor contributing to the expansion of credit supply, although we believe more research is needed on this precise mechanism.
>
> (Mian and Sufi, 2009: 1454)

Engel and McCoy (2007: 2043) speak about what happened in the 2002–2005 period as a textbook case of what they refer to as "predatory lending." Today, lenders securitize "almost eighty percent of subprime mortgages" (Engel and McCoy, 2007: 2043), and as a consequence, "thinly capitalized lenders" and fly-by-night capital firms can actively participate in the construction e.g., subprime home mortgage markets. In addition, these firms benefit the most from securitizing their "receivables" (Engel and McCoy, 2007: 1279). In Engel and McCoy's (2001) account, the development of a global securities market, where MBS, and, on the "second-floor" (Lysandrou and Nesvetailova, 2015), Collateralized Debt Obligations (CDOs) can be traded, is a *sine qua non* for the expansion of predatory lending activities: "Most subprime lenders are nonbank entities that emerged as the result of securitization" (Engel and McCoy, 2001: 1279). Engel and McCoy (2001) explicate their position:

> Securitization, by making possible a constant flow of money to the home-mortgage market, has dramatically altered the business of mortgage lending. Banks and other lenders do not suffer from liquidity restraints and more funds are available to lend. Securitization also has created opportunities for nonbank lenders to enter the home-mortgage market . . . [Now] thinly capitalized mortgage bankers and finance companies can originate loans for sale on the secondary market.
>
> (Engel and McCoy, 2001: 1274)

While securities have traditionally been used in the finance industry to spread risks and to enhance the overall efficiency of its operations, the uses of securities in new areas and to serve new customer segments on the contrary have led to leveraged risk taking, Engel and McCoy (2001) argue:

> Before the 1970s, investments in securities were largely the preserve of the wealthy. For middle- and lower-income people, simpler and safer financial products such as life insurance and bank accounts, certificates of deposit, and government bonds were the savings vehicles of choice.
> (Engel and McCoy, 2001: 1329)

Engel and McCoy (2001: 1330) argue that the "the popularization of mutual funds" led to the insurance industry facing new competition from securities firms, and therefore, "individuals of modest means began shifting their savings out of life-insurance policies and bank accounts into mutual funds that offered the risks and rewards of equities." With the expansion of the subprime mortgage loan market in the 2002–2005 period, the presence of securities issued by thinly capitalized subprime lenders could, thanks to weak incentives to monitor these firms and their assets, blend with more robust securities, Engel and McCoy (2007: 2040) argue. In the 2002–2005 period, Wall Street firms securitize subprime home loans "[w]ithout determining if loan pools contain predatory loans," leading to the leveraged risk that the "secondary market actors" (e.g., firms trading securities) cannot handle through their risk management routines. Consequently, securitization and substandard risk management have "actively facilitated abusive lending"; "due diligence by the secondary market, particularly by the private secondary market, has been lax to date and has failed to deter capital flows to predatory lenders," Engel and McCoy (2001: 1364) remarked a few years before the subprime market expansion take off, a comment that arguably would have saved significant money and efforts if taken seriously by finance market actors.

As the home mortgage loan market is characterized by informational asymmetry as e.g., borrowers are likely to have only limited understanding of the home mortgage market and the securities market, the borrowers are in a subordinate position vis-à-vis the lenders. In George Akerlof's (1970) seminal paper, the term *lemon* (American vernacular for an overpriced used car) is introduced as a term that denotes how a seller can systematically overprice certain assets on basis of informational asymmetry at their advantage as the costs to acquire the information needed to assess the quality and pricing of the asset in question are considerable. Thus, the presence of "lemons" (in this case, subprime home mortgage loans contracts) in securities packages induced costs that were passed on to the borrowers:

> Evidence . . . suggests that investors extract price concessions as recompense for the lemons problem, which pushes up the cost to borrowers of

> subprime loans. As a result, investors can safely invest in top-rated subprime mortgage-backed securities without worrying about losses, even when the underlying loan pools are replete with questionable loans.
>
> (Engel and McCoy, 2007: 2041)

In such situations, Engel and McCoy (2007: 2041) contend, "securitization inflicts negative externalities on subprime borrowers in at least four ways": First, securitization funds "[s]mall, thinly capitalized lenders and brokers, thus enabling them to enter the subprime market"; second, securitization "[d]ilutes incentives by lenders and brokers to avoid making loans with excessive default risk by allowing them to shift that risk to the secondary market, which has other ways to protect itself"; third, securitization "[d]enies injured borrowers legal recourse against assignees" on basis of specific conditions prescribed in the contract; fourth, and finally, securitization drives up the price of subprime loans because "[i]nvestors demand a lemons premium for investing in subprime mortgage-backed securities" (Engel and McCoy, 2007: 2041). In addition, Engel and McCoy (2007: 2043) argue that numerous subprime loans "charge fees and interest rates that are exorbitant compared to the risk that the borrowers present." As indicated by the empirical material reported by Fligstein and Roehrkasse (2016), the combination the expansion of predatory lending and securitization did not only result in "negative externalities" (i.e., costs carried by someone else than the issuer of securities) but in downright "white-collar crime."

Consequences of Predatory Lending and Securitization

Fligstein and Roehrkasse (2016) examine white-collar crime in home-mortgage securitization for the 2001–2008 period. They (2016: 620) suggest that the mortgage securitization industry demonstrates opportunistic behaviour that results in fraud, defined as "behavior that manipulates or falsifies information for gain." In the period, there is substantial evidence of corporate crime related to securitization: "32 of the largest 60 financial firms operating in the markets for mortgage origination and MBS issuance and underwriting have reached regulatory settlements over alleged malfeasance" (Fligstein and Roehrkasse, 2016: 618). They (2016) provide further evidence of escalating malfeasance:

> Evidence overwhelmingly suggests that mortgage fraud and predatory lending became a systemic problem only in the years immediately preceding and concurrent with the mortgage crisis. Between 2003 and 2008, for example, mortgage fraud related 'suspicious activity reports' from financial institutions to the Federal Bureau of Investigation increased from 6,936 to 63,713, and the Bureau's mortgage fraud investigations increased from 436 to 1,644 (Federal Bureau of Investigation 2007, 2008). Between 2006 and 2008, an estimated $60 billion in fraudulent

> loans were originated (Federal Bureau of Investigation 2010). Evidence strongly supports a similar narrative at the level of securities fraud. For example, between 2005 and 2008, the percentage of financial firms listed on the Standard and Poor's 500 index who were newly subject to securities-related class action lawsuits rose from 2 to 31 percent—weighted by market capitalization, an increase from 8 to 55 percent (Cornerstone Research 2015).
>
> (Fligstein and Roehrkasse, 2016: 638, Note 4)

In the law and economics literature, competitive markets are postulated to generate disciplinary mechanisms that curb illegal activities. More specifically, there are three distinct mechanisms identified. First, competition "[c]ompels fair dealing because transaction partners can eschew exchange with fraudulent actors in favor of honest ones" (Fligstein and Roehrkasse, 2016: 625). Second, when "repeated transactions are desirable or necessary," actors are assumed to play fair "to maintain the benefits of trust-based relationships." Third, and finally, if these two first mechanisms fail to impose disciplinary mechanisms or incentives counteracting opportunistic behaviour and fraud more specifically, victims may turn to the legal system to "recognize and recoup damages through litigation"—an action that theoretically speaking "will militate against fraud" (Fligstein and Roehrkasse, 2016: 625). As a consequence and on basis of deductive reasoning, the law and economics literature objects to external regulation and even the most elementary prohibition against fraud as such regulatory control are portrayed as unnecessary complications that just the same are likely to fail to prevent malfeasance.

In contrast to this optimistic view of free-market self-regulation, Fligstein and Roehrkasse's (2016: 632) empirical data show that rather than being blocked and tarnished by relevant actors, a substantial share of the mortgage securitization industry participated in illegal behaviour. More specifically, the vertical integration of the finance industry actively promoted fraud rather than to overrule such behaviour: "[V]ertical integration accentuated criminogenic tier effects by increasing motivations to perpetuate 'origination sin' upward through the MBS value chain" (Fligstein and Roehrkasse, 2016: 632). Once fraud became part of the game, all actors participating in securities trade were anxious to avoid carrying the cost, which enticed widespread fraudulent behaviour. In other words, when large sums of money is on the table, relevant actors were less concerned about their reputation than law and economics scholars assume and predict: "Our evidence is most inconsistent with accounts emphasizing that firms care about their reputations enough that they tend not to engage in fraud" (Fligstein and Roehrkasse, 2016: 635). Instead of locating opportunistic behaviour at the fringes of the industry, where fly-by-night and thinly capitalized finance firms participated in culpable activities, Fligstein and Roehrkasse (2016: 635) provide evidence of an industry-wide presence of predatory lending and accompanying securities fraud activities. In the end, illicit behaviour materialized into considerable fines being paid *ex post facto* to federal agencies by finance industry actors to clear the record and to ensure that regulatory authorities would not intervene further into the lucrative trade:

> The view that small and marginal firms did not care about their reputations and were more likely to commit fraud (i.e., there were a few bad apples) is untrue. The related view that firms who were involved in only one market segment had perverse incentives to pass on 'bad' mortgages to unsuspecting customers down the line is also refuted. Instead, predatory lending and securities fraud were pursued by the largest and most integrated financial firms.
>
> (Fligstein and Roehrkasse, 2016: 635)

This empirical data are daunting for anyone postulating that free markets can operate efficiently and with prudence devoid of regulatory control. In addition, the data are embarrassing for theorists who assume that the market of necessity institute mechanisms that punish fraudulent behavior, a finding that has substantial implications for policy-making and finance industry regulation, Fligstein and Roehrkasse (2016) suggest:

> [L]ax regulation and technical opacity were necessary but not sufficient conditions of opportunism in the mortgage securitization industry. Here, we have to look to how the structure of firms and markets caused fraud. Increased scarcity and competition within markets pushed vertically integrated firms to commit crime in order to keep their securities businesses going.
>
> (Fligstein and Roehrkasse, 2016: 635)

That is, neither technical opacity, nor "the fraudulent behavior in the fringes" explanations (nor any other proposition introduced to save the "free markets regulate themselves" hypothesis) passed to the trial of empirical data. Instead, the organizational structure of the finance industry—Fligstein and Roehrkasse (2016) stress its "vertical integration" (see also Pistor, 2013)—provide an explanation for the widespread white-collar crime in mortgage securitization of the period.

The Role of MBS Rating Failures and the 2008 Bailout

"By spring 2010, 93 percent of subprime mortgage-backed securities issued in 2006 were downgraded to junk status," Tabb (2012: 138) writes. In the quite voluminous post-2008 literature, there are numerous accounts of how CRAs failed to estimate the value of financial assets issued:

> [A]s of June 30, 2009, 90% of the Collateralized Debt Obligations (CDOs) that were issued between 2005 and 2007 and were rated AAA

> by S&P had been downgraded, with 80% graded below investment grade; even the more simple MBS that were issued during those years and were originally rated AAA, 63% had been downgraded, with 52% downgraded below investment grade.
>
> (White, 2013: 105)

Alp's (2013) study of the credit rating standard over the period from 1986 to 2007 provide further evidence that CRAs have done a poor job in neutralizing speculative finance, a finding that supports, for example, Engel and McCoy's (2007) claim that "thinly capitalized" and predatory firms were able to operate in the subprime mortgage loan market on basis of the use of securitization. Not the least, the standard to "let the issuer pays" for the CRAs' services (Alp, 2013: 2455; Cornaggia and Cornaggia, 2013: 2265; White, 2013: 109; Clark and Newell, 2013) is a key factor that undermined the CRA's integrity and the credit rating quality:

> The percentage of speculative-grade firms in the sample increases from 37.3% in 1985 to 47.8% in 2002 and 53.2% in 2007 . . . The agency problems caused by the issuer-pays rating model could play a role here. First-time issuers create a flow of revenues for rating agencies. Hence, rating agencies have incentives to provide more issuer-friendly ratings in order to attract further business in this fast growing asset class.
>
> (Alp, 2013: 2455)

More important, by examining the rating of bonds, which deteriorated over the period, Alp (2013: 2467) argues that the changes in standards "cannot be fully justified by changes in the economic environment." The deteriorating rating standards are an endogenously generated process that speaks against the auto-regulation of finance markets model. As White (2013) remarks, "quite optimistic" ratings propelled the risk leverage in the global economy:

> Unfortunately, these ratings turned out to be quite optimistic, especially for the securities that were issued and rated during 2005–2007, when increase in housing prices were slowing (housing prices would start falling after mid-2006) and the average quality of mortgages had deteriorated even from the looser standards of the early 2000s.
>
> (White, 2013: 105)

In the end, when the finance industry short-circuited in 2008, the federal government (and, by implication, the American taxpayers), otherwise instructed to not meddle with market matters by free-market protagonists, had to carry the consequences, and the Bush Administration initiated the Troubled Asset Relief Program (TARP) to bail out and re-stabilize the finance industry (Barofsky, 2012). "[T]he decision to infuse banks with capital under the

2008 Troubled Asset Relief Program was made in part to encourage banks to continue lending and to refrain from dramatically reducing their lending capacity," Peek and Rosengren (2016: 85) say, with formidable moral hazard problems being tolerated out of hand. The TARP initiative and the bailout of major finance industry actors could have been avoided if finance markets had been more strictly monitored or if credit rating standards would not have deteriorated, Peek and Rosengren (2016: 93–94) claim:

> Had stricter capital rules and stress tests been in place prior to the financial crisis, banks would have had far larger capital cushions to protect them from emerging problems. An additional innovation has been the substantial attention given to liquidity at large financial institutions. Liquidity issues emerged as a major problem at a number of the largest banks that experienced funding problems during the crisis.
>
> (Peek and Rosengren, 2016: 93–94)

After some US$700 billion of tax money was transferred to close-to-failing finance conglomerates, which jointly brought global competitive capitalism to the brink of collapse, the *ancien régime* was quickly restored as many finance industry institutes were anxious to leave this embarrassing story behind. Unfortunately, such amnesties were not bestowed on all actors being part of the tragedy. For some of the subprime mortgage loan borrowers, arguably to considerable degree being victims of predatory lending and exposed to market forces they could not be reasonably expected to fully oversee, the story took another turn, Barofsky (2012) says:

> [I] found it beyond ironic that Treasury [Department] was now emphasizing moral hazard with respect to homeowners. Though some home owners might try to take advantage of the program by intentionally not making mortgage payments in order to qualify—that risk paled in comparison to that created by Treasury by the way it had rescued the too-big-to-fail banks. Rather than requiring those executives to suffer the consequences of their failures, Treasury had handsomely rewarded those who had failed to do their jobs, saving the banks and making sure that almost all of them kept their jobs and the enormous bonuses they had taken home before the crisis stuck.
>
> (Barofsky, 2012: 197)

In the end, it was as if the French revolution would have ended by the late summer in 1789, before it even really started, and with no Robespierres or guillotines ever playing any historical role, but with a new king or queen being installed from the ranks of royalties and aristocracy, and with the French monarchy living happily ever after. *Plus ça change, plus ça la même chose* was the principal learning from the events of 2008 and beyond.

Implications for Policy-Making and Regulation

Taken together, securitization provides the lender with the opportunity to bundle good loans and riskier loans to sell them off to global investors, which, in turn, justifies (as substantiated by Mian and Sufi, 2009) a relaxed creditworthiness check on part of presumptive borrowers. Engel and McCoy (2007: 2048) question the long-term well-being effects of this arrangement:

> [W]hy should investors buy mortgage-backed securities when lenders can deceive them about the quality of the loans in the loan pool? Lenders have incentives to cherry-pick their loans and sell the worst ones to investors. And knowing that they can unload the worst loans onto investors, lenders have less reason to underwrite loans carefully.
>
> (Engel and McCoy, 2007: 2048)

The obvious answer to these questions from the vantage point of the free-market protagonists is that the role of securities is to provide also the subprime market segment with capital (again the recurrent narrative about the "democratization of credit") and that the financial yield made by the issuer of securities would be justified on basis of the "risks carried" and as a premium rewarding the ingenuity needed to be able to develop and issue such financial instruments. Regarding the harm done to borrowers, the counterargument would be that free contracting is a constitutional right in liberal and democratic states. The question of who should be held accountable for the commotion caused by the collapse of the subprime market and the default of outstanding securities is a more thorny one, but hard-core free marketeers tend to claim that any attempt of the state to save market actors from the problem they themselves have caused (i.e., in the case of bailouts) are illegitimate as it engender moral hazard problems, which in turn leads to "too big to fail" problems (Strahan, 2013; Suárez and Kolodny, 2011; Sorkin, 2009), where the state has to save multimillionaire finance industry professionals from the mess they themselves have created and greatly benefitted from. However, such an uncompromising attitude turn a blind eye to the economic consequences for the wider economy, not being politically tolerable and therefore justifying "statutory resolution systems" (Levitin, 2011), including the bailout option. This hard-nosed attitude is easier to maintain when one can be assured that the sovereign state else is actually to picking up the bill when all is said and done to "save competitive capitalism from itself."

More moderate free-market protagonists tend to accept the moral hazard and the free-rider problem where upside risks are privatized and benefit individual actors, while downside risks are transferred to taxpayers—a practice that Princeton economist Paul Krugman refers to as "lemon socialism," where "taxpayers bear the cost if things go wrong, but stockholders and executives get the benefit if things go right" (cited in Palma, 2009: 863). At least this is the attitude that the by then Federal Reserve chairman Ben Bernanke represented after the immediate 2008 crisis was solved on basis of a bailout:

> 'In think we did the right thing to try to preserve financial stability,' [Ben Bernanke] said of the Bear [Stearns] interventions.' That's our job. Yes, it's moral hazard-inducing, but the right way to address this question is not to let institutions fail and have a financial meltdown.'
>
> (Ben Bernanke, former Fed Chairman, in an interview with Cassidy, 2009: 320)

The bundling of the subprime home-mortgage loan market and securitization, justified by the acts of 1999 and 2000, giving *carte blanche* to a variety of thinly capitalized firms to issue both credit and securities, is nevertheless indicative of the new brave world of global finance where market illiquidity is a major problem, yet it is systematically overlooked. In the price theory and efficient market models, liquidity is a conditional factor enabling market prices to constantly accommodate and reflect, for example, managerial decision-making quality, while in the new millennium, when free-market activities is essentially protected by law, regardless of the liquidity of the financial assets issued by finance market actors, such strict theoretical propositions are downplayed. The shift in free-market advocacy policy is significant but surprisingly overlooked. Nevertheless, the consequences of the trade of illiquid assets in unregulated markets were disastrous, even in the eyes of hard-core free marketeers:

> [Subprime mortgages] were explicitly devised to make previous criteria of credit assessment irrelevant because of the purported power of those who bundled them in derivate instruments to parcel out risk. Mortgage-backed securities held the promise of erasing inequalities in risk and increasing homogenization; instead, they created a conflict over creditworthiness, indeed a crisis over what constitutes the moral authority of money. This conflict implicated and destabilized local circuits of money in perhaps unprecedented ways, representing a victory for wildcat banking of epic proportions.
>
> (Polillo, 2011: 457)

One of the key explanatory factors for this failure of "epic proportions" was that the market-based monitoring of the securities market, executed by CRAs, failed to uphold standards for prudence and moderate risk taking (Bolton, Freixas and Shapiro, 2012: 86). The doctrine of "markets are regulating themselves" thus sadly disappointed its proponents, who overrated finance industry actors' ability self-reflexively assess and monitor their risk exposure. CRAs did not live up to their role as shepherds of finance capitalism, but instead, they let its sheep to run amok until the finance market collapse temporarily.

Further Finance Industry Malfeasance: Off-Balance-Sheet Activity and Shadow Banking

Another consequence of the rapid growth of derivative instrument and securitization after the turn of the millennium was that the new free-market ideology gave credence to any market-based activity. Finance institutions started to remove some of their assets from its balance sheets to veil its actual risk leverage for market participants and the remaining regulatory agencies. This new practice was referred to as "shadow banking" or "off-balance-sheet activity" (Adrian and Ashcraft, 2012), and both implied that finance institutions were now in a position to define its own rules of the game: "Importantly, securitization also went hand-in-hand in hand with the growth of 'shadow banking,' in which key functions of traditional banking are provided by a host of non-bank financial entities" (Greenwood and Scharfstein, 2013: 21. See also Philippon and Reshef, 2013: 78–79). Greenwood and Scharfstein (2013: 21) define shadow banking as "financial intermediaries that conduct maturity, credit, and liquidity transformation without explicit access to central bank liquidity or public sector credit guarantees." That is, shadow banking constitutes a parallel financial system operating without the access to a lender-of-last-resort, which served to supply credit but also to leverage systemic risks:

> [T]he shadow banking system that facilitated this expansion [of mortgage credit] made the financial system more fragile. This runs counter to the traditional 'functional' view of finance, which suggests that a primary function of the financial sector is to dampen the effects of risk by reallocating its efficiently to parties that can bear risks the most easily.
> (Greenwood and Scharfstein, 2013: 26)

The combination of securitization and off-balance-sheet activity was an explosive combination, which unsurprisingly led to "greater financial fragility" (Chick, 1997: 358). Previously conservative financial institutions such as banks were now abandoning its traditional prudence, and not the least more financially venturesome companies with lower levels of capitalization, left also the more moderate core of the finance industry with little choice than to participate in the "race to the bottom" when it came to risk management and the inflating of the off-the-balance-sheet credit: "To circumvent [regulatory] restrictions, banks procured capital from non-traditional sources . . . Because shadow banking consisted of commercial banks speculating in highly complex securities, many cite the practice of being one of the most significant causes of the [2008] crisis," Tillman (2012: 1610–1611) argues. Philip Mirowski shares this assessment and points at the faulty assumptions made regarding the self-regulating nature of markets:

> Shadow banking is predicated on the neoliberal notion that borrowers and lenders can be trusted to police the rules of their own market con-

> structs. Right up to the crash, the whole system was predicated upon a lie, which is that if any part of the system runs into trouble, there exists a subset of actors who can pull out by being first in the bankruptcy queue to claim their collateral, and thus not be harmed.
>
> (Philip Mirowski, cited in Lash and Drago, 2016: 16)

All things considered, the new free-market legislation establish an upward shift in risk assessment activities which contaminated the entire financial system with an excessively leveraged risk-appetite. Whether that risk appetite was fuelled by a widespread belief that the sovereign state now tolerated moral hazard and anticipated the "too big to fail" problem as one of its responsibilities to handle (i.e., the sovereign state was ready to circumvent its otherwise well-entrenched free-market policy) remains disputed. Cynics tend to support this case, while, for example, behavioural theories of human decision-making emphasize that finance industry actor demonstrated herd behavior to the extreme; that is, they acted as anyone else did as long as the conventional wisdom and justified true beliefs were not challenged or other changes in the environment suggested otherwise. If behavioural theory carry any explanatory value, the role of legislation and risk management deserves some scholarly attention.

Long-Term Implications: A New Risk Culture

As demonstrated earlier, the CRAs did a substandard work in curbing risk leverage on aggregated industry level. In addition, CRAs rate financial assets being issued only once while traders need to monitor their holdings continuously. Between these two end positions, firm-level risk management practices (see, e.g., Hardy and Magire, 2016; Poon, 2009; Millo and Mackenzie, 2009; Power, 2005; Spira and Page, 2002) serve to monitor the risk leverage on firm level. Ellul (2015: 281) uses the term *risk culture* to denote a "set of unwritten rules that guide risk-taking behavior" in corporations. If this more general culture is to be translated into operative protocols and guidelines, there are significant challenges involved in measuring and monitoring risks in finance markets: "Value at risk (VaR) is a measure widely used by financial institutions, but its correct application is notoriously difficult," Ellul (2015: 282) exemplifies. He continues:

> [R]isk management failures can be of three types: (*a*) when the measurement of risks is not done properly, (*b*) when the level of enterprise-wide risks are not communicated or communicated inappropriately to an institution's senior management, and (*c*) when risks are not monitored and managed appropriately. If these failures occur, enterprise-wide risk taking can move away from an optimal risk profile.
>
> (Ellul, 2015: 284)

The VaR model, Ellul (2015: 284) says, "perform well when risk managers have sufficient historical data that can be used to assess risks under the working assumption that a future return-generating process is not too different from the one that generated the historical data." However, the meteorologist's epistemic shortcut, the "easy way out prediction," to assume and predict that tomorrow's weather will be quite similar to today's (Fine, 2007)—which, after all and statistically speaking, is the most rational prediction *ceteris paribus*—does not qualify as a legitimate procedure in finance market trading. What Fine (2007: 102) refers to as the meteorologist's "futurework"—otherwise sharing many characteristics with the finance trader's work—is instead riddled by uncertainty (i.e., non-parametric risk), non-linear processes, and emergence: "The dark heart of prediction is defining controlling, and presenting uncertainty as confident knowledge. *To forecast* is to strip uncertainty, responding to the demands for surety, eschewing ambiguity" (Fine, 2007: 102). Therefore, Ellul (2015: 284) continues, whenever there is incomplete data series, "[t]here is a fine line between objective failures due to model limitations and organizational failures that occur when model limitations are used as reasons to underweight the opinion of risk." This was precisely the factual condition when MBSs were rated in the 2002–2005 period, Ellul (2015: 285) emphasizes:

> Because these [MBS] were new financial products, statistical analyses based on historical data faced severe limitations. A risk manager would have needed not only an analysis of the behavior of real estate prices across different states and its effect on the balance sheet, but crucially also about the likelihood of a sharp downturn of real estate prices correlated across several geographical states.
>
> (Ellul, 2015: 285)

More important, the individual finance trader's decision-making do not occur in a social and economic vacuum but is today more likely to be made under the influence of shareholder value objectives (Rajan, 2010, 2006). With the enforcement and widespread recognition of the legitimacy of shareholder primacy governance, finance traders are commonly incentivized to leverage risk, simply because, Ellul (2015: 284) says, "maximizing shareholder value means management has to take risks and technically complex trading strategies have to be entered into." Unfortunately, Ellul (2015: 284) continues, "such activities are opaque even to directors, let alone to shareholders and debtholders, and they need to be monitored by financial experts who are in short supply." Therefore, directors and managers in finance industry firms can only monitor their co-workers activities indirectly and on the basis of protocols and guidelines developed in-house if the CRAs fail to do their job in predictable ways or are issuing ratings that quickly become relatively unimportant for the finance trader's day-to-day work. This leads Elul to the conclusion that the *risk culture* of finance industry firms is a key to the regulation of risk leverage in the industry (see also MacKenzie and Spears, 2014: 428).

For orthodox neoclassical economic theory, a term such as *culture*, carrying excessive exogenous baggage and cannot therefore inform risk management practices in any meaningful way; for dyed-in-the-wool economists, a term like *culture* is a quite useless sociological term that does not make sense within a rational choice theory framework. Regardless of such criticism, Ellul (2015: 292) justifies the use of this term in the analysis on basis of its ability to down-pitch the risk-appetite that easily leads excessive speculation on basis of contamination: "Banks with a conservative risk culture will simultaneously take lower risks and decide to have stronger risk management structures. Similarly, banks with a more aggressive risk culture will elect to take higher risks and put in place weaker risk management structures." For instance, Ellul (2015: 289) reports that the presence of independent directors with financial expertise on the board "[p]ositively correlates with several measures of risk taking in the precrisis period." This is a result that "[r]un counter to the popular claim that financially knowledgeable directors will unambiguously reduce risk taking" (Ellul, 2015: 289). In a firm with moderate-risk culture, independent directors should preferably not be recruited from the finance industry (an industry where "financial expertise" is most likely to be acquired[9]) while for a firm with an amplified risk culture should actively recruit such directors.

By and large, that Ellul (2015), a finance economics theorist, recourses to a sociological term such as culture is indicative of how the rational choice theory and free-market ideology is approaching its outer limits where it can no longer explain, for example, illiquidity in finance markets. Mehran and Mollineaux (2012) suggest that "[f]inancial institutions remain frustratingly inscrutable":

> Despite nearly a century of concerted research and periodic financial crises, the connections between the governance of banks, their individual performance, and the long-run stability of the financial system are not well understood. Many questions remain unanswered about the causes of the crisis.
>
> (Mehran and Mollineaux, 2012: 216)

This somewhat-dour statement echoes Morgan's (2002: 888) call for regulatory oversight in the finance industry, simply because of the elusive nature of the finance assets per se: "The relative opacity of banks provides some justification for government intervention in the banking market, since runs, contagion, and other strains of systemic risk stem ultimately from the opacity of banks' assets" (Morgan, 2002: 888). The lack of regulatory oversight is partially explained by the absence of non-business civil society groups engaging in the debate over the role of the finance industry in contemporary capitalism, Pagliari and Young (2016) argue. In this view, the authority of the finance industry and its ability to operate in a de-regulated milieu not only derive from the sheer economic power of the industry, but also from the fact that "it frequently finds itself relatively uncontested" (Pagliari and Young, 2016: 310). Pagliari and Young (2016: 312) provide empirical data that reveal that "financial regulatory politics" is dominated by business groups, either in the finance industry or in the non-financial industry: "Non-business civil society groups certainly express divergent preferences towards the regulated financial industry; however, their infrequent mobilization means that they seldom represent a significant share of mobilized dissent." In addition, "interest group plurality" is both low and variable, and consequently, the role of non-business civil society groups in what Pagliari and Young (2016: 328) refer to as "the political economy of financial regulation" is quite marginal: "[W]hile non-business civil society groups largely mobilize in opposition to the financial industry, their role as a countervailing force to the financial industry targeted for regulation is constrained by their limited mobilization." As business groups contribute "significantly more to interest group plurality than do civil society organizations," and largely represent a sceptical view of finance industry regulation, the externalities of a de-regulated finance industry are addressed only to limited extent. The absence of plurality of views in finance industry regulation has resulted in a trend in financial regulatory policy-making, where "transgovernmental networks" of independent regulators such as the Basel Committee and the International Organization of Securities Commissions lead the way and collaborate with national regulatory bodies and agencies (Pagliari and Young, 2016: 314). This confinement of finance industry regulation to institutions that suffers from a democratic deficit is indicative of what Slaughter (2004) refer to as the "new world order" and Kingsbury, Krisch, and Stewart (2005) discuss in terms of the growing importance of "global administrative international law." When the financed industry is globalized, is it seemingly separated from its national and regional context, at least as a regulatory matter.

Morgan (2002: 888) advises the legislators and reformers to "remember what they are dealing with": "Banks may be the black holes at the centre of the financial universe, powerful and influential, but are to some degree, unfathomable." Perhaps such mysticism is a poor basis for adequate regulatory control, but Morgan's admonition points at how the finance industry has today become, not least on basis of the re-entrenchment of regulatory control, a sort of man-made black hole that strongly shape and structure everyday life of millions of people worldwide. This unprecedented level of opaqueness of the contemporary finance industry is reflected in Weiss and Huault's (2016) study of the post-2008 attempts to re-regulate the over-the-counter (OTC) finance trade in Europe. When encountering the risk of being subject to increased regulatory control, finance industry actors contested the re-regulation attempts along two main lines: By invoking "market nature" and by "leveraging on the inertia of practices" (Weiss and Huault, 2016: 999). The former argument explicitly rejected the traditional Efficient

Market Hypothesis (EMH) and the price theory model being at the very heart of the post-World War II free-market argument. Rather than being transparent, market prices are now portrayed as convoluted, coded information, ultimately determined by the illiquidity of the assets being traded, which demand significant expertise to operate on. In fact, market prices are no longer what economists and finance theorists have assumed for decades but are now a considerably more complex matter, concealed by hard-to-earn expertise of the finance trader. As a consequence, the regulators' ambition to create *transparency* in the OTC market was dismisses as what negatively affected the "efficiency" of the finance trade. This position was articulated by one of the finance market actors:

> In general terms, transparency in markets can help to build confidence, by ensuring that participants have access to information. However, there are products and markets which are so illiquid that revealing trade information could actually be detrimental to buyers and sellers. We have to balance the benefits of transparency versus the potential downsides.
>
> (Citi—MiFID consultation, cited in Weiss and Huault, 2016: 1002)

In order to defend their license to operate and to defend alleged "market efficiencies" vis-à-vis the regulators' transparency ideal, opponents of finance industry regulation "drift further and further away from the traditional theory of market efficiency and end up maintaining that the absence of pre-trade transparency, not to say opacity in OTC markets, actually provides an incentive to trade on them" (Weiss and Huault, 2016: 1003). The illiquidity of the assets traded over the counter and the virtues of "market efficiency" was persistently invoked to portray "mandatory transparency" as wielding a detrimental impact on finance market efficiency, and, by implication, economic well-being. Apparently, both the classic definition of EMH and the very idea of prices as vehicles of available market information were retired to evade the threat of regulatory control, thereby casting further doubt on the robustness of these propositions in the first place.

Second, despite recognizing muddy price mechanisms and the illiquidity of the finance assets being traded, opponents of finance industry regulation defended existing market practices on basis of what Weiss and Huault (2016: 1003) refer to as "a kind of Darwinian argument," according to which "the current market form has emerged naturally and survived because it best fits the interest of 'clients' or 'customers.'" This argument was put forth as a justification of status quo (i.e., a lenient regulatory oversight):

> Opponents attempt to convey that the market form proposed by regulators does not fit OTC markets, depicting the proposed reform items as irrelevant, nonoperational or, more generally, impossible to implement on OTC markets, and by insisting on differentiating between types of

> market and product. If standardization, liquidity or complexity cannot be adequately measured on OTC markets, if they do not exist in OTC markets in ways that are comparable to organized markets, then the transformation intended by the regulator is not only potentially detrimental—it also becomes unachievable.
>
> (Weiss and Huault, 2016: 1004–1005)

The two arguments objecting to and undermining the validity and feasibility of regulatory control of the OTC industry, that is, (1) the illiquidity of assets and the opaque nature of market pricing and market prices per se, and (2) the Panglossian belief that the current OTC market is the most efficient market available, were unified by the idea that the assets traded are in fact *incommensurables*, "things that are defined as so unique that they cannot be expressed in terms of a standardized measure," Weiss and Huault (2016: 1005) argue. Incommensurables are thus goods or services that defy standardization and processes of rationalization (i.e., the use of a single quantitative common metric; see, for example, Karpik, 2010), two elementary propositions supportive of regulatory control. This claim is part of the strategies available for actors who want to maintain their jurisdiction and their license to act as they wish; the creation of incommensurables "relies on constructing insularity, on erecting a fence around a territory of exception where the institutional change proposed is demonstrated to be irrelevant," Weiss and Huault (2016: 1007) summarize.

It is little wonder that finance market actors seek to evade regulatory control to maintain professional autonomy and their license to trade, but the rejection of elementary, even *foundational*, neoclassical propositions regarding market efficiency and the transparency of the pricing mechanism represent a noteworthy deviation from the post–World War II free-market model advocacy. It is worth remarking that one key term remains at the very centre of the free-market argument, *efficiency*. Yet, the concept of efficiency is commonly invoked as a defense against regulatory control and represents a situated and interested use of the term, conspicuously assuming that what is beneficial for and in the interest of finance traders and their clients is of necessity attractive and a sustainable model for the wider society. After the events of 2008, such self-assertive claims, a standing theme in finance theory and finance market communication, carry significantly less weight—apparently, this is one of the reasons for the regulatory control being back on the political agenda—but for finance industry representatives, there was still no acceptance for or recognition of the need to return to more strict regulation, very much to the surprise of Weiss and Huault (2016):

> [W]e were struck by the relative convergence of the answers provided by various members of the industry. There was no apparent dissent among the actors; banks, bank associations, hedge funds, financial services providers or corporates all seemed to subscribe to general criticism of the

> proposed regulation, describing it as useless, ill-suited, difficult to enforce and potentially detrimental to the functioning of financial markets.
> (Weiss and Huault, 2016: 999)

This apparent lack of ability to zoom out and examine the role and position of the finance industry in the 2008–2011 period (when Weiss and Huault's empirical data were collected) is arguably indicative of an insular and parochial industry culture wherein there are few possibilities to transcend the concern for individual self-interests and short-term gains, being a form of perceptual and ideological blind-folding that constitute a substantial challenge for, for example, regulators. This insularity of the "financial universe" and the attitudes it promotes and justifies is an element of what Morgan (2002: 888) portray as the "unfathomable" nature of the finance industry.

Summary of Arguments

The de-regulation of the securities market was based on two premises: (1) the ability to securitize holdings increases the supply of capital and thus serves to "democratize capital supply," and (2) increased securitization serves to stabilize the finance market as local risks are distributed nationally, or even globally, through the issuance of securities. The latter assumption proved itself to be fatally mistaken by 2008. Instead of imposing prudence on finance market traders, the ability to securitize illiquid holdings led to speculative activities that the credit rating agencies either had no incentive or lacked sufficient integrity to discipline, or, equally unflattering for the CRAs, contained risks that they failed to detect (Rom, 2009). What is also noteworthy is that despite overwhelming evidence of the externalities of the unregulated securities market, politicians and policy-makers essentially failed to re-regulate the trade after 2008. "[W]e have seen only a modest adjustment of capital market regulation, marked by the new Basel III capitalization rules and a gradual reform of banking oversight in the EU," Münnich (2016: 284) argues. Using the two cases of Germany and the U.K., Münnich (2016: 284) argues that "the lack of fundamental regulatory reforms" can be explained on basis of how "[i]nstitutionally privileged normative ideas influence the change of those institutions that carry them" (Münnich, 2016: 285). In both Germany and the UK, the "credit crunch" was essentially understood in moralist terms (and not as an evidence of systematic risk), and being explained on basis of a "contagion from the outside" narrative, wherein "failed American house credit policy was blamed, as well as the unwillingness of the US administration to support international financial regulation" (Münnich, 2016: 296). This narrative served to sort out the bad seeds from the finance industry with "greed" (in Germany) and "irrationality" or "incompetence" (in the UK) being the most favoured *ex post facto* explanation among politicians and policy-makers. Not treating the collapse of the global finance industry as systematic and structural effects, for example, UK politicians acted to further strengthen "the market principles of competition and meritocracy" (Münnich, 2016: 285), principles that per se were very likely to have contributed to the present situation. "Boards should be sacked, fraudsters punished and shareholders made to suffer," conservative *Daily Telegraph's* business editor Bill Emmott thundered in an editorial published October 4, 2008 (cited in Münnich, 2016: 298).

Unfortunately, being guided by institutionalized ideas, German and British politicians and policy-makers were turning a blind eye to the fact that their national, financialized economies were thoroughly shaped by securitization. In Germany, the widespread image of long-term "investors" and short-term "speculators," drifting apart, was an inaccurate image of the situation; instead the German banking sector had become "vital parts of the global securitization dynamics" (Münnich, 2016: 296). In the UK, Münnich (2016: 300) continues, "the British financialization boom was fueled by a steep increase in the indebtedness of private households, with a growing degree of securitized loans in mortgage lending. Outstanding debt in mortgage increased to 80% of GDP in 2007." According to Münnich (2016), the lack of regulatory reform after 2008 derives from the fact that policy-makers failed to examine the brute facts that were presented, and instead they took refuge to institutionalized ideas that imposed moral boundaries that protected the core institutional principles of the finance industry. Taken together and after minor adjustment of the existing system, the finance industry was by and large left unregulated:

> Facing uncertainty at the onset of the crisis, policymakers oriented their crisis perception along the assumption that it had been caused by financial actors pursuing illegitimate, immoral forms of profit. Policymakers and public commentators from all camps in Germany agreed that the crisis had been caused by bankers engaging with speculative activities rather than providing real economy investment. In the British debate, a major cause of the crisis was seen in traders gaining profits without being able to secure an effective management of economic risks. This moral filtering of the public debates left policymakers blind for the domestic structural and organizational dimensions of the crisis in both countries. The core problem of the boom years was the explosion of leverage and a growing interdependence of all financial corporations. For both countries, this meant that the largest parts of their financial sectors had been fully engaged in or even driven the international securitization process.
> (Münnich, 2016: 303)

Institutionalized ideas thus "distorted the political learning process" (Münnich, 2016: 303) to the point where its long-term consequences are yet to be determined.

The second proposition, that securitization would benefit the "little guy" as promised by, for example, Texas Senator Phil Gramm, was partially correct but in several cases materialized in the form of predatory lending (Engel and McCoy, 2001, 2007). If the de-regulation of the securities market had any long-term implication, it was to further amplify the levels of debt in American household, reaching critical levels in the first decade of the new millennium (Zinman, 2015; Hyman, 2011; Peñaloza and Barnhart, 2011; Barba and Pivetti, 2009). "Total household debt roughly doubled between 2000 and 2007 alone, and US household debt/GDP has grown about four-fold over the post—World War II period (fivefold if we measure the ratio at its peak in 2009)," Zinman (2015: 254) says. Montgomerie (2009) associates securitization and soaring household debt levels:

> [A]sset-backed securities facilitated widespread private credit creation by consumer credit issuers. The process of securitisation brought about the credit boom which made easy credit available to households, but also made credit issuers dependent on individuals who already have outstanding balances (called revolvers) in order to fund their business model.
>
> (Montgomerie, 2009: 2)

In many cases, large consumer credit issuers were thinly capitalized market actors who "[d]epended on securitization to fund up to 70 percent of their business model" (Montgomerie, 2009: 7). The euphemism democratization of capital thus served to fill the hole that declining real wages and reduced benefits and retirement funds brought, consequences of the shareholder welfare model, and therefore, there is evidence of a sharp growth of both secured debt (e.g., home mortgage loans) and unsecured debt (e.g., credit-card debt) burdening American households and households elsewhere:

> [S]tagnating real wage growth and receding non-wage benefits combined with dwindling state support and rising costs of living costs . . . constrain household's budgets. As credit became easily available, households used unsecured debt to plug the gap between income and expenditure.
>
> (Montgomerie, 2009: 4)

The democratization of capital mediated the decline of economic welfare but, inevitably, served to transfer economic risks from the employers (that employers carry a substantial share of social risks is one of the key propositions in welfare capitalism, see Jacoby, 1997; Quadagno, 1984; Brandes, 1976) to the households (Cobb, 2015; Bidwell, Briscoe, Fernandez-Mateo, and Sterling, 2013; Sullivan et al., 2006; Hacker, 2004).

In this view, it is hard to see how the de-regulated securitizes market benefitted few constituencies other than finance markets actors and their shareholders. The idea that securitizes was a financial innovation that would serve to self-stability finance markets and institute prudence among investors was counterintuitive already when the new legislation was enacted, and empirical evidence disappointed the proponents of the reform. In the end, securities market served many ends and in accordance with its textbook models, but their externalities overshadowed the benefits. "[I]f we are to have securities markets, they must be organized in such a way as *to promote arbitrage and learning* rather than simply assuming that they will operate effectively," Zuckerman (2010: 371) argues. Many moderate commentators would today endorse such a statement. In addition, Levitin (2016: 364) remarks, financial markets are "not organic developments steered by the invisible hand." Instead, financial markets are "marionettes, manipulated by the strings of the government"; market forces "operate within the framework created by the government" (Levitin, 2016: 364). Yet, finance markets are currently based on a tolerance for moral hazard, operationalized as the "asymmetry between the banks' privatized gains and their socialized losses" (Levitin, 2016: 361). This moral hazard encourages banks to "overproduce money" (Strange, 1996, uses the term *overbanking*), a condition that have profound socio-economic consequences (Levitin, 2016: 361).

Despite its shortcomings and its fragility, this state-governed financial market is an issue for democracy, Levitin (2016: 364) insists: "Because the government shapes financial markets and because finance determines distributions of wealth and power in society, finance should be subject to democratic control." Democratic institution should therefore re-claim their authoritative role as regulators and the lender-of-last-resort. Unfortunately, as Fox, Fox, and Gilson (2016) demonstrate, such regulatory authority is complicated to maintain on basis of legislation and court rulings as the magnitude of so-called idiosyncratic risk observed during economic crises undermine the statistical reliability of the empirical data used in fraud-on-the-market cases. The regulation and governance of financial markets thus pose a formidable challenge for policy-makers and legislators.

Final Remarks: "Capitalism May Survive Only in a Compromised Form"

In the debate between Adolf A. Berle and E. Merrick Dodd during the 1930s and in the era of the New Deal rescue and recovery activities, when the very economic system of competitive capitalism seemed corrupt and potentially unable to survive in its present form, the Harvard Law School professor Dodd (1932: 1151–1152) argued that the privately held corporation had a responsibility to treat the "economic security of the worker as one of its obligations." Consistently following the corporate law view that business charters is a contract between the business promoter and the state (i.e., society), Dodd (1932) claimed that competitive capitalism could survive only if the decision-makers in corporations, salaried managers and directors, recognize their wider social responsibilities beside making profits benefitting its investors. As a consequence, Dodd argued, the owners of the stock of public corporations could not be entrusted with such responsibilities; such duties befall only managers and directors: "stockholders who have no contact with business other than to derive dividends from it should become imbued with a professional spirit of public service is hardly thinkable," Dodd (1932: 1153) writes. "If incorporated business is to become professionalized, it is to the managers, not to the owners, that we must look for the accomplishment of this result," Dodd (1932: 1153) concludes. Writing more than eight decades later, Jones et al. (2016) addresses exactly the same theme that Dodd was concerned about, that of how competitive capitalism are capable of producing "public service" (Dodd, 1932) and "social welfare," defined as "[t]he well-being of a society as a whole, encompassing economic, social, physical, and spiritual health" (Jones et al., 2016: 217). In Jones et al.'s (2016) critique of the shareholder welfare governance model, the inability of orthodox neoclassical economic theory to apprehend real-world economies is a key concern:

> [T]he characteristics of modern market capitalism bear little resemblance to the conditions under which the perfect competition model assures social welfare. This divergence of conditions strongly suggests that the model's prescriptions—in particular, laissez-faire governmental policy and a shareholder wealth maximization objective for corporations—are unlikely to lead us to ever-increasing levels of social welfare.
>
> (Jones et al., 2016: 217)

More specifically, while Jones et al. (2016: 217) argue that the "market-oriented economic system" has an "an enviable record of making its citizens collectively richer," it is questionable whether this economic system is capable of addressing "[s]ome other urgent social welfare problems that have emerged from the relationships between the economy and the rest of society." For instance, equating shareholder welfare and social welfare is simply not right, Jones et al. (2016: 221) argue: "[M]anagement cannot simply maximize shareholder returns and expect social welfare gains to emerge; improving social welfare has become a much more complex and less well-understood undertaking." Despite eight decades of economic development and reform, Dodd's (1932) concerns regarding the interests of the investors in the corporate system remain an acute corporate governance issue.

Dodd's key question whether competitive capitalism "is worth saving" and how to do so became re-actualized after the events of 2008. Richard Posner, a libertarian law and economics scholar, a most successful legal practitioner, and an ardent protagonist of free-market reform, was one of these "conservatives" that Dodd speaks about who arrived at the point where they had to revise some of their most deep-seated beliefs after 2008. For Posner (2009: 234), the magnitude and breadth of the 2008 finance industry collapse indicate that "capitalism may survive only in a compromised form." The concern is just that what this "compromised form" actually means. To date, close to a decade after the finance industry cardiac arrest, there has been preciously little reform that have counteracted the previous three decades of free-market policy (Block, 2014: 4; Mian and Sufi, 2014: 186; Barofsky, 2012: 229). Instead, the "end of finance capital supply" has led to a "business as usual" attitude among finance industry actors, and austerity policies for the rest of us (Major, 2014; Konzelmann, 2014; Schui, 2014; Blyth, 2013). And yet competitive capitalism continues to operate, now even more volatile and fragile than before, limping by, so to speak, with higher levels of unemployment and with a retrenchment of welfare state provisions on basis of austerity measures, and in some cases economies are running on basis of *negative* central bank interest rate (as in the case of Sweden in 2015–2017) as a desperate attempt to bring back the inflation to desirable levels.[10] When the free-market theorist Posner (2009) published his pervasive criticism of the failing free-market capitalist system that he himself have actively promoted and held in esteem as the highest human accomplishment, securing economic freedom, he possibly meant something else than such outcomes when he concluded that a "compromised form" would be the only way forward. But perhaps even Richard Posner himself was not really capable of apprehending how far the free-market model had pushed competitive capitalism, in many cases undermining the institutional framework that created various markets and mechanisms for value creation and extraction. When competitive capitalism today is examined more clear-sightedly and predatory practices and dysfunctional activities can anew be addressed as what they actually are, it may be that the institutional re-structuring have gone too far and that the best we can now hope for is considerable periods of austerity and continuing finance market expansion. "Compromised form" is thus a term that includes few new reforms or other new ways of thinking when it comes to the regulation of competitive capitalism. The triumph of free-market thinking cannot be more clearly manifested than this: after at least four decades of free-market advocacy, its images of competitive capitalism and its insistence on the virtues of economic freedom constitute a hegemony which cannot be escaped; we foresee no other ways to organize economic matters, and there is little critical thinking in policy-making quarters moving beyond the imperative to simply carry on and hope for the best. In addition, the policy-makers themselves tend to represent economic interests that benefit from de-regulatory policies in combination with the sovereign state as a steadfast lender-of-last-resort:

> By one recent calculation 44 percent of the members of the U.S. Congress are millionaires. More prosaically, all members of Congress, by dint of their congressional salaries alone, are solidly in the top decile of the American income distribution. Perhaps one reason public policy tends to reflect the preferences of the affluent, then, is simply that policy makers who are themselves affluent pursue policies that reflect their personal values and interests.
>
> (Gilen, 2012: 255)

Also former president Barack Obama aired these concerns in his *The Audacity of Hope*, writing, "I know as a consequence of my fund-raising I became more like the wealthy donors I meet" (cited in Frank, 2012: 181). Empirical fact confirms the accuracy of this observation. While the number of individuals making campaign contributions in the U.S. political system roughly grew 14-fold between 1980 and 2012 (Bonica, McCarty, Poole, and Rosenthal, 2013: 111), the share of campaign contributions made by the top 0.01 percent income group was more than 40 percent in 2012. Perhaps more worrying (given that Democrats and Republicans do, in fact, receive relatively even amount of campaign contributions), the campaign contributions made by organized labour is outnumbered by a factor of 4 to 1 by the top 0.01 percent contributions. Until the early 1990s, these two types of donations were roughly in parity, but the sharp growth in economic inequality amassed more capital in a smaller economic stratum at the top of the income pyramid. In addition, voting is significantly more common in high-income groups than in the groups making less than $15,000 annually: In the former group, "over four-fifths of those with incomes over $150,000 reported voting" in 2008 (Bonica et al., 2013: 111), whereas only half of the under-$15,000-income voters turned out.

What is perhaps even more perplexing than unequal campaign contributions and relatively weak participation in democratic elections among certain groups is the apparent lack of concern in the wider public regarding the growth and consequences of economic inequality. A survey study conducted in July 2010 indicated that Internet entrepreneurs are viewed as deserving their fortunes but also bankers, less than two years after the system-wide finance industry collapse, "found some support" (Bonica et al., 2013: 109), despite campaigns such as Occupy Wall Street being very visible in the media in the period (which, Bonica et al., 2013 noticed, did not have to compete with any "Occupy Silicon Valley" or "Occupy Walmart" initiatives). Taken together, such responses are "hardly a smoking gun of widespread public resentment over rising income inequality," Bonica et al. (2013: 109) suggest. To the contrary, Bonica et al. (2013: 109) continues, "[t]here is no widespread sense that high incomes are illegitimate per se." Executive compensation, highly debated among scholars and political commentators, "went essentially unscathed in the Dodd-Frank financial regulation legislation passed in 2010," and "entrepreneurial wealth derived from providing valued goods and services is admired, even revered" (Bonica et al., 2013: 109). Clearly, Bonica et al. (2013: 108) say, efforts to reduce inequality "are not especially popular": "There has been no groundswell of political support for sharp reforms of the financial sector, nor for actions to reduce mortgage foreclosures substantially, nor for expanding investment in the human capital of children from low-income households" (Bonica et al., 2013: 108). In other words, American voters and the American public seem either relatively unconcerned about economic inequality or have become conspicuously cynical about the political system's ability to amend the situation.

Posner's (2009) account of the events of 2008 are highly illustrative of Hegel's saying that the owl of Minerva takes its flight only when the shades of night are gathering; that is, wisdom can only be formulated with the benefit of hindsight. Still, historians, who are after all a profession trained to think within the temporal horizon fathomed by mankind, have emphasized that as being a man-made economic system, we learn from history, Fernand Braudel (1977: 75) says, that capitalism is "the later-comer" that "arrives when everything is ready." That is, it was not capitalism that invented *hierarchies, the market, production*, or *consumption*—those where societal innovations, Braudel (1977: 75) claims. When such socio-economic conditions were already in place, competitive capitalism enters the scene. Again, this was the case with the corporate system, promoted by corporate law and developed by the state to support venturing while reducing the risk of harmful conflicts between business promoters and business partners (Simmons, Dobbin, and Garrett, 2008; Dobbin and Dowd, 2000; Roy, 1997; Evans, 1995; Dobbin, 1994). Therefore, Braudel (1977: 63–64) continues, very much in direct opposition to the orthodox neoclassical economic theory doctrine and its axiomatic belief in the market as the "supreme and beneficent arbitrator" (Berle, 1962: 442) and the source of all economic activities and ventures, "[c]apitalism is unthinkable without society's active complicity"; capitalism is "[o]f necessity a reality of the social order, a reality of the political order, and even a reality of civilization" (Braudel, 1977: 63–64). Moreover, to be able to operate properly and without producing overbearing externalities, "society as a whole must more or less consciously accept capitalism's values" (Braudel, 1977: 63–64). As in the case of the glorious early capitalist city-states on the Italian Peninsula in the medieval and Renaissance periods, in Venice, Genoa, and Florence, "[c]apitalism only triumphs when it becomes identified with the state, when it is the state," Braudel (1977: 64) says. This insight is illustrated by Berle (1962) in this acrimonious response to Henry G. Manne's (1962) early argument in favour of the market for management control. Speaking with the benefit of hindsight, when the table is already made and the dinner is ready to be served, is something entirely different than to have been part of the process to secure, from this new vantage point, such seemingly trivial accomplishments:

> Professor Manne and his contemporaries did not live through World War I and the decade of the twenties, and the crash of 1929, culminating in the breakdown of the American economic system in 1933. They have not experienced a corporate and financial world without the safeguards of the Securities and Exchange Commission, without systemization and enforced publicity of corporate accounting, without (more or less) consistent application of antitrust laws, without discouragement of financial pyramiding, and which tolerated conflicts of interest to a degree unthinkable now.
>
> (Berle, 1962: 433)

Berle (1962: 433) does however recognize that as a scholarly matter, "pioneer work usually does (and invariably should) come in for critical rake-over a generation later." In many cases, he continues, the author is usually dead and therefore unable to respond to the criticism, but, Berle, adds, "I am not." Thus, Berle is in the position to speak on basis of first-hand experience as a legal scholar and as former a former member of the New Deal policy-making community to avert the criticism of Henry G. Manne and other followers of the free-market orthodoxy.

To make the corporation the key entity for capitalist venturing and economic value creation, the corporation needs to be treated as what is granted the right to operate by the sovereign state as prescribed by corporate law. This view was systematically discredited by law and economics scholars, refusing the accept the legal concepts of fiduciary duties, to recognize the autonomy and discretion of the board of directors and their assigned managers, to tolerate the regulatory oversight of the state, and to grant legitimacy to other stakeholders than the shareholders. In his *Philosophy of Right*, Hegel (1999: 379) proposes that, "the *family* is the first ethical root of the state; the *corporation* is the second, and it is based in civil society." Such declarations cannot be farther away from the orthodox free-market view, substituting the central role of the state and civil society in Hegel's and Braudel's view with the free market and putting the faith in market pricing as the elementary mechanism to ensure efficiency and economic well-being.

"Your theory is crazy, but not crazy enough to be true," the quantum mechanics physicist Niels Bohr said in a response to Albert Einstein's relativity theory (cited in Tasić, 2001: 88). Something similar can be said about the orthodox neoclassicist view of the market and market pricing: it could have been true that unregulated market pricing brought all the benefits its protagonists claimed, but sadly it did not. Following from this proposition, it could have been that in an era of what Michael C. Jensen (2002) calls "enlightened value maximization," unrestricted shareholder enrichment, would have benefitted the *entire* economic system, but it proved not to do so. It could also have been, in the best of possible worlds, that an unregulated market would have been able to stabilize itself and impose penalties on excessive risk taking, leading to moderation and more a sober view of risk exposure, but again, that scenario did never materialize. What free marketeers failed to do (and what Richard Posner, 2009, came to realize but only when the music had stopped) was to recognize the inner nature of capitalism, that is, that the most agile, dynamic, flexible, and adaptable economic system invented by mankind[11] is closely entangled with and dependent on its surrounding society. The market is and will remain one of the key mechanisms within the capitalist economic system, but to assume on a propositional level, as the free-market theorists have done and still do, that the state (and by implication, society at large) is counteracting and distorting the efficiency potential of the unregulated market transaction is beside the point. Such a view of capitalism as some kind of autonomous astral body, floating freely in space and only connected to its wider, surrounding society on basis of the economic wealth it pipes back into the social system. is an inadequate and misleading image of the capitalist system. What orthodox neoclassical economists took great pride in and regarded as their principal contribution to contemporary scholarship, their parsimonious and allegedly elegant and consistent conceptual analytical framework, taking into account no more no less than what is absolutely necessary (in fact, almost nothing beside self-interest and utility-based calculation) and being self-referentially defined as being "rational" (and yet being little more than representing an highly idiosyncratic "economic theory of rationality") was not the *cause* but the *effect* of the institutionalization of markets and an differentiated economic system. Consistency in argumentation may be a good thing, but it could also represent deceiving dogma that mislead the analyst astray and thus fall prey to self-inflicted analytical blindness. The crucial properties of the world, as Geertz (1975: 22) says (as he was cited in the preface), are "invisible only to the clever"; the virtues of parsimonious analytical models and consistency can be disputed. Consistency may be helpful, but it is not all there is. The free-market model justifying a pure and uncompromising shareholder primacy governance prescription, was certainly crazy, but it was not crazy enough to be to be true, demonstrating sustainability and coherence. Only when it was almost too late, at dusk, Richard Posner, Alan Greenspan, and some other hard-core free-market acolytes realized that was the case. Hence, the claim that "capitalism may survive only in a compromised form," that is, as a form wherein society and the state are not excluded but granted a key role in monitoring and stabilizing the inherently volatile investor capitalism, inherited from the free-market crusaders and their collaborators.

Summary and Conclusion

The historian Peter Burke (1994) notices that the economic powers of Venice and Amsterdam started to stagnate when the economic elites turned from being entrepreneurs to become rentiers. In 1612, the British ambassador Dudley Carleton described the Venetian nobility accordingly:

> Their former course of life was merchandising; which is now quite left and they look landward buying houses and lands, furnishing themselves with coach and horses, and giving themselves the good time with more show and gallantry than was wont . . . their wont was to send their sons upon galleys into the Levant to accustom them to navigation and to trade. They now send them to travel and to learn more of the gentleman than the merchant.
>
> (Dudley Carleton, cited in Burke, 1994: 128)

A similar change was visible in Amsterdam, with the merchant classes now living off what the Dutch called *renten*. Perhaps the increased reliance on rent-generating financial systems is not an indication of leveraged market efficiency, but, quite the contrary, an indication of waning economic inventiveness and ingenuity? Perhaps the shareholder welfare society represents the final stages of American dominance in the capitalist economy? If we believe historians are capable of unveiling patterns that are possible to discern only in hindsight, such questions are worthy of some contemplation. As Burke (1994) argues, historical epochs rarely end because entire civilizations collapses but because its key actors lose some of their self-discipline and creativity, and suddenly find themselves being bypassed by more dynamic and venturesome societies.

The hypotheses that free markets are capable of maximizing efficiency and to self-regulate are both bold and intriguing. If it would have been a correct conjecture, much of the constitutive law of corporate legislation and the law enforcement that followed (e.g., antitrust enforcement) would potentially come at unnecessary costs. But real-world economics have revealed that these hypotheses are incomplete, not the least because finance market actors are always at risk to move towards illiquid, high-risk assets, which makes speculation turn into systemic risk and finance market instabilities. The idea of the perfectly functioning free market is a beautiful image, like the biblical image of paradise where the lambs lie down with the lions, but sadly that is not the world we inhabit and have to navigate within. As Demsetz (1969) remarks in his scathing critique of what he calls the "nirvana fallacy" of neoclassical economic theory (with Kenneth Arrow's work being his key target), "the basic problem facing public and private policy" is to design "institutional arrangements" that provide "incentives to encourage experimentation" (including the development of "new products, new knowledge, new reputations, and new ways of organizing activities"), but without "overly insulating these experiments from the ultimate test of survival" (Demsetz, 1969: 20). A healthy economy is dynamic and encourages change and inventiveness, yet expose economic actors, such as entrepreneurs, to market forces that value and price the new product and service offerings. Outside of ideal economic scenarios, lifted straight out from Economics 101 textbooks, Demsetz (1969: 20) says, "no known institutional arrangement can simultaneously maximize the degree to which each of these objectives is achieved," and neither is orthodox neoclassical economic theory capable of prescribing remedies to such policy issues:

> A difficult-to-achieve balance is sought between the returns that can be earned by additional experimentation, by giving directional guidance to investment in experimentation, and by reducing the cost of producing goods through the use of existing knowledge. The concepts of perfect competition and Pareto optimality simply are unable at present to give much help in achieving this balance.
>
> (Demsetz, 1969: 20)

Given these difficulties, Demsetz (1969: 1) rejects the view that he believes now pervades much "public policy economics," which "implicitly" presents policy choices *as if* such choices could be made between "an ideal norm" (as prescribed by formalist economic theory) and an "existing 'imperfect' institutional arrangement." Such choice alternatives do not exist in real-world economics, Demsetz (1969: 1) insists; that choice is delusional. What *does exist* in fact is instead the choice "between alternative real institutional arrangements." As a consequence, Demsetz (1969) concurs, much public policy economics unflatteringly succumb to the nirvana fallacy to assume that perfectly rational (i.e., efficiency-optimal) institutional arrangement can be found outside of textbook and economics seminars.

The epistemic realism of orthodox neoclassical economic theory subscribe to a contrived, even extreme Cartesian belief in the sheer power of human thinking: if economists, the primary and self-declared guardians of reasons in the advanced, contemporary society (Offer and Söderberg, 2016; Fourcade et al., 2015; Fourcade, 2009), only sit down and think hard enough, they would be able to penetrate and lay bare the innermost workings of intricate and emergent economic systems, and thus, their statements and declarations are to be accepted regardless of the empirical substantiation of their theorems, propositions, and, assumptions. Legal scholars for instance, do not of necessity rejects such bold claims—while they are not of necessity need impressed by the acumen of economists either—but as a legal fact, such neoclassical declarations regarding the nature of the economy needs to be compared to exiting legislation. It may be, or it may be not, that these propositions prove to be correct, but unsubstantiated by evidence, they cannot be claimed to justify legal reform simply because the legislators have reached conclusions differing from that of economists. The economists' claim to speak the truth under the aegis of reason and rationality is contrasted against the law as it is written, as a juridical and practical fact, and thus legal scholars proceed accordingly. As have been demonstrated in this volume, most, if not all, of the primary arguments in favour of shareholder primacy governance have been rejected by legal scholars, not because they do not think the bold hypotheses regarding market pricing efficacy and shareholder investment skills are of necessity mistaken, but because they are not yet proven to be correct. Until such evidence is properly presented, the extant legislation, carefully balancing a variety of interest articulated by many stakeholders whom the legislators serve in a democratic society, stand fast. By the end of the day, the power of economic thinking may be impressive and innovative, but it is not impressive and innovative to the point where statements made *ex cathedra* are accepted as a legitimate source of legal reform out of hand. In the eyes of legal scholars, economic theory is nothing more than yet another factor to consider when enacting laws and enforcing legislation, and no particular privileges can be granted this scholarly and professional community vis-à-vis other communities.

This leaves us with the question how the shareholder welfare society could be instituted when the economics argument are (as have been argued in this volume) incomplete and poorly supported by robust empirical evidence.[12]

The persistent critique of the welfare state and an active sovereign state that intervenes into supposedly self-regulating markets among conservative and libertarian economists during the post–World War II decades paid off when the business community mobilized in the 1970s to secure its interests. Economics and business school research were generously financed by business tycoons to advance their ideas, and therefore, the principal explanation is that scholarly and financial activism joined hands during the entire period, but after 1970s, in particular. As Berlin (1958) remarks, the concern for "economic freedom" that unified these two groups of activists, that is, the *negative freedom* of escaping regulatory control and other forms of imposed control is threatened by the *positive freedom* of the paternalist state:

> The liberals of the first half of the nineteenth century correctly foresaw that liberty in this 'positive' sense could easily destroy every 'negative' liberty they held sacred. They pointed out that the sovereignty of the people could easily destroy that of individuals.
>
> (Berlin, 1958: 48)

In the eyes of free-market theorists, negative freedom of unregulated competitive capitalism trumps the positive freedom of the welfare state, also, as Kalecki (1943) makes clear, when welfare state provisions benefit *all* of the economic actors within an economy. This is because, for free-market theorists, the ideal of prudence and the ethics of self-reliance of the economic actor cannot be compromised: "The fundamentals of capitalist ethics require that 'You shall earn your bread in sweat'—unless you happen to have private capital" (Kalecki, 1943: 326). By implication, rising wages and full employment remain unattractive for free-market protagonists, even in the case in which such conditions would benefit their interests:

> [T]he rise in wage rates resulting from the stronger bargaining power of the workers is less likely to reduce profits than to increase prices, and thus affects adversely only the *rentier* interests. But 'discipline in the factories' and 'political stability' are more appreciated by the business leaders than profits. Their class instincts tell them that lasting full employment is unsound from their point of view and that unemployment is an integral part of the 'normal' capitalist system.
>
> (Kalecki, 1943: 326)

Within this line of reasoning, where all benefits generated by the state are by definition a failure to uphold competition over wages, which the core group of capital owners regards as the "natural state of the market," the "liberty of the strong" (Berlin, 1958: 55), derived from either physical or economic strength, is of necessity restrained, and negative freedom of the few is lost for the benefit of the positive freedom of the many. As Berlin (1958: 55) says, "that we cannot have everything is a necessary, not a contingent truth," and therefore free-market protagonists choose the left hand path where free-market discipline is treated as an end in itself, even though such normative statements have failed to recognize the economic growth and welfare developed on basis of positive freedoms (with Hayek's *The Road to Serfdom*, 1944, as an exemplary piece of advocacy that failed to anticipate—or actively ignored—the benevolent outcomes from state-led economic growth; Schui, 2014: 134).

The tragedy of post–World War II economic theory is that not even the two classes of freedom can co-exists and mutually support one another. When the negative freedom of the few gains the upper hand, the positive freedom of the many is losing, and *vice versa*. The struggle over the authority to define the virtues and vices of the two freedoms is not likely to be resolved anytime soon. The final question regarding who are entitled to the fruits of hard and diligent labour and the economic value generated by the team production efforts in corporations and elsewhere still remains to be solved. For the time being, an economic theory that exclusively favours negative freedom seems unsustainable as it benefits the few at the expense of the many, and that, in the long run, we learn from Michał Kalecki (1971), only preys on the future returns of the capitalist class' investments. By implication, the shareholder welfare society, whose intellectual, ideological, theoretical, and legislative roots have been examined in this volume, unaccompanied by initiatives from the sovereign state to buffer its externalities, needs to be questioned as a sustainable economic model.

Notes

1. Landes and Posner (1978) is an exemplary piece of how neoclassical economic theory colonialize various spheres of human life. First, children are, *arguendo*, understood strictly in economic terms by Landes and Posner (1978: 327), saying that "the thousands of children in foster care . . . are comparable to an unsold inventory stored in in a warehouse." Next, Landes and Posner (1978: 343) propose that both the "stock" of children in foster care and the amount of abortions in the U.S. are social concerns that free-market models would be capable of resolving: "In a free adoption market, some of the 900,000 fetuses aborted in 1974 would have been born and placed for adoption." It is hard to see any more far-driven application of rational choice theory and free market advocacy than Landes and Posner's paper, relocating the question of reproduction and children, born or unborn, within what Zelizer (2011: 41) refers to as the "cash nexus," all for the benefit of constructing a case of free market efficiency.
2. Redbird and Grusky (2016) provide robust evidence of the devastating medium to long—term effects of the Great Recession. Regarding unemployment, by January 2007, the years the finance industry turmoil began, 88 percent of men 25 to 54 years old were employed. Three years later, when the finance industry crisis had passed its zenith and when its consequences translated into actual economic effects, only 80 percent of men were employed, representing a decline of 8 percent (Redbird and Grusky, 2016: 191). In addition, by November 2015, more than seven years after the bankruptcy of Lehman Brothers, the largest bankruptcy in U.S. history with Lehman reporting assets valued to $691 billion, "roughly twice as much as the second-largest bankruptcy" (Conti-Brown, 2016:

84), the long-term unemployment rate comprised 26% of the unemployed, which is a figure "well over the rate that prevailed in prior recessions" (Redbird and Grusky, 2016: 189). Needless to say, unemployment is accompanied with growing economic inequality: "The official poverty rate increased from 12.5% in 2007 to 15.1% in 2011 and has since declined only moderately (to 14.5% in 2013)"; "[f]or poverty and prime-age employment alike, the effect of [the Great Recession] has been substantial and enduring" (Redbird and Grusky, 2016: 191–192). It is also worth noticing that there is a social class component playing a decisive role in the economic recovery: The percentage loss was "much greater" for the bottom 90 percent than the top 1 percent, and there is "no evidence of a post-2009 recovery in the wealth of the bottom 90%, yet the top 1% has almost fully recovered their lost wealth" (Redbird and Grusky, 2016: 194). As a consequence, the average real wealth of the bottom 90 percent of families was no higher in 2012 than it was in 1986, but for the average real wealth of the top 1 percent things look more promising, with approximately 2.7 times greater average real wealth than in 1986 (Redbird and Grusky, 2016: 194). In summary, the Great Recession made the top 1 percent families substantially better off than the 90 percent below. Despite this outcome, the growing economic inequality did not stimulate the activism appetite in the U.S. public opinion. On the contrary, "the recession in fact reduced overall support for government activism on such major social problems as poverty, racism, health care, and income inequality" (Redbird and Grusky, 2016: 199).

3. Engel and McCoy (2001: 1260) define predatory lending as "[a] syndrome of abusive loan terms or practices that involve one or more of the following five problems": "(1) loans structured to result in seriously disproportionate net harm to borrowers; (2) harmful rent seeking; (3) loans involving fraud or deceptive practices; (4) other forms of lack of transparency in loans that are not actionable as fraud; and (5) loans that require borrowers to waive meaningful legal redress."
4. The term *fundamental value* is a complicated term in the finance theory vocabulary. Gerding (2005: 397) proposes two definitions, one being theoretically derived and one being more pragmatic: the former is stated as follows: "[T]he fundamental value of a security, according to most definitions in the economic literature, represents the present value of all future cash flows (i.e., dividends) from that security" (Gerding, 2005: 397). As this theoretical definition fails to account for the volatility of e.g., stock prices, a more pragmatic definition of fundamental value has been proposed, being "[t]he price a rational investor would pay for a security if she held it to 'horizon'"(Gerding, 2005: 397–398). It is noteworthy that neither definition explains the presence of bubbles in the economy, which Gerding (2005: 397) defines as "[a] pronounced and prolonged deviation in the prices of securities from their fundamental values."
5. As a matter of fact, some widely traded derivatives, such as the notorious Collateralized Debt Obligations (CDO) are so complex that they demand, Bluhm and Wagner (2011: 217) claim "a certain repertoire that includes valuation teams, booking capabilities, monitoring facilities, etc." to be properly priced. Unless such a repertoire is in place and being fully functional, "then it is not recommended to invest in CDOs," Bluhm and Wagner (2011: 217) write. Bluhm and Wagner (2011: 218) continue: "[I]t takes a lot to be successful in the CDO investor space. There are countless examples of investors whose CDO investment got them into trouble in the course of the crisis."
6. A bubble form whenever "[s]tock prices rise for a prolonged period above what investors would be willing to pay if they were to hold their securities for the long term" (Gerding, 2005: 398). As a conceptual matter, it is complicated to determine what a heterogeneous and geographically dispersed collective of finance

traders and investors "would be willing to pay" for an asset, and especially under the hypothetical proposition that they would all hold the asset for a longer period of time." Consequently, bubbles are complicated to anticipate until they materialize, but at that point, as we learn from history, it is mostly too late to mitigate their effects. Bubbles are therefore essentially an *ex post* construct and by definition, with Downer's (2011: 748) term, epistemic accidents—accidents, derailment, and similar events that can be explained only in hindsight when new information reveals itself to the investigator.

7. "As of the end of the first quarter of 2014, 70 percent of all home mortgages were funded by entities *other* than depositories and credit unions or the government," Levitin (2016: 420) reports. Depositories and credit unions held "only 28 percent of outstanding home mortgages by dollar volume" (Levitin, 2016: 420). These figures indicate how attractive the MBS market was for finance market institutions.
8. After the events of 2008 erupted, many conservative and free-market protagonists claimed it was the federal agencies Freddie Mac and Fannie Mae that have served to destabilize the home mortgage market and thus, *eo ipso* the global finance markets, now closely bound up with the American subprime housing market. But as several moderate commentators have made clear, this is a simplistic model that turn a blind eye to a series of interrelated factors that brought global finance to a standstill (see, e.g., Blinder, 2013: 80).
9. Even though, for example, energy companies or any other industry that securitizes holdings provide such expertise, the finance industry is still the key industry of finance capitalism.
10. "[T]he rise of finance at the firm level is a nontrivial cause of weakened employment growth, net of other macro explanations," Lin (2016: 973) remarks (see also Dünhaupt, 2017).
11. "Capitalism is essentially conjunctural," Braudel (1977: 61) suggests, "that is, it flourishes according to the dictates of changes in the economic situation. Even today one of capitalism's greatest strengths remains its ability to adopt and to change."
12. Despite recent legal initiatives such as the benefit corporation business charter (Hasler, 2014; Collins and Kahn, 2016). There is little evidence of any attempt to abandon the shareholder primacy model. Hasler (2014: 1297) suggests that the shareholder primacy model "offers a clear, simple mandate that is easy for shareholders to track, for directors to follow, and for the media to report on." Second, Hasler (2014: 1297) continues, if the shareholder primacy norm would be abandoned, "it is not clear what would replace it." The lack of ability to think outside of a hegemonic model is one of the foremost challenges for social reformers, demanding both theoretical understanding, legal competence, and political courage and stamina. Hasler (2014: 1298) claims that the third reason explaining the persistency of the shareholder primacy model is related to the lack of incentives, inasmuch as perceived shortcomings and negative consequences are either muted or one step removed; too many has simply too much to gain form maintaining the legitimacy of the shareholder primacy corporate governance model. Fourth and finally, in the U.S., shareholder-value thinking persists since "the federal government has embraced the norm" (Hasler, 2014: 1298). The Securities and Exchange Commission has for instance implemented legal reforms benefitting shareholder interests.

    Recent ideas such as the benefit corporation is thus facing strong headwinds, and unsurprisingly the legal reform do not "involve new codes of conduct or obligatory standards," Collins and Kahn (2016: 334) suggest. Instead, the benefit corporation charter merely "increases the discretion of managers and corporate boards, allowing them to establish their own vision of socially desirable outcomes as the company's mandated 'material positive impact.'"

Bibliography

Adelstein, Richard P., (1991), "The nation as an economic unit": Keynes, Roosevelt, and the managerial ideal, *Journal of American History*, 78(1): 160–187.

Adrian, Tobias, and Ashcraft, Adam B., (2012), Shadow banking regulation, *Annual Review of Financial Economics*, 4: 99–140.

Aguilera, Ruth V., and Jackson, Gregory, (2003), The cross-national diversity of corporate governance: Dimensions and determinants, *Academy of Management Review*, 28(3): 447–465.

Akerlof, George A., (1970), The market for "lemons": Quality uncertainty and the market mechanism, *Quarterly Journal of Economics*, 84(3): 488–500.

Akerlof, George A., and Shiller, Robert J., (2015), *Phishing for phools: The economics of manipulation and deception*, Princeton: Princeton University Press.

Akhigbe, Aigbe, and Whyte, Ann Marie, (2004), The Gramm-Leach-Bliley Act of 1999: Risk implications for the financial services industry, *Journal of Financial Research*, 27(3): 435–446.

Alchian, Armen, and Demsetz, Harold, (1972), Production, information costs and economic organization, *Amercian Economic Review*, 62(5): 777–795.

Alderson, Arthur S., and Nielsen, François, (2002), Globalization and the great u-turn: Income inequality trends in 16 OECD countries, *American Journal of Sociology*, 107(5): 1244–1129.

Almandoz, Juan, (2014), Founding teams as carriers of competing logics: When institutional forces predict banks' risk exposure, *Administrative Science Quarterly September*, 59(3): 442–473.

Alp, Aysun, (2013), Structural shifts in credit rating standards, *The Journal of Finance*, 68(6): 2435–2470.

Amadae, Sonia M., (2016), *Prisoners of reason: Game theory and neoliberal political economy*, Cambridge: Cambridge University Press.

Amadae, Sonya Michelle, (2003), *Rationalizing capitalist democracy: The Cold War origins of rational choice liberalism*, Chicago and London: The University of Chicago Press.

Amihud, Yakov, (2002), Illiquidity and stock returns: Cross-section and time-series effects, *Journal of Financial Markets*, 5(1): 31–56.

Andrade, Gregor, Mitchell, Mark, and Stafford, Erik, (2001), New evidence and perspectives on mergers, *Journal of Economic Perspectives*, 15(2): 103–120.

Appleby, Joyce Oldham, (2010), *The relentless revolution: A history of capitalism*, New York: Norton.

Asen, Robert, (2009), Ideology, materiality, and counterpublicity: William E. Simon and the rise of a conservative counterintelligentsia, *Quarterly Journal of Speech*, 95(3): 263–288.

Atkinson, A.B., Piketty, Thomas, and Saez, Emmanuel, (2010), Top income in the long run of history, in Atkinson, A.B., and Piketty, Thomas, eds., *Top income: A global perspective*, Oxford and New York: Oxford University Press, pp. 664–759.

Augustin, Patrick, Subrahmanyam, Marti G., Tang, Dragon Y., and Wang, Sarah Q., (2016), Credit default swaps: Past, present, and future, *Annual Review of Financial Economics*, 8: 175–196.

Avolio, Bruce J., Walumbwa, Fred O., and Weber, Todd J., (2009), Leadership: Current theories, research, and future directions, *Annual Review of Psychology*, 60: 421–449.

Bain, Joe S., (1952), *Price theory*, New York: Wiley & Sons.

Baker, George P., and Smith, George David, (1998), *The new financial capitalists: Kohlberg, Kravis and Roberts and the creation of corporate value*, Cambridge: Cambridge University Press.

Barba, Aldo, and Pivetti, Massimo, (2009), Rising household debt: Its causes and macroeconomic implications—a long-period analysis, *Cambridge Journal of Economics*, 33(1): 113–137.

Barofsky, Neil M., (2012), *Bailout: An inside account of how Washington abandoned main street while rescuing Wall Street*, New York: Free Press.

Baumol, William J., (1959), *Business behavior, value and growth*, New York: Macmillan.

Bebchuk, L., and Fried, J., (2004), *Pay without performance: The unfulfilled promise of executive compensation*, Cambridge: Harvard University Press.

Bebchuk, Lucian, and Grinstein, Yaniv, (2005), The growth of executive pay, *Oxford Review of Economic Policy*, 21(2): 283–303.

Becker, Gary S., (1968), Crime and punishment: An economic approach, *Journal of Political Economy*, 76(2): 169–217.

Becker, Gary S., and Stigler, George J., (1974), Law enforcement, malfeasance, and compensation of enforcers, *Journal of Legal Studies*, 3(1): 1–18.

Ben-Menahem, Yemima, (2006), *Conventionalism*, Cambridge and New York: Cambridge University Press.

Bennis, W.G., and O'Toole, J., (2005), How business schools lost their way, *Harvard Business Review*, 83(5): 33–53.

Bergson, H., (1999), *An introduction to metaphysics*, Indianapolis: Hackett.

Berle, Adolf A., (1962), Modern functions of the corporate system, *Columbia Law Review*, 62: 433–449.

Berle, Adolf A., and Means, Gardiner C., (1934/1991), *The modern corporation & private property*, New Brunswick: Transaction Publishers.

Berlin, Isaiah, (1958), *Two concepts of liberty: An inaugural lecture*, delivered before the University of Oxford on 31 October 1958, Oxford: Clarendon Press.

Bertrand, Marianne, and Mullainathan, Sendhil, (2003), Enjoying the quiet life? Corporate governance and managerial preferences, *Journal of Political Economy*, 111(5): 1043–1075.

Bhagat, Sanjai, and Black, Bernard, (2002), The non-correlation between board independence and long-term firm performance, *Journal of Corporation Law*, 27: 231–274.

Bidwell, Matthew, Briscoe, Forrest, Fernandez-Mateo, Isabel, and Sterling, Adina, (2013), The employment relationship and inequality: How and why changes in employment practices are reshaping rewards in organizations, *Academy of Management Annals*, 7: 61–121.

Black, Fisher, and Scholes, Myron, (1973), The pricing of options and corporate liabilities, *Journal of Political Economy*, 81(3): 637–654.

Blair, Margaret M., and Stout, Lynn A., (1999), A team production theory of corporate law, *Virginia Law Review*, 247–328.

Blinder, Alan S., (2013), *When the music stopped: The financial crisis, the response, and the work ahead*, New York: Penguin.

Block, Fred, (2014), Democratizing finance, *Politics and Society*, 42(1): 3–28.

Bluestone, Harry, and Harrison, Bennett, (1982), *Deindustrialization of America: Plant closings, community abandonment, and the dismantling of basic industry*, New York: Basic Books.

Bluhm, Christian, and Wagner Christoph, (2011), Valuation and risk management of collateralized debt obligations and related securities, *Annual Review in Financial Economics*, 3: 193–222.

Blyth, Mark, (2002), *Great transformations: Economic ideas and institutional change in the twentieth century*, New York: Cambridge University Press.

Blyth, Mark, (2013), *Austerity: The history of a dangerous idea*, Oxford and New York: Oxford University Press.

Bolton, Patrick, Freixas, Xavier, and Shapiro, Joel, (2012), The credit ratings game, *Journal of Finance*, 67(1): 85–112.

Bonica, Adam, McCarty, Nolan, Poole, Keith T., and Rosenthal, Howard, (2013), Why hasn't democracy slowed rising inequality, *Journal of Economic Perspectives*, 27(3): 103–124.

Bork, Robert H., (1966), Legislative intent and the policy of the Sherman Act, *The Journal of Law & Economics*, 9, 7–48.

Bork, Robert H., (1967), The goals of antitrust policy, *The American Economic Review*, 57(2): 242–253.

Bork, Robert H., (1978), *The antitrust paradox: A policy at war with itself*, New York: Free Press.

Bork, Robert H., and Bowman, Ward S., (1965), The crisis in antitrust, *Columbia Law Review*, 65(3): 363–376.

Boyle, James, (2003), The second enclosure movement and the construction of the public domain, *Law and contemporary problems*, 66(1/2): 33–74.

Brandes, Stuart D., (1976), *American welfare capitalism, 1880–1940*, Chicago and London: The University of Chicago Press.

Bratton, William W., and Wachter, Michael L., (2010), The case against shareholder empowerment, *Pennsylvania Law Review*, 160(1): 653–728.

Braudel, Fernand, (1977), *Afterthoughts on material civilization and capitalism*, trans. by Patricia M. Ranum, Baltimore: Johns Hopkins University Press.

Braudel, Fernand, (1992), *The wheels of commerce: Civilization & capitalism 15th-18th century*, Vol. 2, Berkeley and Los Angeles: The University of California Press.

Brudney, Victor, (1982), The independent director—Heavenly city or Potemkin village? *Harvard Law Review*, 95(3): 597–659.

Brudney, Victor, (1985), Corporate governance, agency costs, and the rhetoric of contract, *Columbia Law Review*, 1403–1444.

Brudney, Victor, (1997), Contract and fiduciary dury in corporate law, *Boston College Law Review*, 38(4): 595–666.

Bryan, Dick, and Rafferty, Michael, (2013), Fundamental value: A category in transformation, *Economy and Society*, 42(1): 130–153.
Bryan, Dick, and Rafferty, Michael, (2014), Financial derivatives as social policy beyond crisis, *Sociology*, 48(5): 887–903.
Bryer, Robert A., (1997), The mercantile laws commission of 1854 and the political economy of limited liability, *Economic History Review*, 50(1): 37–56.
Burke, Peter, (1994), *Venice and Amsterdam: A study of seventeenth-century elites*, 2nd ed., Oxford: Polity Press.
Burns, James MacGregor, (1978), *Leadership*, New York: Harper.
Calomiris, Charles W., and Haber, Stephen H., (2014), *Fragile by design: The political origins of banking crises and scarce credit*, Princeton and Oxford: Princeton University Press.
Cappelli, Peter, (1999), Career jobs are dead, *California Management Review*, 42(1): 146–167.
Carruthers, Bruce G., and Stinchcombe, Arthur L., (1999), The social structure of liquidity, flexibility, markets and states, *Theory and Society*, 28(3): 353–382.
Cassidy, John, (2009), *How markets fail: The logic of economic calamities*, New York: Picador.
Chandler, A.D., (1977), *The visible hand: The managerial revolution in American business*, Cambrdige: Harvard University Press.
Charles, Sébastien, (2016), Is Minsky's financial instability hypothesis valid? *Cambridge Journal of Economics*, 40(2): 427–436.
Cheung, Steven N.S., (1983), The contractual nature of the firm, *Journal of Law and Economics*, 1–21.
Chick, Victoria, (1997), Some reflections on financial fragility in banking and finance, *Journal of Economic Issues*, 31(2): 535–541.
Choi, Seong-Jin, Jia, Nan, and Lu, Jiangyong, (2015), The structure of political institutions and effectiveness of corporate political lobbying, *Organization Science*, 26(1): 158–179.
Chordia, Tarun, Sarkar, Asani, and Subrahmanyam, Avanidhar, (2005), An empirical analysis of stock and bond market liquidity, *Review of Financial Studies*, 18(1): 85–129.
Christophers, Brett, (2015), *The great leveler: Capitalism and competition in the court of law*, Cambridge: Harvard University Press.
Clark, Cynthia E., and Newell, Sue, (2013), Institutional work and complicit decoupling across the U.S. capital markets: The work of rating agencies, *Business Ethics Quarterly*, 23(1): 1–30.
Clark, Robert C., (1989), Contracts, elites, and traditions in the making of corporate law, *Columbia Law Review*, 89(7): 1703–1747.
Coase, R.H., (1937/1991), The nature of the firm, in Williamson, Oliver E., and Winter, Sidney G., eds., *The nature of the firm: Origin, evolution, and development*, New York and Oxford: Oxford University Press.
Coase, Ronald H., (1960), The problem of social cost, *Journal of Law & Economics*, 3(1): 1–44.
Cobb, Adam J., (2015), Risky business: The decline of defined benefit pensions and firms' shifting of risk, *Organization Science*, 26(5): 1332–1350.
Coffee, John C., (1984), Regulating the market for corporate control: A critical assessment of the tender offer's role in corporate governance, *Columbia Law Review*, 84(5): 1145–1296.

Coffee, John C., (1986), Shareholders versus managers: The strain in the corporate web, *Michigan Law Review*, 85(1): 1–109.

Coffee, John C., (1991), Liquidity versus control: The institutional investor as corporate monitor, *Columbia Law Review*, 91(6): 1277–1368.

Coffee John C., (2006), *Gatekeepers: The professions and corporate governance*, New York and Oxford: Oxford University Press.

Coffee, John C. Jr., (2009), What went wrong? An initial inquiry into the causes of the 2008 financial crisis, *Journal of Corporate Law Studies*, 9(1): 1–22.

Coffee, John C. Jr., and Palia, Darius, (2016), The wolf at the door: The impact of hedge fund activism on corporate governance, *Journal of Corporation Law*, 41(3): 545–607.

Cohan, William D., (2011), *Money and power: How Goldman Sachs came to rule the world*, London: Allen Lane and New York: Anchor Books.

Cole, Rebel A., and White, Lawrence J., (2012), Déjà vu all over again: The causes of U.S. commercial bank failures this time around, *Journal of Financial Services Research*, 42: 5–29.

Collins, Jane L., and Kahn, Walker N., (2016), The hijacking of a new corporate form? Benefit corporations and corporate personhood, *Economy and Society*, 45(3–4): 325–349.

Commons, John R., (1924), *Legal foundations of capitalism*, New York: MacMillan.

Conti-Brown, Peter, (2016), *The power and independence of the Federal Reserve*, Princeton: Princeton University Press.

Cornaggia, Jess, and Cornaggia, Kimberly J., (2013), Estimating the costs of issuer-paid credit ratings, *Review of Financial Studies*, 26(9): 2229–2269.

Cremers, Martijn K.J., and Sepe, Simone M., (2016), The shareholder value of empowered boards, *Stanford Law Review*, 68(1): 67–148.

Crilly, Donal, Zollo, Maurizio, and Hansen, Morten T., (2012), Faking it or muddling through? Understanding decoupling in response to stakeholder pressures, *Academy of Management Journal*, 55(6): 1429–1448.

Crotty, James, (2012), The great austerity war: What caused the US deficit crisis and who should pay to fix it? *Cambridge Journal of Economics*, 36: 79–104.

Cusumano, M.A., (1985), *The Japanese automobile industry: Technology and management at Toyota and Nissan*, Cambridge: Harvard University Press.

Cyert, Richard M., and March, James G., (1963), *A behavioral theory the firm*, Englewood Cliffs: Prentice-Hall.

Daily, Catherine M., Dalton, Dan R., and Cannella, Albert A., Jr., (2003), Corporate governance: Decades of dialogue and data, *The Academy of Management Review*, 28(3): 371–382.

Davies, William, (2010), Economics and the "nonsense" of law: The case of the Chicago antitrust revolution, *Economy and Society*, 39(1): 64–83.

Davis, Gerald F., (1991), Agents without principles? The spread of the poison pill through the intercorporate network, *Administrative Science Quarterly*, 36(4): 583–613.

Davis, Gerald F., (2010), After the ownership society: Another world is possible, *Research in the Sociology of Organizations*, 30B: 331–356.

Davis, Gerald F., (2013), After the corporation, *Politics and Society*, 41(2): 283–308.

Davis, Gerald F., Diekmann, Kristine A., and Tinsley, Catherine, (1994), The decline and fall of the conglomerate firm in the 1980s: The deinstitutionalization of an organization form, *American Sociological Review*, 59: 547–570.

Davis, Gerald F., and Greve, Henrich R., (1997), Corporate elite networks and governance changes in the 1980s, *American Journal of Sociology*, 103(1): 1–37.
Davis, Gerald F., and Stout, Suzanne K., (1992), Organization theory and the market for corporate control: A dynamic analysis of the characteristics of large takeover targets, 1980–1990, *Administrative Science Quarterly*, 37(4): 605–633.
De Rond, Mark, and Miller Alan N., (2005), Publish or perish: Bane or boon of academic life? *Journal of Management Inquiry*, 14(4): 321–329.
Decker, Ryan, Haltiwanger, John, Jarmin, Ron, and Miranda, Javie, (2014), The role of entrepreneurship in US job creation and economic dynamism, *The Journal of Economic Perspectives*, 28(3): 3–24.
DeMott, Deborah A., (1988), Beyond metaphor: An analysis of fiduciary obligation, *Duke Law Journal*, 37(5): 879–924.
Demsetz, Harold, (1969), Information and efficiency: Another viewpoint, *Journal of Law & Economics*, 12(1): 1–22.
Desan, Christine, (2005), The market as a matter of money: Denaturalizing economic currency in American constitutional history, *Law & Social Inquiry*, 30(1): 1–60.
Dittmar, Amy K., (2000), Why do firms repurchase stock? *Journal of Business*, 73(3): 331–355.
Djelic, Marie-Laure, (2013), When limited liability was (still) an issue: Mobilization and politics of signification in 19th-century England, *Organization Studies*, 34(5–6): 595–621.
Djelic, Marie-Laure, and Bothello, Joel, (2013), Limited liability and its moral hazard implications: The systemic inscription of instability in contemporary capitalism, *Theory and Society*, 42(6): 589–615.
Dobbin, Frank, (1994), *Forging industrial policy*, Cambridge: Cambridge University Press.
Dobbin, Frank, and Dowd, Timothy J., (2000), The market that antitrust built: Public policy, private coercion, and railroad acquisitions, 1825 to 1922, *American Sociological Review*, 65(5): 631–657.
Dodd, Merrick E. Jr., (1932), For whom are corporate managers trustees? *Harvard Law Review*, 45(7): 1145–1163. doi:10.2307/1331697
Dore, Ronald, Lazonick, William, and O'Sullivan, Mary, (1999), Varieties of capitalism in the twentieth century, *Oxford Review of Economic Policy*, 15(4): 102–120.
Downer John, (2011), "737-Cabriolet": The limits of knowledge and the sociology of inevitable failure, *American Journal of Sociology*, 117(3): 725–762.
Dünhaupt, Petra, (2017), Determinants of labour's income share in the era of financialisation, *Cambridge Journal of Economics*, 41(1); 283–306.
Dyer, Geoff, (1997), *Out of sheer rage: In the shadow of D.E. Lawrence*, Edinburgh and London: Canongate.
Easterbrook, Frank H., and Fischel, Daniel R., (1993), Contract and fiduciary duty, *Journal of Law and Economics*, 36(1): 425–446.
Easterbrook, Frank H., and Fischel, Daniel R., (1996), *The economic structure of corporate law*, Cambridge: Harvard University Press.
Eisenberg, Melvin Aron, (1976), *The structure of the corporation*, Boston: Little, brown and Company.
Eisenberg, Melvin Aron, (1989), The structures of corporate law, *Columbia Law Review*, 89: 1461–1152.
Ellickson, Robert C., (1989), Bringing culture and human frailty to rational actors: A critique of classical law and economics, *Chicago-Kent Law Review*, 65: 23–55.

Ellul, Andrew, (2015), The role of risk management in corporate governance, *Annual Review of Financial Economics*, 7: 279–299.

Elzinga, K.G., (1977), The goals of antitrust: Other than competition and efficiency, What else counts? *University of Pennsylvania Law Review*, 125(6): 1191–1213.

Engel, Kathleen C., and McCoy, Patricia A., (2001), A tale of three markets: The law and economics of predatory lending, *Texas Law Review*, 80(6): 1255–1381.

Engel, Kathleen C., and McCoy, Patricia, A., (2007), Turning a blind eye: Wall Street finance of predatory lending, *Fordham Law Review*, 75(4): 2039–2103.

Erickson, Paul, Klein, Judy L., Daston, Lorraine, Lemov, Rebecca, Sturm, Thomas, and Gordin, Michael D., (2013), *How reason almost lost its mind: The strange career of Cold War rationality*, Chicago and London: The University of Chicago Press.

Erturk, Ismail, Froud, Julie, Johal Sukhdev, and, Williams, Karel, (2004), Corporate governance and disappointment, *Review of International Political Economy*, 11(4): 677–713.

Evans, Peter, (1995), *Embedded autonomy*, Priceton and London: Priceton University Press.

Fahlenbrach, Rüdiger, and René Stulz M., (2011), Bank CEO incentives and the credit crisis, *Journal of Financial Economics*, 99(1): 11–26.

Fama, Eugene F., (1980), Agency problems and the theory of the firm, *Journal of Political Economy*, 88: 288–305.

Fama, Eugene F., and Jensen, Michael, (1983), Separation of ownership and control, *Journal of Law and Economics*, 26(2): 301–325.

Farre-Mensa, Joan, Michaely Roni, and Schmalz, Martin, (2014), Payout policy, *Annual Review in Financial Economics*, 6: 75–134.

Fernandez, Rodrigo, and Wigger, Angela, (2016), Lehman Brothers in the Dutch offshore financial centre: The role of shadow banking in increasing leverage and facilitating debt, *Economy and Society*, 45(3–4): 407–430.

Fine, Gary-Alan, (2007), *Authors of the storm: Meteorologists and the culture of prediction*, Chicago and London: The University of Chicago Press.

Fischel, Daniel R., (1978), Efficient capital market theory, the market for corporate control, and the regulation of cash tender offers, *Texas Law Review*, 57(1): 1–46.

Fiss, Peer, Kennedy, Mark T., and Davis, Gerald F., (2012), How golden parachutes unfolded: Diffusion and variation of a controversial practice, *Organization Science*, 23(4): 1077–1099.

Flaherty, Eoin, (2015), Top incomes under finance-driven capitalism, 1990–2010: Power resources and regulatory orders, *Socio-Economic Review*, 13(3): 417–447. doi:10.1093/ser/mwv011

Fligstein, Neil, and Choo, Jennifer, (2005), Law and corporate governance, *Annual Review of Law and Social Science*, 1: 61–84.

Fligstein Neil, and Roehrkasse, Alexander F., (2016), The causes of fraud in the financial crisis of 2007 to 2009: Evidence from the mortgage-backed securities industry, *American Sociological Review*, 81(4): 617–643.

Fourcade, Marion, (2009), *Economists and societies: Discipline and profession in the United States, Britain, and France, 1890s to 1990s*, Princeton and London: Princeton University Press.

Fourcade, Marion, and Khurana, Rakesh, (2013), From social control to financial economics: The linked ecologies of economics and business in twentieth century America, *Theory and Society*, 42(2): 121–159.

Fourcade, Marion, Ollion, Etienne, and Algan, Yann, (2015), The superiority of economists, *The Journal of Economic Perspectives*, 29(1): 89–113.
Fox, Edward G., Fox, Merritt B., and Gilson, Ronald J., (2016), Economic crisis and integration of law and finance: The impact of volatility spikes, *Columbia Law Review*, 116(2): 325–407.
Frame, Scott W., and White, Lawrence J., (2004), Empirical studies of financial innovation: Lots of talk, little action? *Journal of Economic Literature*, 42(1): 116–144 .
Frank, Thomas, (2012), *Pity the billionaire: The hard times swindle and the unlikely comeback of the Right*, New York: Metropolitan Books/Henry Holt.
Frankel, Tamara, (1983), Fiduciary law, *California Law Review*, 71(3): 795–836.
French, E.A., (1990), The origin of general limited liability in the United Kingdom, *Accounting and Business Research*, 21(81): 15–34.
Froot, Kenneth A., Scharfstein, David S., and Stein, Jeremy C., (1992), Herd on the street: Informational inefficiencies in a market with short-term speculation, *The Journal of Finance*, 47(4): 1461–1484.
Froud, Julie, Johal, Sukhdev, Papazian, Viken, and Williams, Karel, (2004), The temptation of Houston: A case study of financialisation, *Critical Perspective on Accounting*, 15(6–7): 885–909.
Frydman, Carola, and Jenter, Dirk, (2010), CEO compensation, *Annual Review of Financial Economics*, 2:75–102.
Funk, Russell J., and Hirschman, Daniel, (2014), Derivatives and deregulation: Financial innovation and the demise of Glass—Steagall, *Administrative Science Quarterly*, 59(4): 669–704.
Galbraith, J.K., ([1967] 1971), *The new industrial state*, 2nd ed., Boston: Houghton-Mifflin.
Gammon, Earl, and Wigan, Duncan, (2015), Veblen, Bataille and financial Innovation, *Theory, Culture & Society*, 32(4): 105–131.
Garvey, Gerald T., and Swan, Peter L., (1994), The economics of corporate governance: Beyond the Marshallian firm, *Journal of Corporate Finance*, 1(2): 139–174.
Geertz, Clifford, (1975), Common sense as a cultural system, *The Antioch Review*, 33(1): 5–25.
Gerding, Erik F., (2005), Next epidemic: Bubbles and the growth and decay of securities regulation, *The Connecticut Law Review*, 38: 393–453.
Gershon, Ilana, (2011), Neolibereal agency, *Current Anthropology*, 52(4): 537–555.
Gilens, Martin, (2012), *Affluence and influence: Economic inequality and political power in America*, Princeton and Oxford: Princeton University Press.
Goldberg, Victor P., (1976a), Regulation and administered contracts, *Bell Journal of Economics*, 7(2): 426–448.
Goldberg, Victor P., (1976b), Toward an expanded economic theory of contract, *Journal of Economic Issues*, 10(1): 45–61.
Goldberg, Victor P., (2013), Contracts: Coordination across firm boundaries, in Grandori, Anna, ed., *Handbook of economic organization: Integrating economic and organization theory*, Cheltenham and Northampton: Eward Elgar, pp. 85–95.
Goldstein, Adam, (2012), Revenge of the managers: Labor cost-cutting and the paradoxical resurgence of managerialism in the shareholder value era, 1984 to 2001, *American Sociological Review*, 77(2): 268–294.
Goody, Jack, (2004), *Capitalism and modernity: The great debate*, Cambridge and Malden: Polity.

Gordon, Jeffrey N., (1989), The mandatory structure of corporate law, *Columbia Law Review*, 89(7): 1549–1598.

Gordon, Jeffrey N., (2007), The rise of independent directors in the United States, 1950–2005: Of shareholder value and stock market prices, *Stanford Law Review*, 59(6): 1465–1568.

Gordon, Robert J., (2015), Secular stagnation: A supply-side view, *The American Economic Review*, 105(5): 54–59.

Gotham, Kevin Fox, (2006), The secondary circuit of capital reconsidered: Globalization and the U.S: Real estate sector, *American Journal of Sociology*, 112(1): 231–275.

Grant, Joseph Karl, (2010), What the financial services industry puts together let no person put asunder: How the Gramm-Leach-Bliley Act contributed to the 2008–2009 American capital markets crisis, *Albany Law Review*, 73(2): 371–419.

Greenwald Bruce C., and Stiglitz, Joseph E., (1986), Externalities in economies with imperfect information and incomplete markets, *Quarterly Journal of Economics*, 90: 229–264.

Greenwood, Robin, and Scharfstein, David, (2013), The growth of finance, *Journal of Economic Perspectives*, 27(2): 3–28.

Greve, Henrich R., Kim, Ji-Yub (Jay) and Teh, Daphne, (2016), Ripples of fear: The diffusion of a bank panic, *American Sociological Review*, 81(2): 396–420.

Grossman, Sanford J., and Stiglitz, Joseph E., (1980), On the impossibility of informationally efficient markets, *American Economic Review*, 70(3): 393–408.

Grullon, Gustavo, and Ikenberry, David L., (2000), What do we know about stock repurchases? *Journal of Applied Corporate Finance*, 13(1): 31–51.

Guillén, Mauro F., and Capron, Laurence, (2015), State capacity, minority shareholder protections, and stock market development, *Administrative Science Quarterly*, 61(1): 125–160.

Hacker, Jacob S., (2004), Privatizing risk without privatizing the welfare state: The hidden politics of social policy retrenchment in the United States, *American Political Science Review*, 98(2): 243–260.

Hacker, Jacob S., and Pierson, Paul, (2010a), Winner-take-all politics: Public policy, political organization, and the precipitous rise of top incomes in the United States, *Politics & Society*, 38(2): 152–204.

Hacker, Jacob S., and Pierson, Paul, (2010b), *Winner-take-all politics: How Washington made the rich richer and turned its back on the middle class*. New York: Simon and Schuster.

Hall, Bronwyn H., (1994), Corporate restructuring and investment horizons in the United States, 1976–1987, *Business History Review*, 68(1): 110–143.

Halliday, Terence C., and Carruthers, Bruce G., (2007), The recursivity of law: Global norm making and national lawmaking in the globalization of corporate insolvency regimes, *American Journal of Sociology*, 112(4): 1135–1202.

Hamel, Gary, (2000), *Leading the revolution*, Boston: Harvard Business School.

Hamel, Gary, and Prahalad, C.K., (1994), *Competing for the future*, Cambridge, MA: Harvard University Press.

Handlin, Oscar, and Handlin, Mary F., (1945), Origins of the American business corporation, *Journal of Economic History*, 5(1): 1–23.

Harcourt, Bernard E., (2011), *The illusion of free markets*, Cambridge: Harvard University Press.

Hardy, Barbara, (1951), Distinction without difference: Coleridge's fancy and imagination, *Essays in Criticism*, 1(4): 336–344.

Hardy, Cynthia, and Magire, Steve, (2016), Organizing risk: Discourse, power and "riskification," *Academy of Management Review*, 41(1): 80–108.

Harnay, Sophie, and Scialom, Laurence, (2016), The influence of the economic approaches to regulation on banking regulations: A short history of banking regulations, *Cambridge Journal of Economics*, 40(2): 401–426.

Harrington, Brooke, (2008), *Pop finance: Investment clubs and the new investor populism*, Princeton and Oxford: Princeton University Press.

Hasler, Jacob E., (2014), Contracting for good: How benefit corporations empower investors and redefine shareholder value, *Virginia Law Review*, 100: 1279–1322.

Hayek, Friedrich A. von, (1944), *The road to serfdom*, Chicago: University of Chicago Press.

Hegel, George Wilhelm Friedrich, ([1820] 1952), *Hegel's philosophy of rights*, trans. by T.M. Knox, London: Oxford University Press.

Hegel, George Wilhelm Friedrich, (1999), *The Hegel Reader*, edited by Steven Houlgate, Oxford: Blackwell.

Heilbron, Johan,Verheul, Jochem, and Quak, Sander, (2013), The origins and early diffusion of "shareholder value" in the United States, *Theory and Society*, 43(1): 1–22.

Hicken, Allen, (2011), Clientelism, *Annual Review of Political Science*, 14: 289–310.

High, Brandon, (2009), The recent historygraphy of American neoconservatism, *The Historical Journal*, 52(2): 475–491.

Hilt, Eric, (2014), History of American corporate governance: Law, institutions, and politics, *Annual Review in Financial Economics*, 6: 1–21.

Hirsch, Paul M., (1986), From ambushes to golden parachutes: Corporate takeovers as an instance of cultural framing and institutional integration, *American Journal of Sociology*, 91(4): 800–837.

Hirsch, Paul, and Pozner, Jo-Ellen, (2005), To avoid surprises, acknowledge the dark side: Illustrations from securities analysts, *Strategic Organization*, 3(2): 229–238.

Hobsbawm, Eric J., (1975), *The age of capital, 1848–1875*, London: Weidenfeld and Nicolson.

Hochfelder, David, (2006), "Where the common people could speculate": The ticker, bucket shops, and the origins of popular participation in financial markets, 1880–1920, *Journal of American History*, 93(2): 335–358.

Hofstadter, Richard, (1963), *Anti-intellectualism in American life*, New York: Vintage.

Hovenkamp, Herbert, (1985), Antitrust policy after Chicago, *Michigan Law Review*, 84(2): 213–284.

Hovenkamp, Herbert, (1995), Law and economics in the United States: A brief historical survey, *Cambridge Journal of Economics*, 19: 331–331.

Howard, John L., (1991), Fiduciary relations in corporate law, *Canadian Business Law Journal*, 19(1): 1–27.

Hunt, John Patrick, (2009), Credit rating agencies and the worldwide credit crisis: The limits of reputation, the insufficiency of reform, and a proposal for improvement, *Columbia Business Law Review*, 109(1): 109–209.

Hyman, Louis, (2011), *Debtor nation: The history of America in Red Ink*, Princeton University Press.

Ingham, Geoffrey, (2008), *Capitalism*, Cambridge: Polity.

Ireland, Paddy, (2010), Limited liability, shareholder rights and the problem of corporate irresponsibility, *Cambridge Journal of Economics*, 34: 837–856.
Jacobs, David, and Myers, Lindsey, (2014), Union strength, neoliberalism, and inequality: Contingent political analyses of U.S. income differences since 1950, *American Sociological Review*, 79(4): 752–774.
Jacoby Sanford M., (1997), *Modern manors: Welfare capitalism since the New Deal*, Princeton and London: Princeton University Press.
James, Simon, (1993), The idea brokers: The impact of think tanks on British government, *Public Administration*, 71(4): 491–506.
Jensen, Michael C., (1986), Agency costs of free cash flow, corporate finance, and takeovers, *American Economics Review*, 76(2): 323–329.
Jensen, Michael C., (1993), The modern industrial revolution, exit, and failure of internal control systems, *Journal of Finance*, 48(3): 831–880.
Jensen, Michael C., (2002), Value maximization, stakeholder theory, and the corporate objective function, *Business Ethics Quarterly*, 12(2): 235–256.
Jensen, Michael C., and Meckling, William H., (1976), Theory of the firm: Managerial behavior, agency costs and ownership structure, *Journal of Financial Economics*, 3(4): 305–360.
Jensen, Michael C., and Ruback, Richard S., (1983), The market for corporate control: The scientific evidence, *Journal of Financial Economics*, 11(1): 5–50.
Jones, Daniel Stedman, (2012), *Masters of the universe: Hayek, Friedman, and the birth of neoliberal politics*, Princeton and Oxford: Princeton University Press.
Jones, Thomas M., Donaldson, Thomas, Freeman, Edward R., Harrison, Jeffrey S., Leana, Carrie R., Mahoney, Joseph T., and Pearce, Jone L., (2016), Management theory and social welfare: Contributions and challenges, *Academy of Management Review*, 41(2): 216–228.
Kahle, Kathleen M., (2002), When a buyback isn't a buyback: Open market repurchases and employee options, *Journal of Financial Economics*, 63(2): 235–261.
Kaldor, Nicholas, (1939), Welfare propositions of economics and interpersonal comparisons of utility, *The Economic Journal*, 49(195): 549–552.
Kaldor, Nicholas, (1972), The irrelevance of equilibrium economics, *The Economic Journal*, 82(328): 1237–1255.
Kalecki, Michał, (1943), Political aspects of full employment, *Political Quarterly*, 14(4): 322–330.
Kalecki, Michał, (1971), *Selected essays on the dynamics of the capitalist economy 1933–1970*, Cambridge: Cambridge University Press.
Kar, Robin, (2016), Contract as empowerment, *The University of Chicago Law Review*, 83(2): 759–834.
Karpik, Lucien, (2010), *Valuing the unique: The economics of singularities*, Princeton: Princeton University Press.
Kaufman, Allen, and Englander, Ernest J., (1993), Kohlberg Kravis Roberts & Co. and the restructuring of American capitalism, *Business History Review*, 67(1): 52–97.
Kaufman, Allen, and Englander, Ernie, (2005), A team production model of corporate governance, *The Academy of Management Executive*, 19(3): 9–22.
Kaufman, Allen, and Zacharias, Lawrence, (1992), From trust to contract: The legal language of managerial ideology, 1920–1980, *Business History Review*, 66(3): 523–572.
Kaufman, Allen, Zacharias, Lawrence, and Karson, Marvin, (1995), *Managers vs. owners: The struggle for corporate control in American democracy*, New York and Oxford: Oxford University Press.

Kaufman, Jason, (2008), Corporate law and the sovereignty of states, *American Sociological Review*, 73(3): 402–425.

Keller, Matthew R., and Block, Fred, (2013), Explaining the transformation in the US innovation system: The impact of a small government program, *Socio-Economic Review*, 11(4): 629–656.

Kelly, Nathan J., and Enns, Peter K., (2010), Inequality and the dynamics of public opinion: The self-reinforcing link between economic inequality and mass preferences, *American Journal of Political Science*, 54(4): 855–870.

Khurana, Rakesh, (2007), *From higher aims to hired hands: The social transformation of American business schools and the unfulfilled promise of management as a profession*, Princeton: Princeton University Press.

Kierkegaard, Søren, (1992), *Unscientific concluding postscript to philosophical fragments*, Vol. 1, Princeton: Princeton University Press.

Kindleberger, Charles P., (2007), *A financial history of Western Europe*, New York and London: Routledge.

Kingsbury, Benedict, Krisch, Nico, and Stewart, Richard B., (2005), The emergence of global administrative law, *Law and Contemporary Problems*, 68(3/4): 15–61.

Klausner, Michael, (2013), Fact and fiction in corporate law and governance, *Stanford Law Review*, 65(6): 1325–1370.

Kogut, Bruce, and Macpherson, Muir J., (2011), The mobility of economists and the diffusion of policy ideas: The influence of economics on national policies, *Research Policy*, 40: 1307–1320.

Konzelmann, Suzanne J., (2014), The political economics of austerity, *Cambridge Journal of Economics*, 38(4): 701–741.

Krippner, Greta R., (2011), *Capitalizing on crisis: The political origins of the rise of finance*, Cambridge and London: Harvard University Press.

Kuhn, Thomas S., (1962), *The structure of scientific revolutions*, Chicago: University of Chicago Press.

Lambert, Susan J., (2008), Passing the buck: Labor flexibility practices that transfer risk onto hourly workers, *Human Relations*, 61(9): 1203–1227.

Lamoreaux, Naomi R., (1998), Partnerships, corporations, and the theory of the firm, *American Economic Review*, 88(2): 66–71.

Lan, Luh Luh, and Heracleous, Loizos, (2010), Rethinking agency theory: The view from law, *Academy of Management Review*, 35(2): 294–314.

Landes, Elizabeth M., and Posner, Richard A., (1978), The economics of the baby shortage, *Journal of Legal Studies*, 7: 323–348.

Lash, Scott, and Dragos, Bogdan, (2016), An interview with Philip Mirowski Forthc, *Theory, Culture & Society*, 33(6): 123–140.

Laverty, Kevin J., (1996), Economic "short-termism": The debate, the unresolved issues, and the implications for management practice and research, *Academic Management Review*, 21: 825–860.

Lazonick, William, (2013), From innovation to financialization: How shareholder value ideology is destroying the U.S-economy, in Wolfson, Martin H., and Epstein, Gerald, A. eds., *Handbook of the political economy of financial crises*, New York and Oxford: Oxford University Press, pp. 491–511.

Lazonick, William, and Mazzucato, Mariana, (2013), The risk-reward nexus in the innovation-inequality relationship: Who takes the risks? Who gets the rewards? *Industrial and Corporate Change*, 22(4): 1093–1128.

Leeson, Peter T., Ryan, Matt E., and Williamson, Claudia R., (2012), Think tanks, *Journal of Comparative Economics*, 40: 62–77.

Lemarchand, Rene, and Legg, Keith, (1972), Political clientelism and development: A preliminary analysis, *Comparative Politics*, 4(2): 149–178.

Levine, Michael E., and Forrence, Jennifer L., (1990), Regulatory capture, public interest, and the public agenda: Toward a synthesis, *Journal of Law, Economics, & Organization*, 6, 167–198.

Levitin, Adam J., (2011), In defense of bailouts, *Georgetown University Law Review*, 99: 435–514.

Levitin, Adam J., (2014), The politics of financial regulation and the regulation of finacial politics: A review essay, *Harvard Law Review*, 127(7): 1991–2068.

Levitin, Adam J., (2016), Safe banking: Finance and democracy, *The University of Chicago Law Review*, 83(1): 357–455.

Levitt, Kari Polany, (2013a), From mercantilism to neoliberalism and the financial crisis of 2008, in Kari Polany Levitt, ed., *From the great transformation to the great financialization: On Karl Polanyi and other essays*, New York: Zed Books, pp. 137–179.

Lin, Ken-Hou, (2016), The rise of finance and firm employment dynamics, *Organization Science*, 27(4): 972–988.

Lindblom, Charles E., (1959), The science of muddling through, *Public Administration Review*, 19(2): 79–88.

Locke, John, ([1690] 2003), *Two treatises of government: And a letter concerning toleration*, New Haven and London: Yale University Press.

Lord, Richard, A., and Siato, Yoshie, (2010), Trends in CEO compensation and equity holdings for S&P 1500 firms: 1994–2007, *Journal of Applied Finance*, 3(2): 40–56.

Lowry, Robert C., (1999), Foundation patronage toward citizen groups and think tanks: Who gets grants? *Journal of Politics*, 61(3): 758–777.

Lysandrou, Photis, and Nesvetailova, Anastasia, (2015), The role of shadow banking entities in the financial crisis: A disaggregated view, *Review of International Political Economy*, 22(2): 257–279.

Mackenzie, Donald, (2006), *An engine, not a camera: How financial models shape markets*, Cambridge, MA and London: The MIT Press.

MacKenzie, Donald, and Spears, Taylor, (2014), "A device for being able to book P&L": The organizational embedding of the Gaussian copula, *Social Studies of Science*, 44(3): 418–440.

Madrick, Jeff, (2011), *Age of greed: The triumph of finance and the decline of America, 1970 to the present*, New York: Alfred A. Knopf.

Major, Aaron, (2014), *Architects of austerity: International finance and the politics of growth*, Stanford University Press.

Mandis, Steven G., (2013), *What happened to Goldman Sachs: An insider's story of organizational drift and its unintended consequences*, Boston and London: Harvard Business Review Press.

Maney, Patrick J., (2016), *Bill Clinton: New gilded age president*, Lawrence: University Press of Kansas.

Manne, Henry G., (1962), The "higher criticism" of the modern corporation, *Columbia Law Review*, 62(3): 399–432.

Manne, Henry G., (1965), Mergers and the market for corporate control, *Journal of Political Economy*, 73(2): 110–120.

Manne, Henry G., (1967), Our two corporation systems: Law and economics, *Virginia Law Review*, 53(2): 259–284.
March, James G., and Simon, Herbert A., (1958), *Organizations*, 2nd ed., Oxford: Blackwell.
Marris, Robin, (1964), *The economic theory of "managerial" capitalism*, London: Macmillan, pp. 1–80
Martin, Randy, (2002), *Financialization of everyday life*, Philadelphia: Temple University Press.
Mayer, Jane, (2016), *Dark money: The hidden history of the billionaires behind the rise of the radical right*, New York: Doubleday.
McDonald, Lawrence G., and Robinson Patrick, (2009), *A colossal failure of common sense: The inside story of the collapse of Lehman Brothers*, London: Ebury Press.
McLevey, John, (2015), Understanding policy research in liminal spaces: Think tank responses to diverging principles of legitimacy, *Social Studies of Science*, 45(2): 270–293.
Medema, Steven G., (2011), Chicago price theory and the Chicago Law and economics: A tale of two transitions, in Van Horn, Robert, and Mirowski, Philip, and Stapleford, Thomas A., eds., *Building Chicago economics: New perspectives on the history of America's most powerful economics program*, Cambridge and New York: Cambridge University Press, pp. 151–180.
Medvetz, Thomas, (2012), *Think tanks in America*, Chicago and London: University of Chicago Press.
Mehran, Hamid, and Mollineaux, Lindsay, (2012), Corporate governance of financial institutions, *Annual Review of Financial Economics*, 4: 215–232.
Mehrling, Perry, (2011), *The new Lombard Street: How the Fed became the dealer of last resort*, Princeton and Oxford: Princeton University Press.
Mian, Atif, and Sufi, Amir, (2009), The consequences of mortgage credit expansion: Evidence from the U.S. mortgage default crisis, *The Quarterly Journal of Economics*, 124(4): 1449–1496.
Mian, Atif, and Sufi, Amir, (2014), *House of debt*, Chicago and London: The University of Chicago Press.
Milberg, William, (2008), Shifting sources and uses of profits: Sustaining US financialization with global value chains, *Economy and Society*, 37(3): 420–451. doi:10.1080/03085140802172706
Millo, Yuval, and Mackenzie, Donald, (2009), The usefulness of inaccurate models: Towards an understanding of the emergence of financial risk management, *Accounting, Organization and Society*, 34: 638–653.
Mirowski, Philip, (2013), *Never let a serious crisis go to waste: How neoliberalism survived the financial meltdown*, London and New York: Verso.
Mizruchi Mark S., (2010), The American corporate elite and the historical roots of the financial crisis of 2008, *Research in the Sociology of Organizations*, 30B: 103–139.
Mizruchi, Mark S., (2013), *The fracturing of the American corporate elite*, Cambridge: Harvard University Press.
Montgomerie, Johnna, (2009), The pursuit of (past) happiness?: Middle-class indebtedness and American financialisation, *New Political Economy*, 14(1): 1–24.
Moore, Marc T., and Rebérioux, Antoine, (2011), Revitalizing the institutional roots of Anglo-American corporate governance, *Economy and Society*, 40(1): 84–111.

Morgan, Donald P., (2002), Rating banks: Risk and uncertainty in an opaque industry *American Economic Review*, 92(4): 874–888.

Münnich, Sascha, (2016), Readjusting imagined markets: Morality and institutional resilience in the German and British bank bailout of 2008, *Socio-Economic Review*, 14(2): 283–307.

Nik-Khah, Edward, (2011), George Stigler, the Graduate School of Business, and the pillars of the Chicago School, in Van Horn, Robert, Mirowski, Philip, and Stapleford, Thomas A., eds., *Building Chicago economics: New perspectives on the history of America's most powerful economics program*, Cambridge & New York: Cambridge University Press, pp. 117–147.

Nik-Khah, Edward, (2014), Neoliberal pharmaceutical science and the Chicago School of Economics, *Social Studies of Science*, 44(4): 489–517.

Nik-Khah, Edward, and Van Horn, Robert, (2012), Inland empire: Economics imperialism as an imperative of Chicago neoliberalism, *Journal of Economic Methodology*, 19(3): 259–282.

Nye, Mary Jo, (1979), The Boutroux circle and Poincaré's conventionalism, *Journal of the History of Ideas*, 40(1): 107–120.

Offer, Avner, and Söderberg, Gabriel, (2016), *The Nobel factor: The prize in economics, social democracy, and the market turn*, Princeton and London: Princeton University Press.

Olson, Mancur, (1965), *The logic of collective action*, Cambridge: Harvard university Press.

Ott, Julia C., (2009), "The free and open people's market": Political ideology and retail brokerage at the New York Stock Exchange, 1913–1933, *Journal of American History*, 96(1): 44–71.

Pagliari Stefano, and Young, Kevin, (2016), The interest ecology of financial regulation: Interest group plurality in the design of financial regulatory policies, *Socio-Economic Review*, 14(2): 309–337.

Palma, José Gabriel, (2009), The revenge of the market on the rentiers: Why neoliberal reports of the end of history turned out to be premature, *Cambridge Journal of Economics*, 33(4): 829–869.

Paredes, Troy A., (2003), Blinded by the light: Information overload and its consequences for securities regulation, *Washington University Law Quarterly*, 81: 417–485.

Partnoy, Frank, (1999), The Siskel and Ebert of financial markets?: Two thumbs down for the credit rating agencies, *Washington University Law Quarterly*, 77(3): 619–714.

Pascale, R.T., and Athos, A.G., (1981), *The art of Japanese management*, Penguin, London.

Peck, Jamie, (2011), Orientation, in Van Horn, Robert, Mirowski, Philip, and Stapleford, Thomas A., eds., *Building Chicago economics: New perspectives on the history of America's most powerful economics program*, Cambridge and New York: Cambridge University Press, pp. 151–180.

Peek, Joe, and Rosengren, Eric, (2016), Credit supply disruptions: From credit crunches to financial crisis, *Annual Review of Financial Economics*, 8: 81–95.

Peñaloza, Lisa, and Barnhart, Michelle, (2011), Living U.S. capitalism: The normalization of credit/debt, *Journal of Consumer Research*, 38(4): S111-S130.

Perrow, Charles, (2002), *Organizing America: Wealth, power, and the origins of corporate capitalism*, Princeton and London: Princeton University Press.

Perrow, Charles, (2010), The metdown was not an accident, *Research in the Sociology of Organizations*, 30B: 309–330.

Philippon, Thomas, and Reshef, Ariell, (2013), An international look at the growth of modern finance, *Journal of Economic Perspectives*, 27(2): 73–96.

Phillips-Fein, Kim, (2011), Conservatism: A state of the field, *Journal of American History*, 98(3): 723–743.

Piketty, Thomas, and Saez, Emanuel, (2003), Income inequality in the United States, 1913–1998, *Quarterly Journal of Economics*, 118(1): 1–39.

Pistor, Katharina, (2013), A legal theory of finance, *Journal of Comparative Economics*, 41(2): 315–330.

Pitluck, Aaron Z., (2011), Distributed execution in illiquid times: An alternative explanation of trading in stock markets, *Economy and Society*, 40(1): 26–55.

Pitofsky, Robert, (1979), The political content of antitrust, *University of Pennsylvania Law Review*, 127(4): 1051–1075.

Poincaré, Henri, (2001), *The value of science: Essential writings of Henri Poincaré*, New York: The Modern Library.

Polillo, Simone, (2011), Money, moral authority, and the politics of creditworthiness, *American Sociological Review*, 76(3): 437–464.

Polillo, Simone, and Guillén, Mauro F., (2005), Globalization pressures and the state: The worldwide spread of central bank Independence, *American Journal of Sociology*, 110(6): 1764–1802.

Poon, Martha, (2009), From new deal institutions to capital markets: Commercial consumer risk scores and the making of subprime mortgage finance, *Accounting, Organizations and Society*, 34(5): 654–674.

Posner, Richard A., (1979), The Chicago school of antitrust analysis, *University of Pennsylvania Law Review*, 127(4): 925–948.

Posner, Richard A., (2009), *A failure of capitalism: The crisis of '08 and the descent into depression*, Cambridge and London: Harvard University Press.

Powell, Lewis E., (1971), Confidential memorandum: Attack of American free enterprise system, to Mr. Eugene B. Sydnor, Jr., Chairman, Education Committee, U.S. Chamber of Commerce. August 23, 1971. (URL: http://law2.wlu.edu/deptimages/Powell%20Archives/PowellMemorandumPrinted.pdf. Accessed March 24, 2016).

Power, Michael, (2005), enterprise risk management and the organization of uncertainty in financial institutions, in Knorr Cetina, Karin, and Preda, Alex, eds., *The sociology of financial markets*, Oxford and New York: Oxford University Press, pp. 250–268.

Prasad, Monica, (2012), *The land of too much: American abundance and the paradox of poverty*, Cambridge and London: Harvard University Press.

Prechel, Harland, and Morris, Theresa, (2010), The effects of organizational and political embeddedness on financial malfeasance in the largest U.S. corporations: Dependence, incentives, and opportunities, *American Sociological Review*, 75(3): 331–354.

Quadagno, Jill, (1984), Welfare capitalism and the Social Security Act of 1935, *American Sociological Review*, 45(5): 632–647.

Rabinow, Paul, Marcus, George E., Faubion, James D., and Rees, Tobias, (2008), *Designs for an anthropology of the contemporary*, Durham and London: Duke University Press.

Rajan, Raghuram G., (2006), Has finance made the world riskier? *European Financial Management*, 12(4): 499–533.

Rajan, Raghuram G., (2010), *Fault lines: How hidden fractures still threaten the world economy*, Princeton and London: Princeton University Press.

Redbird, Beth, and Grusky, David B., (2016), Distributional effects of the Great Recession: Where has all the sociology gone? *Annual Review of Sociology*, 42: 185–215.

Rhee, Eunice Y., and Fiss, Peer, C., (2014), Framing controversial action: Regulatory focus, source credibility, and stock market reactions to poison pill adoption, *Academy of Management Journal*, 57(6): 1734–1758.

Riles, Annelise, (2011), *Collateral knowledge: Legal reasoning in the global financial markets*, Chicago: The University of Chicago Press.

Riskin, Jessica, (2015), Striving machinery: The romantic origins of a historical science of life, *Intellectual History Review*, 25(3): 293–309.

Rizzo, Mario J., and Whitman, Douglas Glen, (2009), The knowledge problem of new paternalism, *Brigham Young University Law Review*, 905(4): 905–968.

Robé, Jean-Philippe, (2012), Being done with Milton Friedman, *Accounting, Economics, and Law*, 2(2): 1–31.

Robert, Dan, (2014), Wall Street deregulation pushed by Clinton advisers, documents reveal, *The Guardian*, Saturday April 19, 2014 (URL: www.theguardian.com/world/2014/apr/19/wall-street-deregulation-clinton-advisers-obama. Accessed August 29, 2016).

Rock, Edward A., (2013), Adapting to the new shareholder-centric reality, *University of Pennsylvania Law Review*, 161(7): 1907–1988.

Roe, Mark J., (1994), *Strong managers, weak owners: The political roots of American corporate finance*, Princeton: Princeton University Press.

Rom, Mark Carl, (2009), The credit rating agencies and the subprime mess: Greedy, ignorant, and stressed? *Public Administration Review*, 69(4): 640–650.

Romano, Roberta, (1985), Law as a product: Some pieces of the incorporation puzzle, *Journal of Law, Economics, & Organization*, 1(2): 225–283.

Rona-Tas, Akos, and Hiss, Stefanie, (2010), The role of ratings in the subprime mortgage crisis: The art of corporate and the science of consumer credit rating is, *Research in the Sociology of Organizations*, 30A: 115–155.

Rosas, Guillermo, (2006), Bagehot or bailout? An analysis of government responses to banking crises, *American Journal of Political Science*, 50(1): 175–191.

Rosett, Joshua G., (1990), Do union wealth concessions explain takeover premiums? The evidence on contract wages, *Journal of Financial Economics*, 27(1): 263–282.

Rowe, Frederick M., (1984), The decline of antitrust and the delusions of models: The Faustian pact of law and economics, *Georgetown Law Journal*, 72: 1511–1570.

Roy, William G., (1997), *Socializing capital: The rise of the large industrial corporation in America*, Princeton: Princeton University Press.

Rueda, David, and Pontusson, Jonas, (2000), Wage inequality and varieties of capitalism, *World Politics*, 52(3): 350–383.

Sanders, Gerard, and Hambrick, Donald C., (2007), Swinging for the fences: The effects of CEO stock options on company risk taking and performances, *Academy of Management Journal*, 50(5): 1055–1076.

Sassen, Saskia, (2014), *Expulsions: Brutality and complexity in the global economy*, Cambridge: The Belknap Press.

Schneper, William D., and Guillén, Mauro F., (2004), Stakeholder rights and corporate governance: A cross-national study of hostile takeovers, *Administrative Science Quarterly*, 49(2): 263–295.

Schui, Florian, (2014), *Austerity: The great failure*, New Haven and London: Yale University Press.

Seeger Matthew W., and Ulmer, Robert R., (2003), Explaining Enron: Communication and responsible leadership, *Management Communication Quarterly*, 17(1): 58–84.

Sen, Amartya, (1988), Freedom of choice: Concept and content, *European Economic Review*, 32(2–3): 269–294.

Shin, Hyun Song, (2009), Securitization and financial stability, *The Economic Journal*, 119(536): 309–332.

Simmons, Beth A., Dobbin, Frank, and Garrett, Geoffrey, eds., (2008), *The global diffusion of markets and democracy*, New York and Cambridge: Cambridge University Press.

Simon, Herbert A., (1957), *Models of man*, New York: Wiley.

Slaughter, Anne-Marie, (2004), *A new world order*, Princeton: Princeton University Press.

Smith, Gordon D., (2002), Critical resource theory of fiduciary duty, *Vanderbilt Law Review*, 55: 1399–1497.

Sorkin, Andrew Ross, (2009), *Too big to fail: The insider story of how Wall Street and Washington fought to save the financial system—and themselves*, New York: Viking.

Sotiropoulos, Dimitris P., Milios, John, and Lapatsioras, Spyros, (2013), *A political economy of contemporary capitalism and its crisis: Demystifying finance*, London and New York: Routledge.

Spira, Laura, and Page, Michael, (2002), Risk management: The reinvention of internal control and the changing role of internal audit, *Accounting, Auditing and Accountability Journal*, 16(4): 640–661.

Stearns, Linda, and Allan, Kenneth D., (1996), Economic behavior in institutional environments: The merger wave of the 1980s, *American Sociological Review*, 61(4): 699–718.

Stein, Judith, (2011), *Pivotal decade: How the United States traded factories for finance in the seventies*, New Haven: Yale University Press.

Steinmetz, George, and Wright, Erik Olin, (1989), The fall and rise of the petty bourgeoisie: Changing patterns of self-employment in the postwar United States, *American Journal of Sociology*, 94(5): 973–1018.

Stigler, George J., (1971), The theory of economic regulation, *Bell Journal of Economics and Management Science*, 2(1): 3–21.

Stillman, Peter G., (1988), Hegel's analysis of property in the *Philosophy of Right*, *Cardozo Law Review*, 10: 1031–1072.

Stockhammer, Engelbert, (2015), Rising inequality as a cause of the present crisis, *Cambridge Journal of Economics*, 39: 935–958.

Stout, Lynn A., (2012), New thinking on "shareholder primacy," *Accounting, Economics, and Law*, 2(2): 1–22.

Stout, Lynn A., (2013), Toxic side effects of shareholder primacy, *University Pennsylvania Law Review*, 161(7): 2003–2023.

Strahan, Philip E., (2013), Too big to fail: Causes, consequences, and policy responses, *Annual Review in Financial Economics*, 5: 43–61.

Strange, Susan, (1996), *The retreat of the state: The diffusion of power in the world economy*, Cambridge: Cambridge University Press.

Suárez, Sandra, and Kolodny Robin, (2011), Paving the road to "too big to fail": Business interests and the politics of financial deregulation in the United States, *Politics & Society*, 39(1): 74–102.

Sullivan, Teresa A., Warren, Elizabeth, and Westbrook, Jay Lawrence, (2006), Less stigma and more financial distress: An empirical analysis of the extraordinary increase in bankruptcy filings, *Stanford Law Review*, 59(1): 213–256.

Swedberg, Richard, (2003), The case for an economic sociology of law, *Theory and Society*, 32(1): 1–37.

Tabb, William J., (2012), *The restructuring of capitalism*, New York: Columbia University Press.

Tasić, Vladimir, (2001), *Mathematics and the roots of postmodern thought*, Oxford and New York: Oxford University Press.

Tichy, N.M., and Ulrich, D.O., (1983), The leadership challenge—A call for transformational leadership, *Sloan Management Review*, 26(1): 59–68.

Tillman, Joseph A., (2012), Beyond the crisis: Dodd-Frank and private equity, *New York University Law Review*, 87: 1602–1640.

Tomaskovic-Devey, Donald, Lin, Ken-Hou, and Meyers, Nathan, (2015), Did financialization reduce economic growth? *Socio-Economic Review*, 13(3): 525–548.

Topham, W.S., (2010), Re-regulating "financial weapons of mass destruction": Observations on repealing the commodity futures modernization act and future derivative regulation, *Willamette Law Review*, 47: 133–160.

Urofsky, Melvin I., (1985), State courts and protective legislation during the progressive era: A reevaluation, *Journal of American History*, 72(1): 63–91.

Useem, Michael, (1990), Business restructuring, management control, and corporate organization, *Theory and Society*, 19(6): 681–707.

Van Arnum, Bradford M., and Naples Michele I., (2013), Financialization and income inequality in the United States, 1967–2010, *American Journal of Economics and Sociology*, 72(5): 1158–1182.

Van Horn, Robert, and Emmett, Ross B., (2015), Two trajectories of democratic capitalism in the post-war Chicago school: Frank Knight versus Aaron Director, *Cambridge Journal of Economics*, 39(5): 1443–1455.

Veblen, Thorstein ([1919] 1964), *The vested interests and the common man*, New York: August M. Kelley.

Vidal, Jord Blanes I, Draca, Mirko, and Fons-Rosen, Christian, (2010), Revolving door lobbyists, *American Economic Review*, 102(7): 3731–3748.

Vogel, David, (1983), The power of business in America: A re-appraisal, *British Journal of Political Science*, 13(I): 19–43.

Vogel, E.F., (1979), *Japan as number one*, New York: Harper & Row.

Vogel, Steve K., (1996), *Freer markets, more rules: Regulatory reforms in advanced industrial countries*, Ithaca and London: Cornell University Press.

Watson, George G., (1953), Contributions to a dictionary of critical terms: Imagination and fancy, *Essays in Criticism*, 3(2): 201–214.

Weber, Max, (1999), *Essays in economic sociology*, edited by Richard Swedberg, Princeton: Princeton University Press.

Weeden, Kim A., and Grusky, David B., (2014), Inequality and market failure, *American Behavioral Scientist*, 58: 473–491.

Weinstein, Olivier, (2013), The shareholder model of the corporation, between mythology and reality, *Accounting, Economics and Law*, 3(1): 43–60.

Weiss, Hélène Rainelli, and Huault, Isabelle, (2016), Business as usual in financial markets? The creation of incommensurables as institutional maintenance work, *Organization Studies*, 37(7): 991–1015.
Western, Bruce and Beckett, Katherine, (1999), How unregulated is the U.S. labor market? The penal system as a labor market institution, *American Journal of Sociology*, 104(4): 1030–1060.
Westphal, James D., and Bednar, Michael K., (2008), The pacification of institutional investors, *Administrative Science Quarterly*, 53(1): 29–72.
Westphal, James D., and Clement, Michael, (2008), Sociopolitical dynamics in relations between top managers and security analysts: Favor rendering, reciprocity and analyst stock recommendations, *Academy of Management Journal*, 51(5): 873–897.
Westphal, James D., and Graebner, Melissa, E., (2010), A matter of appearance: How corporate leaders manage the impressions of financial analysis about the conducts of their boards, *Academy of Management Journal*, 53(1): 15–44.
White, Lawrence J., (2013), Credit rating agencies: An overview, *Annual Review in Financial Economics*, 5:93–122.
Whitley, Richard, (1986), The transformation of business finance into financial economics: The role of academic expansion and changes in the U.S. capital markets, *Accounting, Organizations, and Society*, 11: 171–192.
Whyte, W.H., (1956), *The organization man*, New York: Simon and Schuster.
Wilde, Oscar, (1999), *De profundis, The ballad of Reading Gaol & Other writings*, London: Wordsworth.
Williamson, Oliver E., (1981), The modern corporation: Origins, evaluations, attributions, *Journal of Economic Literature*, 19: 1537–1568.
Wisman, Jon D., (2013), Wage stagnation, rising inequality and the financial crisis of 2008, *Cambridge Journal of Economics*, 37(4): 921–945.
Wolff, Edward N., (2003), What's behind the rise in profitability in the US in the 1980s and 1990s? *Cambridge Journal of Economics*, 27(4): 479–499.
Wood, Dan B., and Anderson, James E., (1993), The politics of U.S antitrust regulation, *American Journal of Political Science*, 37(1): 1–39.
Wray, Randall, and Pigeon, Marc-Andre, (2000), Can a rising tide raise all boats? Evidence from the Clinton-era expansion, *Journal of Economic Issues*, 34(4): 811–845.
Yates, JoAnne, (1989), *Control through communication*, Baltimore and London: The Johns Hopkins University Press.
Zaleznik, Abraham, (1977), Management and leaders: Are they different? *Harvard Business Review*, 55(3): 67–78.
Zelizer, Viviana A., (2011), *Economic lives: How culture shapes the economy*, Princeton and Oxford: Princeton University Press.
Zelner, Bennet A., Henisz, Witold, and Holburn, Guy L.F., (2009), Contentious implementation and retrenchment in neoliberal policy reform: The global electric power industry, 1989–2001. *Administrative Science Quarterly*, 54(3): 379–412.
Zhang, Yu, and Gimeno, Javier, (2016), Earnings pressure and long-term corporate governance: Can long-term-oriented investors and managers reduce the quarterly earnings obsession? *Organization Science*, 27(2): 354–372.
Zinman, Jonathan, (2015), Household debt: Facts, puzzles, theories, and policies, *Annual Review of Economics*, 7: 251–276.
Zuckerman, Ezra W., (2010), What if we would have been in charge? The Sociologist as builder of rational institutions, *Research in the Sociology of Organizations*, 30B: 359–378.

Index

For Product Safety Concerns and Information please contact our EU
representative GPSR@taylorandfrancis.com
Taylor & Francis Verlag GmbH, Kaufingerstraße 24, 80331 München, Germany

www.ingramcontent.com/pod-product-compliance
Ingram Content Group UK Ltd.
Pitfield, Milton Keynes, MK11 3LW, UK
UKHW020939180425
457613UK00019B/465

* 9 7 8 0 3 6 7 8 8 6 4 4 8 *